Facts
about Germany

1992

Facts
about Germany

Societäts-Verlag

Contents

Contents

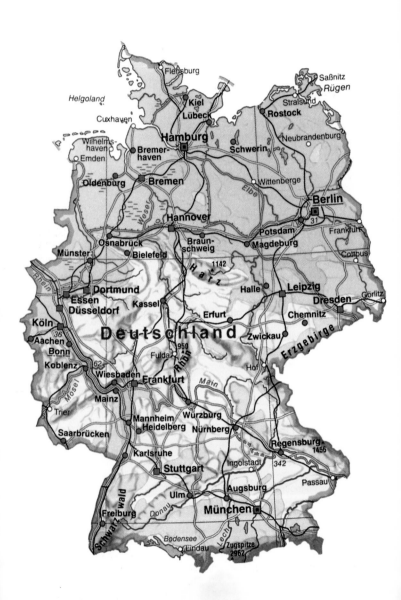

The country

The Federal Republic of Germany is situated in the heart of Europe. It has nine neighbours: Denmark in the north, the Netherlands, Belgium, Luxembourg and France in the west, Switzerland and Austria in the south, and the Czechoslovakia as well as Poland in the east. This central location has been more pronounced since 3 October 1990 when Germany was reunited. The Federal Republic is more than ever a link between east and west, but also between Scandinavia and the Mediterranean. As an integral part of the European Community and NATO, Germany is a bridge to the countries of Central and Eastern Europe.

The Federal Republic of Germany covers an area of 357,000 sq km. The longest distance from north to south as the crow flies is 876 km, from west to east 640 km. Its extremities are List on the island of Sylt in the north, Deschka, Saxony, in the east, Oberstdorf, Bavaria, in the south, and Selfkant, North-Rhine/Westphalia, in the west. The total length of the country's borders is 3,767 km.

Germany has a population of approximately 79.1 million. Next to Russia, the Federal Republic is the most densely populated country in Europe, followed by Italy (population 58 million), the United Kingdom (57 million) and France (56 million). In size, however, Germany is smaller than France (552,000 sq km) and Spain (505,000 sq km).

Geographical features. Germany has many different and charming landscapes. Low and high mountain ranges intermingle with upland plains, terrace country, hilly regions and lakelands, as well as wide, open lowlands. From north to south Germany is divided into five regions with different topographical features: the North German Plain, the Central Upland Rift, the terrace landscape of the southwest, the alpine foothills in the south, and the Bavarian Alps.

In the north we find the dry, sandy lowland with many lakes as well as heath and moors. There is also the fertile land south of the Central Upland Range. These lowland penetrations include the Lower Rhenish Bight, the Westphalian Bight and the Saxon-Thuringian Bight. The marshes along the North Sea coast extend as far as the geest. Characteristic features of the Baltic Sea coastline are, in Schleswig-

Europe today (april 1992)   ——— Border of State   ○ Capital

Holstein, the fjords, in Mecklenburg-Western Pomerania the lakes and the counterbalancing coastline. The main islands are, in the North Sea, the East Frisian Islands such as Borkum or Norderney, the North Frisian Islands of Amrum, Föhr, Sylt and the Halligen, Helgoland in the Helgoland Bight, as well as Rügen and Fehmarn in the Baltic Sea. Some parts of the Baltic coast have flat, sandy shores, others steep cliffs. Between the North and Baltic Seas lies the low-hill country called "Holsteinische Schweiz" (Holstein Switzerland).

The Central Upland Rift divides north Germany from the south. The central Rhine valley between Bonn and Bingen and the Hessian depressions serve as the natural north-south traffic arteries. The Central Uplands include the Rhenish Slate Mountains (Hunsrück, Eifel, Taunus, Westerwald, Bergisches Land and Sauerland), the Hessian Mountains, the Weser and Leine Mountains in western and central Germany. Right in the centre of Germany are the Harz Mountains. In the eastern region are the Rhön Mountains, the Bavarian Forest, the Upper Palatinate Forest, the Fichtelgebirge, the Frankenwald, the Thuringian Forest and the mountains of the Erzgebirge.

The terrace landscape of the Central Uplands in the south-west embrace the upper Rhine valley with the adjacent mountain ranges of the Black Forest, the Odenwald and Spessart, the Palatinate Forest with the Haardt and the Swabian-Franconian terrace country with the Alb.

In a narrow valley between Bingen and Bonn the river Rhine, the main north-south axis, slices through the Rhenish Slate Mountains,

Mountains, rivers, islands

Zugspitze (nothern Alps)	2962 m
Watzmann (northern Alps)	2713 m
Feldberg (Black Forest)	1493 m
Großer Arber (Bavarian Forest)	1456 m
Fichtelberg (Erzgebirge)	1214 m
Brocken (Harz)	1142 m
Rivers within Germany:	
Rhine	865 km
Elbe	700 km
Main	524 km
Weser	440 km
Spree	382 km
Shipping canals:	
Mittellandkanal	321 km
Dortmund-Ems Canal	269 km
North Sea-Baltic Canal	99 km
Lakes and Dams:	
Lake Constance (total area)	538 sq. km
Lake Constance (German part)	305 sq. km
Müritz	115 sq. km
Schwammenauel	205 cubic metres
Eder Dam (Lake Eder)	202 cubic metres
Islands:	
Rügen	926 sq. km
Usedom (German part)	354 sq. km
Fehmarn	185 sq. km
Sylt	99 sq. km

whose not very fertile highland areas (Hunsrück, Taunus, Eifel, Westerwald) are considerably less densely populated than the sheltered wine-growing areas on both sides of the Rhine which are very popular with tourists.

The alpine foothills embrace the Swabian-Bavarian highlands and lakes, the broad, gravel plains, the hilly landscape of Lower Bavaria, and the Danube valley. Characteristic features of this region are the moors, dome-shaped hill ranges and lakes (Chiemsee, Starnberger See) as well as small villages.

The German part of the Alps between Lake Constance and Berchtesgaden is limited to the Allgäu, the Bavarian Alps and the Berchtesgaden Alps. In this alpine world lie picturesque lakes, such as the Königssee near Berchtesgaden, and popular tourist resorts such as Garmisch-Partenkirchen or Mittenwald.

Climate. Germany is situated in the temperate zone between the Atlantic Ocean and the eastern part of the European continent. Sharp changes in temperature are rare. There is precipitation all the year round. In winter the average temperature is between 1.5°C in the lowland areas and minus 6°C in the mountains. In the warmest month of the year, July, temperatures are between 18°C in low-lying regions and 20°C in the sheltered valleys of the south. Exceptions are the Upper Rhine Trough with its extremely mild climate, Upper Bavaria with its warm alpine wind (Föhn) from the south, and the Harz Mountains, a climatic zone of its own with cold winds, cool summers and heavy snow in winter.

The people

Germany has a population of over 79 million (including 5.6 million foreigners) and is one of the most densely populated countries in Europe (222 people per sq km). Only Belgium and the Netherlands have a higher population density.

The population is distributed very unevenly. Greater Berlin, which has been growing rapidly since Germany's unification and now has 3.4 million inhabitants, will probably have eight million by the end of the millennium. More than four million people (about 5,500 per sq km) live in the Rhein-Ruhr industrial agglomeration where towns and cities are so close together that there are no distinct boundaries between them.

Other concentrations are to be found in the Rhein-Main area around Frankfurt, Wiesbaden and Mainz, and the Rhein-Neckar region focusing on Mannheim and Ludwigshafen, the industrial area around Stuttgart, as well as the catchment areas of Bremen, Dresden, Hamburg, Cologne, Leipzig, Munich and Nuremberg/Fürth. These contrast with the thinly populated moorlands of the North German Plain, parts of the Eifel Mountains, the Bavarian Forest, the Upper Palatinate, the March of Brandenburg, and large parts of Mecklenburg-Western Pomerania.

The western part of Germany is much more densely populated than the five new states in the east, where only about a fifth of the population (16 million) live on roughly 30% of the national territory. Of the 20 cities with more than 300,000 inhabitants, four are in the eastern part of Germany.

Nearly one third of the population live in the 85 cities (more than 100,000 inhabitants). They number about 26 million. But the great majority live in villages and small towns: over 7 million in municipalities with a population of less than 2,000. 46 million live in towns with between 2,000 and 100,000 inhabitants.

The population in both the old and new federal states began to decline in the 70s because the birth rate was falling. In the west, however, there has been a slightly upward trend since 1990. With eleven births a year to every 1,000 inhabitants (in West Germany prior to unification) Germany has one of the lowest birth rates in the world. The population increase after the Second World War was mainly due to

Age structure of the population of Germany on 1 Jan. 1990

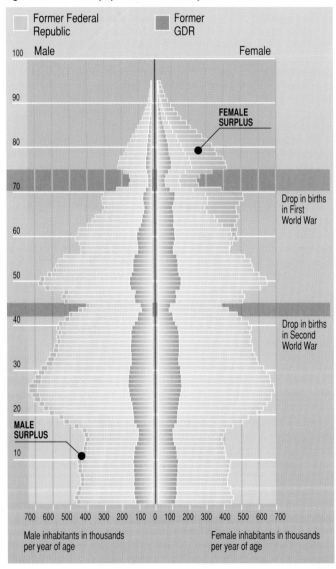

Former Federal Republic · Former GDR

Male · Female

FEMALE SURPLUS

Drop in births in First World War

Drop in births in Second World War

MALE SURPLUS

700 600 500 400 300 200 100 0 0 100 200 300 400 500 600 700

Male inhabitants in thousands per year of age

Female inhabitants in thousands per year of age

immigration. Some 13 million German refugees and expellees entered the present German territory from the former German eastern provinces and Eastern Europe. There was a continuous strong flow of people who fled from East to West Germany until the Berlin wall was erected by the communist regime in East Germany in 1961 which hermetically sealed the border. From the early 60s large numbers of foreign workers came to the Federal Republic of old whose expanding economy needed additional labour which was not available at home.

Regional disparities. Over the past thousand years or so the German nation has grown out of a number of tribes, such as the Franks and Saxons, Swabians and Bavarians. They have of course long since lost their original character, but their traditions and dialects live on in their respective regions.

Those ethnic regions are not identical to the present federal states (Länder), most of which were only formed after the Second World War in collaboration with the occupying powers. In most cases the boundaries were drawn without much consideration for old traditions. Furthermore, the flows of refugees and the massive post-war migrations, but also the mobility of the modern industrial society, have more or less blurred the ethnic boundaries.

What remains are the regional characteristics. The natives of Mecklenburg, for instance, are reserved, the Swabians thrifty, the Rheinländer happy-go-lucky, and the Saxons hardworking and canny, and so on.

The German language. German is one of the large group of Indo-Germanic languages, and within that one of the Germanic languages. It is thus related to Danish, Norwegian and Swedish, Dutch and Flemish, but also to English. The emergence of a common High German language is attributed to Martin Luther's translation of the Bible.

Germany has a wealth of dialects but it is usually possible to determine a person's native region. If, on the other hand, a Frisian or a Mecklenburger and a Bavarian were to speak to one another in pure dialect they would have great difficulty understanding one another. Moreover, whilst the country was divided the two German states developed a different political vocabulary. New words were also coined which were not necessarily understood in the other part of the country. But basic vocabulary and grammar remained the same in east and west. The common language was one of the links which held the divided nation together.

German is also spoken as the native language in Austria, Liechtenstein, large parts of Switzerland, South Tirol (northern Italy) and in small parts of Belgium, France (Alsace) and Luxembourg along the German border. And the German minorities in Poland, Romania and the republics of the former Soviet Union have partly retained the German language.

German is the native language of more than 100 million people. About one in every ten books published throughout the world has been written in German. As regards translations into foreign languages, German is third after English and French; as regards translations into German, it heads the list.

Foreign nationalities. Well over five million foreign workers and their families live in the Federal Republic of Germany (including Turks 30%, Yugoslavs 12%, Italians 10%). Nearly 60% of them have been there for at least ten years and more than two thirds of their children were born there.

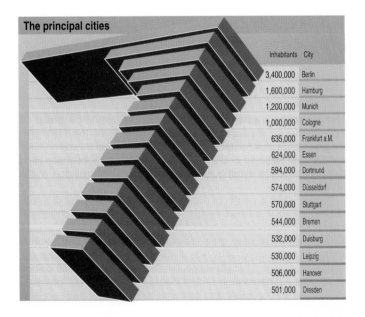

The principal cities

Inhabitants	City
3,400,000	Berlin
1,600,000	Hamburg
1,200,000	Munich
1,000,000	Cologne
635,000	Frankfurt a.M.
624,000	Essen
594,000	Dortmund
574,000	Düsseldorf
570,000	Stuttgart
544,000	Bremen
532,000	Duisburg
530,000	Leipzig
506,000	Hanover
501,000	Dresden

The Federal Republic has much to be grateful to them for. They have made a large contribution to the country's economic growth and every year add roughly DM 100 billion to the gross national product. Most Germans and foreigners try to develop a harmonious relationship. Nonetheless, racial tensions do occur, as in all parts of the world, especially in some large cities where foreigners account for 20% or more of the population. This is only natural since it is not easy for workers from a different cultural region to adapt to an unfamiliar way of life. The second generation, the children of foreign workers who have grown up in Germany, are in a better position. Special efforts are being made to ensure they receive a good school and vocational education.

The German Government's policy is to try and integrate those foreigners and their families who have been living in Germany for many years. The aim is to enable them to play a full part in the country's economic, social and cultural life whilst preserving their native traditions and ties.

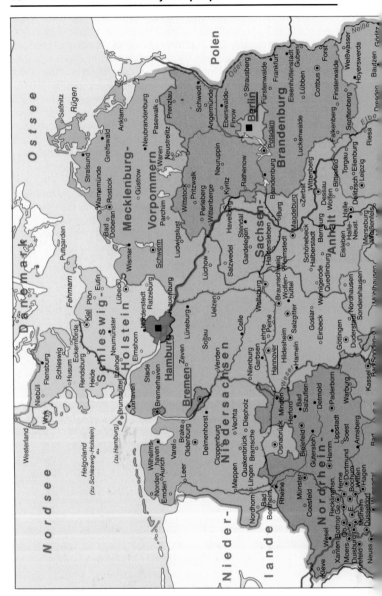

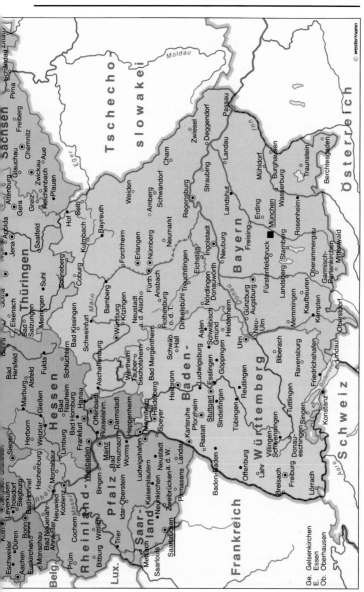

The 16 federal states

The Federal Republic of Germany consists of 16 states (Länder): Baden-Württemberg, Bavaria, Berlin, Brandenburg, Bremen, Hamburg, Hesse, Mecklenburg-Western Pomerania, Lower Saxony, North-Rhine/Westphalia, Rhineland-Palatinate, Saarland, Saxony, Saxony-Anhalt, Schleswig-Holstein and Thuringia.

Germany has always been divided into states but the map has changed its shape over the centuries. The most important changes in the modern age resulted from the Napoleonic wars at the beginning of the 19th century, the Austro-Prussian war of 1866, the First World War, and Germany's defeat in the Second World War. After the latter Germany was occupied and divided and the country's largest state, Prussia, dissolved. Most of the federal states as we know them today were established after 1945, but they have largely retained their ethnic traditions and characteristics and some of the old boundaries.

Until Germany was reunited the Federal Republic consisted of eleven states which had been created in the former western occupation zones and had adopted democratic constitutions between 1946 and 1957.

In the Soviet-occupied zone, which later became the German Democratic Republic, five states were formed, partly along the traditional lines, but as early as 1952 this structure was smashed by the east German regime and replaced by a centralized administration. Soon after the successful peaceful and democratic revolution in Germany in October 1989 the people began to demand the restoration of those former states. At mass rallies they called for freedom and German unification, waived the flags and coats of arms of the old states, and carried banners demanding the establishment of Brandenburg, Thuringia, Saxony and Saxony-Anhalt, Mecklenburg and Western Pomerania. Following the first free election in the former GDR on 18 March 1990, the parliament created five federal states. They replaced the 14 districts that had been formed by the communist regime in 1952 and were for the most part restored to the boundaries that existed prior to that date.

Then, on 3 October 1990, the German Democratic Republic, and hence the states of Brandenburg, Mecklenburg-Western Pomerania, Saxony, Saxony-Anhalt and Thuringia, acceded to the Federal Republic of Germany. At the same time East Berlin was merged with West Berlin.

State election 1992:	
CDU	39.6 %
SPD	29.4 %
Republicans	10.9 %
The Greens	9.5 %
FDP/DVP	5.9 %

Baden-Württemberg

Population	9.6 mill.
Area	35,751 sq km
Capital	Stuttgart

Baden-Württemberg

High-tech and cuckoo clocks. The landscape of Baden-Württemberg is as varied as its economic structure. This region has some of the country's most charming countryside. It embraces not only the Black Forest, a very popular recreational area in the central uplands, or Lake Constance, known locally as the "Swabian Sea", but also the green valleys of the Rhine and the Danube, the Neckar and the Tauber, the rugged Schwäbische Alb and the gentle Markgräflerland with its vineyards.

Not only blessed by nature, it is also ideal crossroads for transport and communications. The inventiveness and business sense of

The New State Gallery in Stuttgart

the people are proverbial, and their intellectual and artistic achievements fill many a chapter of German cultural and literary history, as testified by such names as the writers Friedrich Schiller (1759-1805) and Friedrich Hölderlin (1770-1843), or the philosophers Georg Wilhelm Friedrich Hegel (1770-1831) and Martin Heidegger (1889-1976).

The central Neckar region with the state capital Stuttgart (population 571,000) is Baden-Württemberg's industrial centre, which is based on traditional local crafts and modern private enterprise.

Half-timbered houses in Urach/Schwäbische Alb

Cars and microchips. Baden-Württemberg is a highly industrialized region and thus, in economic terms, one of Germany's most powerful states. Precision engineering, which is concentrated in the Black Forest of cuckoo clock fame, and the automotive industry have the longest tradition.

In and around Stuttgart are to be found the headquarters of such world famous firms as Daimler Benz, Bosch, IBM, SEL and the sports car manufacturer Porsche. Here, as everywhere else in Baden-Württemberg, there is a highly organized network of small and medium-sized firms who supply state-of-the-art parts and equipment to the big companies.

The strongest party is the CDU, which has supplied the minister-president since 1953. The south-west has long been a liberal stronghold and the FDP's share of the vote is now much the same as in the other federal states.

Adjacent to the central Neckar industrial region are Karlsruhe (265,000) with its oil refineries, Mannheim (300,000) and Heidelberg (131,000), which make buses and printing machinery respectively, but also Freiburg (183,000) and Ulm (106,000) with their extensive service industries.

Science and research. Among Baden-Württemberg's numerous academic and scientific institutions is the Nuclear Research Centre at Karlsruhe, the German Cancer Research Centre in Heidelberg, as well as several Max Planck Institutes and nine universities. Heidelberg University, founded in 1386, is the oldest in Germany, whereas Karlsruhe is home to Germany's oldest technical college. That city is also the seat of Germany's supreme courts, the Federal Court of Justice and the Federal Constitutional Court.

State election 1990:	
CSU	54.9 %
SPD	26 %
The Greens	6.4 %
FDP	5.2 %

Population	11.2 mill.
Area	70,554 sq km
Capital	Munich

The Free State of Bavaria

A white-and-blue tradition with a future. Bavaria is by far the largest of Germany's states and has the longest political tradition, there having been a Bavarian tribal dukedom as early as the 6th century. Bavaria owes much of its reputation as a tourist's paradise to its cultural heritage. Its charming landscapes provide the perfect background: the Alps, with Germany's highest mountain the Zugspitze (2,963 m), the picturesque lakes in the hilly alpine foreland, the Bavarian Forest with the first German national park, the Danube and Main valleys, a region of beautiful scenery and towns through which passes a "Romantic Route".

Bavaria is Germany's largest farming area. In former times Munich was considered the rural capital. After the Second World War it enjoyed calling itself "Germany's secret capital" and became the focal point of a rapidly growing industrial region (automobiles and aircraft, electrical engineering and electronics industry, insurance and publishing). And with its university and other institutions of higher education, the Max Planck Institute and its nuclear reactor, Bavaria's capital (population 1.2 million) is also a major academic and research centre.

Nuremberg (486,000) lies at the intersection of Europe's future motorway network stretching from Naples to Stockholm and from Lisbon via Prague to Warsaw. Together with Fürth and Erlangen, Nuremberg forms an industrial agglomeration focussing on engineering and the electrical and toy industries. Nuremberg's annual International Toy Fair is the most important of its kind. Augsburg (248,000) is home to the engineering and textile industries. Regensburg (119,000) has a young electrical and an even younger automobile industry (BMW). East Bavaria's glassworks (Zwiesel) and porcelain factories (Rosenthal, Hutschenreuther) carry on the region's famous crafts. Large parts of Bavaria, especially the Alps and the alpine foothills, are mainly

Munich against the background of the Bavarian Alps

farming areas. There are also hundreds of breweries which produce Bavaria's famous beer.

Culture from all ages. Regensburg has retained most of its medieval townscape. Nuremberg, the city of Albrecht Dürer (1471-1528), has some of the finest examples of late medieval treasures in its churches and museums, whereas Augsburg has the purest Renaissance heritage. The churches in Banz, Vierzehnheiligen, Ettal and Steingaden, whose "Wieskirche" appears in UNESCO's list of world cultural assets, as well as Würzburg, former residence of the prince-bishops, are outstanding examples of baroque and rococo architecture.

In Munich we find not only Germany's largest university but also the Deutsches Museum, the world's biggest exhibition of science and technology. The city also boasts numerous historic buildings, famous art galleries and theatres. The Herrenchiemsee, Linderhof and Neuschwanstein castles built by the "fairytale king" Ludwig II in the 19th

Modern architecture: Hypobank in Munich

century are tourist magnets. So too are the towns of Rothenburg, Nördlingen and Dinkelsbühl with their traditional semi-timbered houses.

State election 1990:	
CDU	40.4 %
SPD	30.4 %
PDS	9.2 %
FDP	7.1 %
Alternative List	5 %
Alliance 90 / Greens	4.4 %

Population	3.4 mill.
Area	883 sq km
Capital	Berlin

Berlin

A metropolis taking off. For decades Berlin was the symbol of Germany's division and of the East-West conflict. During the Cold War it was a flashpoint in the relationship between the western victorious powers and the Soviet Union. In 1948 only the unforgettable airlift enabled the West Berliners to survive an 11-month blockade of the city by the Soviet Union. Aircraft of the American Air Force, supported by the British and French allies, kept the people of West Berlin

Charlottenburg Palace

The Technology Centre of the Fraunhofer Society

ported by the British and French allies, kept the people of West Berlin supplied with vital necessities.

The three western sectors and East Berlin grew more and more apart. The city's partition seemed to be cemented for ever when the East Germans began to build that infamous wall on 13 August 1961. With his famous call "Ich bin ein Berliner" in 1963, US President John F. Kennedy endorsed his support for the city and its people. And in 1987 President Ronald Reagan, in a speech near the Brandenburg Gate, appealed to the Soviet Union to "tear down this wall". The wall was indeed opened - on 9 November 1989 - in the wake of the peaceful revolution in East Germany. That marked the beginning of a new chapter in the history of the 750-year-old city.

Germany's capital and a European cultural centre. Prior to its spiritual and cultural decline under the nazi dictatorship, and prior to the destruction caused by the Second World War, Berlin was not only the hub of German industry but, in the "golden twenties", also one of Europe's cultural capitals.

The capital of reunited Germany and the future seat of government continues to grow and it is estimated that by the year 2000 the metropolitan area will have a population of eight million.

Berlin is still Germany's largest industrial centre, focusing mainly on engineering, food and beverages, textiles and especially electrical goods. Two world famous companies were established there in the 19th century: Siemens and AEG. With Berlin as their base they have successfully coped with the transition to the information age.

There are many indications that the city will reestablish itself in the 90s as the largest window on German culture. For with Germany's division now a thing of the past, cultural roots, severed for decades, can grow together again and complement each other. Berlin boasts three opera houses (Deutsche Oper, Deutsche Staatsoper Unter den Linden, Komische Oper), several major orchestras and dozens of theatres, and it continues to be one of the world's greatest museum cities.

Berlin today has three large universities. In the eastern part of the city is the one named after the von Humboldt brothers, Wilhelm, the scholar and politician, and Alexander, a famous naturalist and traveller who lived from 1769 to 1859. In the western part are the Free University and the Technical University, both founded in 1948. Berlin also has many famous research establishments, such as the Hahn-Meitner Institute of Nuclear Physics, the Heinrich Hertz Institute of Communications Technology, and the Technology Centre of the Fraunhofer Society.

The reunited city faces tremendous challenges. The people in both parts of Berlin have to grow accustomed to one another again and the economic disparity will have to be overcome. Hundreds of thousands of flats, especially in the eastern districts, have to be brought up to standard. Unification has sparked an economic boom but it will have to be supported with social measures. Added impetus came from the decision of the Federal Parliament to make the capital the seat of government as well.

The Brandenburg Gate is open again

State election 1990:	
SPD	38.2 %
CDU	29.4 %
PDS	13.4 %
Alliance 90 / Greens	9.3 %
FDP	6.6 %

Population	2.6 mill.
Area	29,060 sq km
Capital	Potsdam

Brandenburg

The legacy of Frederick II, history and architecture. The state of Brandenburg encircles the German capital. Just outside Berlin lies the state capital of Potsdam (140,000), venue of the Potsdam Conference where, in the summer of 1945, the leaders of the United States, the United Kingdom and the Soviet Union took decisions which greatly affected the future of conquered Germany. Potsdam had been deliberately chosen for the conference because of its close association with Prussian-German history, King Frederick II (1712-1786) having made it his residence. Frederick's architectural masterpieces in Potsdam, especially those in the beautiful park of Sanssouci, outlived Prussia's existence as a state. It was there that the

Tourist attraction: Sanssouci Palace and park

Lübbenau, a typical village in the Spreewald

Prussian king held philosophical discussions with his friends, who included Voltaire (1694-1778). And there he also received other famous guests such as Johann Sebastian Bach (1685-1750).

Of Dutchmen and Huguenots. For a long time the thinly populated Brandenburg remained economically undeveloped. In order to rectify this situation its rulers opened the borders to large numbers of foreigners in the 17th and 18th centuries. Dutch immigrants as well as Protestants who had been expelled from France and Bohemia brought their knowledge and skills and contributed largely to the region's development. We are still reminded of this by such names of the "Dutch Quarter" and the "French Church" in Potsdam.

The countryside around Berlin has been impressively described by Theodor Fontane (1819-1898), a descendant of French Huguenots, in his famous "Walks in the March of Brandenburg".

Rye and steel. Agriculture and forestry are important branches of Brandenburg's economy. This region grows rye and wheat, potatoes and sugarbeet and, in a belt around Berlin, fruit and vegetables. The region's industrial centres are around Eisenhüttenstadt (steel) and Cottbus, where the lignite mines provide the raw materials for the chemical industry and energy. Mercedes Benz recently opened a truck assembly works in Ludwigsfelde to the south of Berlin. The company proposes to invest one billion marks there.

The old university town of Frankfurt on the Oder acquires a new significance now that visas are no longer required for travel between Germany and Poland.

Brandenburg is currently undergoing an economic and social transformation. It sees good prospects of sharing in Berlin's economic boom. There is talk of merging Brandenburg and Berlin into one federal state with Potsdam as the capital so as to facilitate the planning and development of Berlin as the federal capital.

The Free Hanseatic City of Bremen

The two-city state. Two cities, one state: Bremen and Bremerhaven are 65 km apart but nonetheless belong together. The old merchant city and the young maritime town constitute the smallest German state in terms of both area and population. Yet this Free Hanse-

The Bremen market square with town hall and cathedral

A view of Bremerhaven port

atic City of Bremen is, next to Bavaria, the oldest body politic in Germany, and after San Marino the second oldest city-republic in the world.

Bremen is also many centuries older than its sister city. Founded as a bishopric in 787, it quickly flourished, thanks to the privileges bestowed upon it as a market town. In the 11th century it was described as the "Rome of the North". In 1358 Bremen became a member of the Hanseatic League, which dominated trade in the North and Baltic Seas until well into the 16th century.

Risk and win. "Outside and in, risk and win", is the motto which tells of this city's growth. And it made it larger still because in 1827, when it seemed that the river Weser would be silted up, mayor Smidt founded a new port a little downstream - Bremerhaven, which, together with other townships, grew into a new city.

Bremen and Bremerhaven are fast transshipment ports. The more profitable small consignments (now transported in containers) are preferred to bulk goods. Bremen almost has a monopoly of imports of tea and coffee, tobacco and cotton. For other freight it competes with Hamburg, though no longer with its own fleet since its Norddeutscher Lloyd was merged with Hamburg's Hapag to form Hapag-Lloyd.

Bremen has explored new avenues in other fields as well. It made itself less dependent on maritime trade and shipbuilding by developping a highly productive aerospace industry. It has also resumed car production and is making its mark in the electronics sector. Whereas in former times all initiative came from the mercantile sector, innovation today is unthinkable without the aid of science. Bremerhaven is the focal point of German polar research. Also afloat there are the old barges and men-o'-war of the German Maritime Museum.

Bremen's "parlour". On the market place stands the Gothic cathedral of St. Peter and the magnificent Renaissance townhall with its very hospitable wine cellar. In front of it is Roland's column, symbol of the city's freedom and a local landmark, like the nearby monument to Bremen's "town musicians". From the market square the visitor enters the Böttcherstrasse, a narrow street full of legend built on the initiative of the merchant Roselius. It is a brick monument to Bremen's civic spirit.

State election 1991:	
SPD	48 %
CDU	35.1 %
GAL	7.2 %
FDP	5.4 %

Population	1.6 mill.
Area	755 sq km
Capital	Hamburg

The Free and Hanseatic City of Hamburg

Germany's gateway to the world. Hamburg is Germany's principal seaport and largest overseas trade and transshipment centre. The port's industrial area encompasses shipyards, refineries and proces-

The traditional warehouses in the port of Hamburg

sing plant for raw materials from abroad. In addition to these port-re-
lated activities, the aerospace, electronics, precision engineering, optical and chemical industries play an increasingly important role in
this city-state.

Hamburg began to flourish as a commercial town in 1189, when it
was granted customs and commercial rights. One of the first members of the Hanseatic League, it soon became the main transshipment port between the North Sea and the Baltic Sea. In 1460, and
then finally in 1510, Hamburg was raised to the status of an imperial

Hamburg, Germany's principal seaport

city - an autonomous status it has retained to this day. However, the devastating fire of 1842 and the Second World War spared but few of this commercial centre's medieval buildings.

A green industrial city. Hamburg is Germany's second largest industrial centre with a population of 2.8 million. Nonetheless the many boulevards and parks have retained its character as a "green city".

As a result of Germany's unification, the port of Hamburg, with its ramified links with the waterway network, has regained its old hinterland. This enhances the city-state's prospects of being the hub of trade, services and communications for the north and east, thus following in its old tradition. Reunification is also having a favourable impact on Hamburg's function as a banking and service centre for the whole of northern Germany. The fact that it is the world's principal consular city after New York underscores its international status. Hamburg's role as a media city is uncontested. It is home to Germany's largest periodicals, the German Press Agency (dpa), and television and radio broadcasting corporations.

Civic pride and passion for art. Hamburg has always been an attractive cultural city. It was here that Germany's first permanent opera house was established in 1678, where Georg Friedrich Händel (1685-1759) began to write operatic works. Later, one of the city's famous sons, the composer Johannes Brahms (1833-1897), though not enhancing the world of opera, produced masterpieces in nearly all forms of classical music: symphonies, chamber music, choral works, songs. In 1767 the Deutsches Nationaltheater was founded. It was linked with the name of Lessing and achieved fame chiefly on account of its performances of Shakespeare. At that time Friedrich Gottlieb Klopstock (1724-1803) and Matthias Claudius (1740-1815) were Hamburg's "literary institutions". In the present century Rolf Liebermann, director of Hamburg's opera house, and Gustaf Gründgens the actor, gave to opera and the theatre respectively a strong international flavour with their avantgard productions. Public generosity stemming from civic pride, and a far-sighted buying policy, have given Hamburg's Kunsthalle, Museum für Kunst und Gewerbe and Völkerkundemuseum, to name only three, outstanding collections.

State election 1991:	
SPD	40.8 %
CDU	40.2 %
The Greens	8.8 %
FDP	7.4 %

Population	5.7 mill.
Area	21,114 sq km
Capital	Wiesbaden

Hesse

The Rhein-Main crossroads. The central location of Hesse in the Federal Republic of Germany prior to the country's unification was a boon to its biggest city Frankfurt (635,000), Germany's main financial centre, and to its industrial fairs. This city is a huge autobahn intersection and railway junction, and it has the vast Rhein-Main airport which handles more passengers than any other European airport. Frankfurt on the river Main accommodates most of Germany's large banks and many branches of foreign banks in Germany. It is also the headquarters of the German Federal Bank, which watches over the stability of the deutschmark.

The market square in Bad Hersfeld/north Hesse

Frankfurt am Main and its skyscrapers

A business centre with cultural flair. The Rhein-Main region is Germany's second largest industrial centre after the Rhein-Ruhr district. It is home to such firms as Hoechst, Opel and Degussa. Other major industries (machinery, locomotives and waggons, automobiles) have established themselves in the northern part of the state around Kassel. This city has an excellent reputation among art lovers owing to its extensive collections of Dutch paintings and its "documenta" exhibitions of contemporary art from all over the world. Southern Hesse is home to the leather industry (Offenbach). This region's centre is Darmstadt with its famous Technical University and the Mathildenhöhe, a picturebook of art nouveau.

Frankfurt, too, birthplace of Johann Wolfgang von Goethe (1749-1832), is a city of art. The new museums on the Main embankment are striking evidence of this. The city also plays host to the theatre and the publishing trade. The International Book Fair, at which the Peace Prize of the German Book Trade Association is awarded annually, is the largest of its kind in the world. Every year the fair focuses on a particular country or region. Its theme in 1991 was Spain.

Amidst charming landscapes are the university towns of Marburg and Giessen, as well as Wetzlar, famous for its optical instruments. The

Bergstrasse and the Rheingau are among the best of Germany's fruit and wine-growing areas. In eastern Hesse is the bishopric of Fulda, a baroque town of considerable historical importance.

Republican tradition. Hesse has existed in its present form only since 1945. In previous centuries it had nearly always been split up. It became a focal point in the 16th century, when landgrave Philipp the Magnanimous became one of the political leaders of the Reformation. Frankfurt was for a long time a free imperial city and the place where German emperors were crowned.

Saint Paul's Church in Frankfurt has become a national monument. It was there in 1848/1849 that the National Assembly convened, the first democratic German Parliament. It failed, however, because of the power wielded by Germany's ruling princes.

The state capital, Wiesbaden, is not only an administrative centre but an elegant spa.

State election 1990:	
CDU	38.3 %
SPD	27 %
PDS	15.7 %
Alliance 90 / Greens	6.4 %
FDP	5.5 %

Population	1.95 mill.
Area	23,835 sq km
Capital	Schwerin

Mecklenburg-Western Pomerania

Land of a thousand lakes. No other German state is as rural, no other has such a varied coastline, and no other is as thinly populated as Mecklenburg-Western Pomerania.

Its striking brick architecture bears the unmistakable characteristics of the Hanseatic trade centres Stralsund and Wismar, and of the old university towns of Greifswald (founded in 1456) and Rostock. All of these Baltic towns have links with Scandinavia which go back centu-

The chalk cliffs of Rügen are a wonder of nature

North German brick architecture in Wismar

ries. Rostock, an old Hanseatic town, is today the region's largest city (250,000). However, it is Schwerin (130,000) which became the state capital after Germany's unification.

Nature and art. Mecklenburg-Western Pomerania is a gently undulating region with hundreds of lakes, a patchwork of fields, woods and livestock enclosures. Mecklenburg's largest lake is the Müritz (117 sq km), which has an extensive nature reserve along its eastern shore. There are countless testimonies to this region's rich cultural history, but most of them are in a state of repair.

A wonder of nature are the chalk cliffs on Rügen, Germany's largest island (926 sq km). Caspar David Friedrich (1774-1840) featured them in his paintings. This romantic from Greifswald inimitably captured the mystery of seascapes on canvas. The writer Fritz Reuter (1810-1874) vividly described the area and its people and in so doing made low German a language of literature. The sculptor and writer Ernst Barlach (1870-1938) spent his productive period in Güstrow. And Uwe Johnson (1934-1984) erected with his novels a literary monument to his native region and its people.

Tourism, the industry of tomorrow. The most important branches of the economy are farming and animal husbandry. The coastal and inland fishing industries are having to readjust to changing consumer demand.

As yet this region has seen little industry, but there are now growth centres like Neubrandenburg, which produces food, building materials and car tyres. The traditional shipbuilding industry on the coast now has to face the test of free competition. One shipyard specializing in the construction of vessels for inland waterways has already seized the opportunity afforded by a free market.

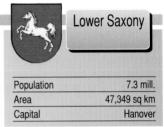

Lower Saxony

Lower Saxony

A variegated landscape. The second largest state in Germany can be subdivided into three main regions: the Harz, the Weserbergland (Weser Highlands) and the North German Lowlands around Lüneburg Heath. A world to themselves are the moors of the Emsland, the marshland behind the North Sea dikes, and the East Frisian islands in the shallow coastal waters.

The major north-south and west-east autobahn and railway arteries intersect in Lower Saxony, and here too the Elbe Canal links up the Rhine, Elbe and Oder, the principal waterways of western and eastern Europe.

Endless lines of cars: the Volkswagen factory in Wolfsburg

Hanover: the town hall on Lake Masch

Mining tradition and Volkswagen. Nearly two thirds of this region is given over to farming. It also has a long mining tradition especially in the Harz. Even in medieval times the imperial town of Goslar owed its wealth to silver mining. In 1775 a school for miners and foundry workers was established in Clausthal which developed into a world-famous mining college. Lüneburg gained prominence because of local salt deposits, and the potash industry is a major branch of Lower Saxony's economy. Salzgitter is the centre of Europe's third largest iron-ore deposit. Significant quantities of local oil and gas are also extracted, providing about 5% of the country's requirements. Emden has Germany's third largest port on the North Sea. Famous companies produce container vessels and automobiles there.

But one town in Lower Saxony epitomized car manufacturing in Germany: Wolfsburg, home of the famous Volkswagen. Volkswagen is the largest company in the region and its foundation the largest non-governmental scientific institution in Germany.

Hanover and the industrial fair, Göttingen and its university. Half a million of this state's 7.3 million inhabitants live in the capital, Hanover. It is the venue for the world famous industrial fair, and more lately for its "Cebit" display of communications technology. Every year they show the present generation the world of tomorrow.

The university town of Göttingen has played an outstanding role in the country's political and scientific history. In 1837 a group of professors, the "Göttingen Seven", protested against the sovereign's decision to annul the constitution. This led to their dismissal, but most of these liberal spirits were deputies to the National Assembly in Frankfurt in 1848. Another famous name associated with Göttingen is that of the mathematician and astronomer Carl Friedrich Gauss (1771-1859), a genius of his century.

In the 20th century Göttingen has been a source of major developments in the field of nuclear physics. Of all those who taught or studied in Göttingen one need only mention the Nobel Prize winners Max Born (1882-1970) and Werner Heisenberg (1901-1976).

Katz Castle overlooks the Rhine at St. Goarshausen

main economic artery. Rhineland-Palatinate's three main cities are also situated on the Rhine: Ludwigshafen (158,000), the chemical centre, Mainz (175,000), the state capital, and Koblenz (107,000), the service centre. A little off the beaten track, as it were, and with a population of just under 100,000 are Kaiserslautern and Trier, the 2,000-year-old city on the Mosel.

One of Germany's most beautiful landscapes is the stretch of the Rhine valley between Bingen and the Siebengebirge near Bonn in North-Rhine/Westphalia. It is steeped in legend and its praises have been sung by countless poets and musicians. At the foot of the Palatinate Forest runs the "German Wine Route". The silver light above this charming hilly area was captured by the painter Max Slevogt (1868-1932). Many of his pictures are to be found in Ludwigshöhe Palace near Edenkoben. Some are also to be found, together with works by Hans Purrmann (1880-1966) who was "ostracized" by the nazi regime, in the Federal Chancellery in Bonn.

Yesterday and today. The Rhineland was settled by Celts, Romans, Burgundians and Franks. In Speyer, Worms and Mainz, all on the Rhine, are to be found the great imperial cathedrals of the Middle Ages. The elector of Mainz was archchancellor of the "Holy Roman Empire of the German Nation". Worms has Germany's oldest synagogue (construction of which began in 1034 in the romanesque style). It was

Relics of Roman times: the Porta Nigra in Trier

in Worms too, at the imperial diet of 1521, that the reformer Martin Luther showed his defiance. In Koblenz the liberal paper "Rheinischer Merkur" opposed Napoleonic rule and censorship of the press, and Hambach Castle was the scene of the first democratic-republican assembly in Germany (1832). The Print Museum in Mainz displays the treasures of Johannes Gutenberg (1400-1468), the inventor of book-printing using movable characters. Trier is the birthplace of Karl Marx (1818-1893), the philosopher and critic of the national economy.

Rhineland-Palatinate was formed in 1946 from parts of Bavarian, Hessian and Prussian territory which previously had never belonged together. In the meantime they have become closely knit and Rhineland-Palatinate has acquired its own identity.

State election 1990:	
SPD	50 %
CDU	36.7 %
FDP	5.8 %
The Greens	5 %

North-Rhine/Westphalia

Population	17.3 mill.
Area	34,068 sq km
Capital	Düsseldorf

North-Rhine/Westphalia

A powerhouse in the heart of Europe. North-Rhine/Westphalia is as large as Belgium and Luxembourg together. Not only is it the most densely populated state in the Federal Republic (17 million), it is also Europe's largest industrial centre. About half of this region's population live in cities with more than 500,000 inhabitants. The Ruhr district is an agglomeration of towns and cities with a total population of about 7.5 million, and it is Germany's, indeed Europe's, largest industrial region. With its 31 huge power stations the Ruhr is Germany's main source of energy.

Tradition and innovation. In a massive effort on the part of industry, the regional and the federal government over many years, North-Rhine/Westphalia has succeeded in restructuring its economy, which is traditionally based on coal and steel. Hundreds of thousands of new jobs have been created through the settlement of innovative industries, with the result that today it is the future-oriented branches that dominate the scene. Proof of the region's economic dynamism is the fact that, apart from heavy industry, there are 450,000 small and medium-sized firms, many of whom have state-of-the-art technology. A traditional yet expanding branch of the service sector is that of insurance, while Dortmund is the location of Germany's largest breweries.

The most visible sign of North-Rhine/Westphalia's dynamic economy is the dense network of autobahns, railways and waterways. It incorporates Europe's traffic arteries and links together the region's principal cities of Cologne, Essen, Dortmund, Düsseldorf, Duisburg, Bochum, Wuppertal, Bielefeld, Gelsenkirchen, Solingen, Leverkusen and Aachen. Duisburg has the largest inland port in the world.

Leisure, culture, and higher education. This coalmining region is undergoing a transformation. Former landscapes of smoking chimney stacks and conveyor belts are turning increasingly green. The open-cast mining areas on the Rhine are now being replaced by lakes fit to swim in. The Sauerland and the Bergisches Land are popular recreational areas, particularly for people on the Rhine and Ruhr. Hardly any other region in Germany can boast so much cultural activity as the Ruhr. Here there are more theatres than in New York.

Cologne, now the region's largest city (over a million) and a major centre since Roman times, is famous for its romanesque churches and Gothic cathedral, but also for its museums (Wallraf Richartz Museum/Museum Ludwig, Roman-Germanic Museum). Düsseldorf (574,000), the state capital, is one of the country's main financial centres. It has made its name as a cultural city through its outstanding collections of paintings, its Deutsche Oper am Rhein (Düsseldorf/ Duisburg), and its famous Schauspielhaus.

Münster in Westphalia, one of Germany's most beautiful cities, has a major university. Together with many other institutions throughout the state, it forms the heaviest concentration of universities, colleges and academies in Europe.

South of Cologne lies Bonn, until 1949 a medium-sized university town, but from that year until the country's unification capital of the Federal Republic of Germany. Although the seat of the Federal Government is to be switched to Berlin, Bonn will continue to play an important role as an administrative centre.

Duisburg has the world's largest inland port

A view of Bonn: the Siebengebirge in the background

North-Rhine/Westphalia was established in 1946. The British, who occupied the region at that time, amalgamated the bulk of the former Prussian Rhine Province with the Province of Westphalia and the state of Lippe-Detmold. Over the years the local population, as in the other newly created states, developed their own regional consciousness.

State election 1991:	
SPD	44.8 %
CDU	38.7 %
FDP	6.9 %
The Greens	6.5 %

Rhineland-Palatinate

Population	3.7 mill.
Area	19,848 sq km
Capital	Mainz

Rhineland-Palatinate

A region of superlatives. One of the smaller German states, it is in one respect the biggest: the vineyards on the Rhine, the Ahr and the Mosel yield two thirds of the country's wine. Initially one of the poorer regions, it is today the state with the largest export quota and seat of Europe's largest chemical corporation, BASF. Every year six million visitors seek recreation in Rhineland-Palatinate, and also curative treatment from the thermal and mineral waters of the region's famous spas. Every third litre of mineral water in Germany gushes from springs in Rhineland-Palatinate.

The Rhine, the region's main artery. 80% of the population live on the "Rhine axis", the 290 km section of the river which is the region's

The main BASF works is on the Rhine in Ludwigshafen

beginning in January 1993, especially in the mechanical engineering, metal-processing and chemical industries.

The Saarland's savoir vivre. Traditional branches of industry of supraregional importance are glass and ceramics. The distinctive features of goods produced by large companies such as Villeroy & Boch are high quality as well as richness of form and colour - a symbiosis, perhaps, of German thoroughness and French charm.

In fact, it seems that the people of this area in general have acquired a touch of the French savoir vivre. They have a partiality for culinary delights and wine, and on a fine day their capital is like an open-air stage. A native of the city, the director Max Ophüls (1902-1957), made film history with such charming though melancholy comedies as "Liebelei".

Saxony

State election 1990:	
CDU	53.8 %
SPD	19.1 %
PDS	10.2 %
Alliance 90 / Greens	5.6 %
FDP	5.3 %

Population	4.8 mill.
Area	18,300 sq km
Capital	Dresden

Saxony

Porcelain, art, microelectronics. Saxony is outstanding among the new German states in three respects: it is the most densely populated, it is the most industrialized, and it was in the vanguard of the peaceful revolution that resulted in German unity.

More than one fifth of Saxony's 4.9 million inhabitants live in Leipzig (530,000) and Dresden (501,000). Leipzig, famous for its international industrial fair and referred to by Goethe as "little Paris", was one of the main centres of non-violent resistance to the Communist regime in East Germany. The "Monday demonstrations" culminated on 9 October 1989 in the chant: "We are the people!" And Dresden, that

The Semper Opera House in Dresden

"pearl of baroque architecture" which was reduced almost to ashes in the inferno of the 1945 bombings, has been made capital of the restored "Free State of Saxony". The Meissen porcelain factory has been producing its famous merchandise continuously since 1710. The year before, Johann Friedrich Böttger (1682-1719) had produced his formula for this "white gold".

Chemnitz, with its Technical University and research institutes, focuses on mechanical engineering and, of late, microelectronics. Zwickau is a car manufacturing centre, though instead of the legendary Trabant ("Trabi") Volkswagen's "Polo" is now produced there.

Leipzig: The new Gewandhaus and the university building

The tradition of car building is continued in Zwickau

Leipzig, once Germany's most important commercial centre and hub of the publishing world, will continue its international trade fair, which makes it a gateway to Eastern Europe. Dresden hopes to be able to live up to its reputation as one of Germany's cultural centres. It is still a leading city in the world of music, with the Semper Opera House which has been restored to its former glory, the Staatskapelle, and its famous choir, the Kreuzchor. It is an El Dorado of the visual arts with its extensive collections of precious stones, pearls and works of art in the Grünes Gewölbe and its paintings by European masters in the Gemäldegalerie Alte Meister.

Creative energy and enterprising spirit. Saxony features in many chapters of German cultural history. The works of Johann Sebastian Bach (born in Eisenach in 1685) are traditionally performed by the Thomasschule in Leipzig where he was cantor from 1723 until his death in 1750. Gottfried Wilhelm Leibniz (1646-1716), philosopher, mathematician and diplomat, discovered the binary number system and – independently of Newton – infinitesimal calculus. Gotthold Ephraim Lessing (1729-1781) extolled in his drama Nathan the Wise the virtues of humanity and tolerance. Other sons of Saxony are the composers Robert Schumann (1810-1856) and Richard Wagner (1813-1883).

Even when eastern Germany had a centrally planned economy the Saxons retained their artistic and business sense, with the result that Saxon enterprise is beginning to reassert itself. Of the new federal states, this one is considered to have the best economic prospects.

State election 1990:	
CDU	39 %
SPD	26 %
FDP	13.5 %
PDS	12 %
Alliance 90 / Greens	5.3 %

Population	2.96 mill.
Area	20,445 sq km
Capital	Magdeburg

Saxony-Anhalt

The Halle-Magdeburg-Dessau triangle. This region is only thinly populated, particularly in the northern parts, Altmark and Magdeburger Börde, which are mainly given over to farming (wheat, sugarbeet and vegetables). Nearly one in five of the state's three million inhabitants live in Halle (235,000), Magdeburg (290,000), and Dessau (104,000).

Halle, Bitterfeld, Leuna, Wolfen, and Merseburg, hitherto centres of the chemical and lignite mining industries, are in a phase of radical

The Bauhaus in Dessau influenced architecture throughout the world

Courtyard in Wernigerode, the "colourful city in the Harz"

change as a result of the misguided policies of the former German Democratic Republic. Extensive investment to reverse environmental pollution and create a new infrastructure will have to be maintained for many years. The nucleus of the region's traditional chemical industry is to be preserved, however.

The decision in 1990 to make Magdeburg, which has a Technical University and a School of Medicine and is a centre of heavy engineering, capital of Saxony-Anhalt, settled the traditional rivalry with Halle, at least in this respect. Both cities have a distinctive medieval past. The cathedral of Magdeburg, seat of emperors and bishops, is one of the largest in Germany. The old salt town of Halle, birthplace of the composer Georg Friedrich Händel (1685-1759), is dominated by the cathedral, the Marktkirche and the Red Tower. The German-American painter Lyonel Feininger (1871-1956) captured the city's landmarks with his fascinatingly modernistic style. His works and those of his contemporaries are to be found in Moritzburg's Staatliche Galerie. But one of the major centres of 20th century art was Dessau, thanks mainly to its Bauhaus school of architecture.

Classical central Germany. Saxony-Anhalt is the classical embodiment of central Germany on the rivers Elbe and Saale, covering the area between the Harz mountains, with Brocken (3,500 ft), the Blocksberg in Goethe's Faust, and the Fläming, a ridge of hills in the east, between the Auwiesen in the north and the vineyards along the Saale and Unstrut. Halberstadt's cathedral, originally built in the romanesque style, and the monument to the "Merseburg spells" which is over a thousand years old, bear witness to a historical continuity from the days of Charlemagne. In many towns the past has lived on. Tangermünde, with its brick architecture, is regarded as the "Rothenburg of the North". Wernigerode, a jewel of semi-timbered buildings, is commonly known as the "colourful town in the Harz region". The medieval figures depicting the founders of Naumburg's cathedral are early examples of realistic representation. Eisleben is where Martin Luther (1483-1546) was born and died. He was buried in Wittenberg's Schlosskirche, to the door of which he nailed his 95 theses in 1517. At the royal court in Köthen Johann Sebastian Bach composed his six Brandenburg concertos, each with a different form and instrumentation but all of equal beauty.

State election 1992:	
SPD	46.2 %
CDU	33.8 %
DVU	6.3 %
FDP	5.6 %
SSW	1.9 %

Population	2.6 mill.
Area	15,700 sq km
Capital	Kiel

Schleswig-Holstein

Forever undivided. Schleswig-Holstein is the only German state bordered by two seas, the North Sea and the Baltic. An ancient deed says that the region's two parts, Schleswig and Holstein, should remain "undivided forever". Consequently, they have long been linked as Schleswig-Holstein - unlike those regions which were "hyphenated" by the occupying powers after 1945.

Schleswig-Holstein is thinly populated (2.6 million inhabitants). The state capital Kiel (244,000) and the Hanseatic City of Lübeck (213,000) owe their importance to their position on the Baltic. Lübeck-Travemünde is one of Germany's principal ferry ports.

The Holstentor: a part of the Lübeck World Cultural Monument

Helgoland: the island of red rock in the German Bight

Farming and commerce. In former times Schleswig-Holstein was an exclusively agricultural area (mainly livestock farming) and this branch of the economy is still predominant in the fertile marshlands along the western coast. The coastal fishing industry on the North Sea and the Baltic is also proud of its tradition.

In the Middle Ages and in early modern times Flensburg had one of the largest sail fleets in the North and dominated the route to the West Indies. Lübeck, on the other hand, owed its prosperity to the grain trade, whereas Kiel grew with the navy.

The region's seafaring tradition led to the development of a major shipbuilding industry. As a result of the crisis in this sector in the late 60s, some companies successfully switched to the construction of special vessels. Another solution was to develop a wide range of small and medium-sized industries. This caused a particularly lively economic upswing in these northern parts of the country around Hamburg.

Tourism – a growth industry. The North Sea island of Helgoland, where Hoffmann von Fallersleben composed his German anthem in 1841, as well as the North Frisian Islands, including the fashionable Sylt and Föhr, a popular family resort, have their regular visitors just like the resorts on the Baltic Sea, the modern Damp being no different from the dreamy town of Hohwacht in this respect. Nature friends are drawn by the Wattenmeer (mud flats) National Park on the North Sea.

Inland, the area known as "Holstein's Switzerland" with its lakes is another tourist attraction. Other towns worth visiting are Mölln and the cathedral town of Schleswig, famous for its late Gothic Bordesholm altar created by Hans Brüggemann between 1514 and 1521, a masterpiece of woodcarving.

World cultural heritage and world literature. Lübeck, whose 500-year-old gate, the Holstentor, bears the inscription in Latin "harmony at home, peace outside", has been entered in UNESCO's world cultural list as a German contribution to world culture.

Thomas Mann (1885-1955), a writer of world fame, was born in Lübeck. He was awarded the 1929 Nobel Prize for literature.

Kiel Week denotes the famous regatta which every year attracts yachtsmen from all over the world.

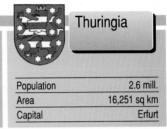

State election 1990:	
CDU	45.4 %
SPD	22.8 %
PDS	9.7 %
FDP	9.3 %
Alliance 90 / Greens	6.5 %

Population	2.6 mill.
Area	16,251 sq km
Capital	Erfurt

Thuringia

Germany's green heartland. On account of its position and extensive forest areas Thuringia is also referred to as "Germany's green heartland".

The state capital is Erfurt (217,000), which was founded in the eighth century and is proud to be called a "garden city". The old part of the city has an unusually large number of Patrician houses, churches and monasteries which make it a kind of architectural museum.

Johann Sebastian Bach was born in Eisenach in 1685, one of a ramified family of musicians. He died in Leipzig in 1750. Martin Luther hid in the nearby Wartburg in 1521/22. There he translated the New

The Wartburg, a popular tourist attraction

Testament into German – a major step in the development of modern written German. And at the same place in 1817 students called for a united Germany.

Territorial fragmentation, culture and barbarity. Thuringia was particularly affected by Germany's much lamented territorial fragmentation. But culturally this proved to be a good thing since the rulers of even small territories were keen patrons of the arts. By far the

The Krämer Bridge, a jewel of the old part of Erfurt

most prominent among them was Duke Karl August of Saxony-Weimar (1757-1828). He brought to his court the romantic poet and translator of Shakespeare Christoph Martin Wieland (1733-1813), the poet and philologist Johann Gottfried Herder (1744-1803), and above all Johann Wolfgang von Goethe (1749-1832).

Thus at that time, around 1800, Weimar was a capital of culture, and not only of German culture. In this city Goethe produced some of his most famous works, including the final version of Faust. Weimar was also home to Friedrich Schiller from 1787 to 1789 and from 1799 to 1805. There he wrote, among other works, his William Tell. Franz Liszt (1811-1886) composed and gave concerts there in the second half of the 19th century. Here the Bauhaus was founded in 1919, a school of architecture which sought to overcome the divisions between art, handicraft and technology. In 1925 the Bauhaus moved to Dessau, and a few years later to Berlin, where, in 1933, it fell victim to the barbarity which followed Hitler's seizure of power. The year 1933 also marked the demise of the first German Republic, the "Weimar Republic", whose constitution had been drafted in Weimar in 1919.

Industry and crafts. In medieval times several Thuringian towns, especially Erfurt, became rich through trade with a blue-dyeing plant, the woad. Other branches of the economy grew up later, including machine tools and precision and optical instruments, which made the city of Jena and the name of Carl Zeiss, the mechanic, world famous. Automobiles have been manufactured in Eisenach for some considerable time (in GDR times a famous make was the "Wartburg"). Since German unification the firm of Opel has been operating there. This region is also famous for its traditional crafts.

A brief German history up to 1945

Up to last century it was a widely held belief that German history began in the year A. D. 9. That was when Arminius, a prince of a Germanic tribe called the Cherusci, vanquished three Roman legions in the Teutoburg Forest (south-east of modern-day Bielefeld). Arminius, about whom not much else is known, was regarded as the first German national hero and a huge memorial to him was built near Detmold in the years 1838-1875.

Nowadays a less simplistic view is taken. The fusing of a German nation was a process which took hundreds of years. The word "deutsch" (German) probably began to be used in the 8th century and initially defined only the language spoken in the eastern part of the Franconian realm. This empire, which reached the zenith of its power under Charlemagne, incorporated peoples speaking Germanic and Romance dialects. After Charlemagne's death (814) it soon fell apart. In the course of various inheritance divisions, a west and an east realm developed, whose political boundary approximately coincided with the boundary between German and French speakers. Only gradually did a feeling of cohesion develop among the inhabitants of the eastern realm. Then the term "deutsch" was transferred from the language to its speakers and ultimately to the region they lived in, "Deutschland."

The German western frontier was fixed relatively early and remained fairly stable. But the eastern frontier moved to and fro for hundreds of years. Around 900 it ran approximately along the Elbe and Saale rivers. In subsequent centuries German settlement, partly peaceful and partly by force, expanded far eastward. This expansion stopped only in the middle of the 14th century. The ethnic boundary then made between Germans und Slavs remained until World War II.

High Middle Ages. The transition from the East Franconian to the German "Reich" is usually dated from 911, when, after the Carolingian dynasty had died out, the Franconian duke Conrad I was elected king. He is regarded as the first German king. (The official title was "Frankish King," later "Roman King," from the 11th century the name of the realm was "Roman Empire," from the 13th century "Holy Roman Empire," in the 15th century the words "of the German Nation" were added.) It was an electoral monarchy, that is to say that the high nobility chose the king. In addition, "dynastic right" also applied and so the new king had to be a blood relation of his predecessor. This principle was broken several times. There was also a number of double elections. The medieval empire had no capital city; the king ruled roving about from place to place. There were no imperial taxes; the king drew his sustenance mainly from "imperial estates" he administered in trust. His authority was not always recognised by the powerful tribal dukes unless he was militarily strong and a skilful forger of alliances. Conrad's successor, Henry I (919-936), was the first to succeed in this, and to an even greater extent his son, Otto (936-973). Otto made himself the real ruler of the realm. His great power found obvious expression when he was crowned Emperor in 962 in Rome.

From then on the German king could claim the title Emperor. The emperorship was conceived as universal and made its incumbent ruler of the entire Occident. However, this notion never became full political reality. For the coronation as emperor by the Pope the king had to make his way to Rome. With that began the Italian policy of the German kings. For 300 years they were able to retain control of upper and central Italy but because of this were diverted from important tasks in Germany. And so Otto's successors inevitably suffered big setbacks. However, under the succeeding Salian dynasty a new upswing occurred. With Henry III (1039-1056) the German kingship and emperorship reached the zenith of its power, maintaining above all a supremacy over the Papacy. Henry IV (1056-1106) was not able to hold this position. In a quarrel with Pope Gregory VII over whether bishops and other influential church officials should be appointed by the Pope or the temporal ruler he was superficially successful. But Gregory retaliated by excommunicating Henry, who thereupon surrendered his authority over the church by doing penance to the pope at Canossa (1077), an irretrievable loss of power by the emperorship. (To this day Germans use the phrase "A walk to Canossa" for someone having to eat humble pie). From then on emperor and pope were equal-ranking powers.

In 1138 the century of rule by the Staufer or Hohenstaufen dynasty began. Frederick I Barbarossa (1115-1190), in wars with the pope, the upper Italian cities and his main German rival, the Saxon duke, Henry the Lion, led the empire into a new golden age. But under him began a territorial fragmentation which ultimately weakened the central power. This weakening continued under Barbarossa's successors, Henry VI (1190-1197) and Frederick II (1212-1250) despite the great power vested in the emperorship. The religious and temporal princes became semi-sovereign territorial rulers. The end of Hohenstaufen rule (1268) meant the end of the universal Occidental emperorship, too. Internal disintegrative forces prevented Germany from becoming a national state, a process just beginning then in other west European countries. Here lies one of the roots for the Germans' becoming a "belated nation."

Late Middle Ages to modern times. Rudolf I (1273-1291) was the first Habsburg to take the throne. Now the material foundation of the emperorship was no longer the lost imperial estates but the "house estates" of the dynasties and house power politics became every emperor's main preoccupation. The "Golden Bull" (imperial constitution) issued by Charles IV in 1356 regulated the election of the German king by seven electors privileged with special rights. These sovereign electors and the towns, because of their economic power, gradually gained influence while that of the small counts, lords and knights declined. The towns' power further increased when they linked up in leagues. The most important of these, the Hanseatic League, became the leading Baltic power in the 14th century. To this day the city-states of Hamburg and Bremen proudly call themselves "Hanseatic cities."

From 1438 the crown — although the empire nominally was an electoral monarchy — practically became the property of the Habsburg dynasty which had become the strongest territorial power. In the 15th century demands to reform the empire increased. Maximilian I (1483 to 1519), the first to accept the imperial title without a papal coronation, tried to implement such a reform but without much success. The institutions newly created or reshaped by him — Reichstag (Imperial Diet), Reichskreise (Imperial Counties), Reichskammergericht (Imperial Court) — lasted until the end of the Reich (1806), but were not able to halt its continuing fragmentation. Consequently, a dualism of "Emperor and Reich" developed: the head of the Reich was offset by various institutions — electoral princes, princes and municipalities. The power ot the emperors was curtailed and increasingly eroded by "capitulations," which they negotiated at their election with the electoral princes. The princes, especially the powerful among them, greatly expanded their rights at the expense of imperial power. But the Reich continued to hold together, the glory of the imperial idea had remained alive and the

Emperor Karl IV and the seven electors
(Armorial, around 1370, Bibliothèque Royale Albert Ier, Brussels)

small and medium territories were protected in the Reich system from attack by powerful neighbours.

The towns became centres of economic power, profiting above all from growing trade. In the burgeoning textile and mining industries, forms of economic activity grew which went beyond the guilds system of the craftsmen and, like long-distance trading, were beginning to take on early capitalistic traits. At the same time an intellectual change was taking place, marked by the Renaissance and Humanism. The newly risen critical spirit turned above all on the church.

Age of religious schism. The smouldering dissatisfaction with the church broke out, mainly through the actions of Martin Luther from 1517, in the Reformation, which quickly spread. Its consequences went far beyond the religious sphere. The entire social structure began to stir with change. In 1522/23 the Reich knights rose up and in 1525 the Peasants' Revolt broke out, the first major revolutionary movement in German history to strive for both political and social change. Both uprisings failed or were brutally quelled. The territorial princes profited most from the Reformation. After changing fortunes of war they were given the right to dictate their subject's religion by the 1555 Peace of Augsburg. This accorded the Protestants equal rights with those of the Catholics. With that, the religious division of Germany was established.

Peasants in revolt (woodcut by Hans Burgkmair, 1525)

On the imperial throne at the time of the Reformation was Charles V (1519-1556), heir to the biggest realm since the time of Charlemagne but also the last Holy Roman emperor to aspire to the medieval ideal of universal empire. His international political interests were too demanding for him to be able to assert himself within Germany. After his abdication the empire was split up. The German territorial states and the west European nation-states together now formed the new European system of states.

At the time of the Peace of Augsburg, four fifths of Germany were Protestant but the struggle between the faiths had not ended with it. In following decades the Catholic church was able to recapture many areas (Counter-Reformation). The differences between the faiths sharpened, religious parties — the Protestant Union (1608) and the Catholic League (1609) — were formed. A local conflict in Bohemia then triggered off the Thirty Years War which widened into a European conflict over religious and political differences. Between 1618 and 1648 much of Germany was devastated and depopulated. The 1648 Peace of Westphalia brought the cession of territories to France and Sweden and confirmed the withdrawal of Switzerland and the Netherlands from the Reich. The Reich estates were accorded all major sovereign rights in religious and temporal matters and the right to enter alliances with foreign partners.

Age of Absolutism. The almost sovereign principalities took over the absolutist form of government modelled on the French.

Absolutism gave the ruler limitless power while at the same time allowing tight administrations to be built up, an organised fiscal policy to be introduced and new armies to be mobilised. Many princes aspired to making their residences cultural focal points. Some of them — representatives of "enlightened absolutism" — encouraged learning and philosophy, albeit within the confines of their power interests. The policy of state control of all economic life also allowed the absolutist states to build up their economic strength. Thus lands such as Bavaria, Brandenburg (the later Prussia), Saxony and Hanover were able to develop into power centres in their own right. Austria, which repelled the attacking Turks and acquired Hungary as well as parts of the formely Turkish Balkan countries, rose to a large power. A rival to it developed in the 18th century in the form of Prussia which,

Fireworks at the Dresden Court
(engraving by Johann August Corvinus, 1719)

under Frederick the Great (1740-1786), grew into a first-rank military power. Both states pursued European big power policies.

Age of the French Revolution. The nudge which brought the crumbling Reich crashing down came from the West. Revolution broke out in France in 1789. Under pressure from the middle classes, the feudal social order which had existed since the early middle ages was swept away; a divison of powers and human rights were to assure the liberty and equality of all. The attempt by Prussia and Austria to intervene by force in the events in the neighbouring country failed ignominiously and triggered a counter-thrust by the revolutionary armies. Under the stormy advances of the forces of Napoleon who had assumed the revolutionary heritage in France the Reich finally collapsed. France took the left bank of the Rhine. To compensate the former owners of these areas for their losses, an enormous territorial reshuffling took place at the expense of the smaller and particularly the religious principalities. By the "Reichsdeputationshauptschluss" of 1803 some four million subjects had changed rulers. The medium-sized states were the beneficiaries. In 1806 most of them grouped together under French protection in the "Rheinbund" (Rhenish League). In the same year Emperor Franz II laid down the crown and with that the Holy Roman Empire of the German Nation ceased to be.

The French revolution did not spread into Germany. Although there, too, various individuals had over the years tried time and again to do away with the barriers between the aristocracy and the common people and although leading thinkers welcomed the overthrow in the west as the start of a new era one major reason why the spark could not catch easily was that, in contrast to the centrally oriented France, the federalistic structure of the Reich hampered the spread of new ideas. Another big reason was that France, the motherland of the revolution, opposed the Germans as an enemy and an occupying power. Indeed, the struggle against Napoleon forged a new national movement which culminated in wars of liberation. But Germany did not remain unaffected by the forces of social change. First in the "Rheinbund" states and then in Prussia (in the latter connected with names like Stein, Hardenberg, Scharnhorst, W. von Humboldt) reforms were begun, aimed at breaking down feudal barriers and creating a society of free, responsible citizens. The objectives were abolition of serfdom, freedom of trade, municipal self-administration, equality before the law, general conscription. But many reform moves were pulled up short. Participation by the populace in legislation was refused almost everywhere. Only hesitantly did some princes grant their states constitutions, especially in southern Germany.

The German Confederation. After the victory over Napoleon the Congress of Vienna (September 1814 to June 1815) redrew the map of Europe. The hopes of many Germans for a free, unitary nation-state were not fulfilled. The "Deutscher Bund" (German Confederation) which replaced the old Reich was a loose association of the individual sovereign states. Its sole organ was the "Bundestag" (Federal Diet) in Frankfurt, not an elected but a delegated diet. It was able to act only if the two great powers, Prussia and Austria, agreed. It saw its main task in the ensuing decades in suppressing all aspirations and efforts aimed at unity and freedom. Press and publishing were subject to rigid censorship, the universities were under close supervision and political activity was virtually impossible.

Meanwhile a modern economic development which worked against these reactionary tendencies had begun. In 1834 the "German Customs Union" (Deutscher Zollverein) was founded, creating a unitary inland market. In 1835 the first German railway line

Frankfurt National Assembly (lithograph)

went into operation. Industrialisation began. With the factories there grew the new class of factory workers. At first they found better incomes; but the rapid growth of the population soon led to a labour surplus. And since there were no social welfare provisions, the mass of factory workers lived in great misery. Tensions exploded violently, for example in the 1844 uprising of the Silesian weavers, which was harshly put down by the Prussian military. Very hesitantly at first, a workers' movement began to form.

The 1848 revolution. In contrast to the revolution of 1789, the French February revolution of 1848 found immediate response in Germany. In March there were uprisings in all states, and these forced many concessions from the stunned princes. In May the National Assembly (Nationalversammlung) convened in Frankfurt's Paulskirche (St. Paul's Church). It elected Austrian archduke Johann Imperial Administrator (Reichsverweser) and set up a Reich Ministry which, however, had no powers or authority. The tune was called in the National Assembly by the Liberal centre, which strove for a constitutional monarchy with limited suffrage. The splintering of the National Assembly from Conservatives to Radical Democrats which already indicated the spectrum of parties to come made it difficult to draw up a constitution. But not even the Liberal centre could overcome the differences between the protagonists of "greater Germany" and "smaller Germany" concepts, that is a German Reich with or without Austria. Hard bargaining produced a democratic constitution which attempted to combine old and new ideas and required a government responsible to parliament. But when Austria insisted on bringing into the future Reich its entire realm, encompassing more than a dozen different peoples, the "smaller Germany" concept won the day and the National Assembly proffered Friedrich Wilhelm IV (Frederick William) of Prussia the hereditary German imperial crown. The king turned it down, not wanting to owe imperial majesty to a revolution. In May 1849 popular uprisings in Saxony, the Palatinate and Baden which aimed at enforcing the constitution "from below" failed. That was the seal on the failure of the whole revolution. Most of the achievements were rescinded, the constitutions of the individual states reactionarily revised. In 1850 the German Confederation was refounded.

The rise of Prussia. The 1850s were years of great economic upswing. Germany became an industrial country. Although its

Roman-German Empire (c. 950)

Holy Roman Empire of the German Nation after the Peace of Westphalie (1648)

Swedish possession

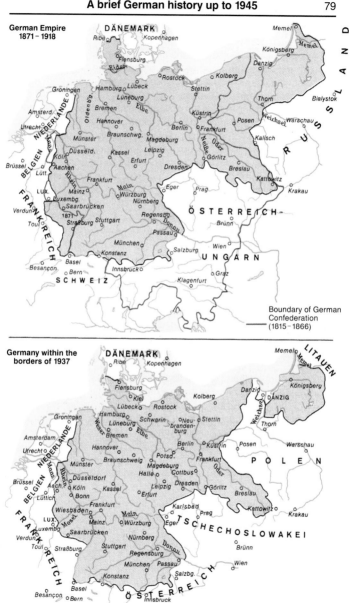

**German Empire
1871 – 1918**

DÄNEMARK

Boundary of German
Confederation
(1815 – 1866)

**Germany within the
borders of 1937**

1:15 000 000

0 100 200 300 400 500

production output still lagged far behind England's it outpaced it in growth rate. Pacemakers were heavy industry and machine manufacture. Prussia also became the predominant economic power of Germany. The economic power strengthened the political self-confidence of the liberal middle class. The German Progress Party (Deutsche Fortschrittspartei), set up in 1861, became the strongest party in the Prussian diet and denied the government the funds when it wanted to make reactionary changes in the structure of the army. The newly appointed Prime Minister (Ministerpräsident), Otto von Bismarck (1862), took up the challenge and for some years governed without parliamentary approval of the budget which was required by the constitution. The Progress Party dared offer no further resistance than parliamentary opposition however.

Bismarck was able to offset his precarious position on the domestic front by foreign policy successes. In the German-Danish war (1864) Prussia and Austria forced the Danes to cede the duchies of Schleswig-Holstein (now forming Federal Germany's northernmost state) which they initially administered jointly. But Bismarck had from the outset pursued the annexation of the two duchies and steered for open conflict with Austria. In the Austro-Prussian War (1866) Austria was defeated and had to leave the German stage. The German Confederation was dissolved and replaced by the North German Confederation (Norddeutscher Bund) of states north of the River Main, with Bismarck as Federal Chancellor (prime minister).

The Bismarck Reich. From then on Bismarck worked towards "smaller German" unity. He broke France's resistance in the war of 1870/71, triggered off by a diplomatic conflict over the succession to the Spanish throne. Defeated France had to cede Alsace-Lorraine and pay huge reparations. In the patriotic enthusiasm of the war, the southern German principalities joined up with the northern confederation to form the German Empire (Deutsches Reich). At Versailles near Paris, on the vanquished enemy's territory, King Wilhelm (William) I of Prussia was proclaimed German Emperor on January 18, 1871.

German unity had not come about by popular decision "from below" but by a treaty between princes, "from above". Prussia's predominance was stifling. To many the new Reich seemed like a "Greater Prussia." The Reichstag (Imperial Diet) was elected by universal and equal suffrage. Although it had no say in the formation of the cabinet, it could influence government by its participation in lawmaking and its budgetary right. Although the Reich Chancellor

Proclamation of William I as German Emperor in the Hall of Mirrors at Versailles 1871 (painting by Anton Werner)

(chief minister) was accountable only to the Kaiser (emperor) and not to parliament he did have to try to get majorities for his policies in the Reichstag. Suffrage in the Länder (states) still varied. In eleven it was still class suffrage, dependent on tax paid; in four there was still the old division into estates. The south German states, with their longer parliamentary tradition, reformed their electoral laws after the turn of the century and Baden, Württemberg and Bavaria made theirs the same as the Reich laws. Although Germany's becoming a modern industrial country strengthened the influence of the economically successful middle class, the people who still called the tune in society were the aristocrats, above all in the army officer corps where they predominated.

Bismarck ruled as Reich Chancellor 19 years. Through a consistent peace and alliance policy he tried to give the Reich a secure position in the new European balance of power. In contrast to this farsighted foreign policy was his home policy. He had no understanding for the democratic tendencies of his time. To him, political opposition was "hostility to the Reich". Bitterly, but ultimately vainly, he fought the left wing of the liberal middle class, political Catholicism and especially the organised labour movement which for 12 years (1878-1890) was practically under a ban by an Anti-Socialists Act (Sozialistengesetz). Hence the vastly growing working class, despite progressive social legislation, were alienated from the state. Bismarck ultimately became a victim of his own system when he was dismissed in 1890 by the young Emperor Wilhelm II.

Wilhelm II wanted to rule himself but he lacked the knowledge and staying power. More by speeches than by actions he created the impression of a peace-threatening dictator. Under him there took place a transition to "Weltpolitik" (world policy), with Germany trying to shorten the lead of the great imperialist powers and thereby becoming more isolated. In his home policies Wilhelm II soon took a reactionary course after his attempt to win the working class over to a "social emperorship" failed to bring the quick success he had hoped for. His chancellors had to rely on changing coalitions of conservatives and national liberals. Social Democrats, although one of the strongest parties, obtaining millions of votes, continued to be excluded from any participation in government.

World War I. The assassination of the heir to the Austrian throne on June 28, 1914, triggered off the outbreak of World War I. The question as to who was to blame for this war remains in dispute. Certainly, Germany and Austria on the one side, France, Russia and Britain on the other, did not consciously seek it but they were prepared to risk it. From the start, all had definite war aims for which military action was at least not unwelcome. The Germans failed in their aim quickly to vanquish France. The fighting in the west after the defeat of Germany in the Battle of the Marne soon froze into trench warfare, ultimately peaking in senseless material attrition with enormous losses on both sides. With the outbreak of war, the Kaiser receded into the background. As it progressed, the weak Reich Chancellors hat to submit more and more to the will of the army supreme command, whose nominal chief was Field Marshal Paul von Hindenburg, and whose real head was General Erich Ludendorff. The entry into the war of the United States in 1917 brought the decision which had long been developing and which could no longer be changed by the revolution in Russia and the peace in the east. Although the country had bled dry, Ludendorff, completely misjudging the situation, continued until September 1918 to insist on "peace through victory" but then surprisingly demanded an immediate armistice. Hand in hand with the military collapse went the civilian. Unresisting, the Kaiser and the princes yielded their thrones in November 1918. Not a hand stirred to defend a monarchy which had lost all credibility. Germany became a republic.

The Weimar Republic. Power fell to the Social Democrats. Their majority had long since abandoned the revolutionary notions of earlier years and saw its mission as securing an orderly transition from the old to the new form of state. Private ownership of industry and agriculture remained untouched. The mostly anti-republican civil servants and judges were taken over without exception. The imperial officer corps retained command of the armed forces. Attempts by radical leftists to drive the revolution on in a socialist direction were quelled militarily. In the National Assembly elected in January 1919, which convened at Weimar and drew up a new Reich constitution, three unconditionally republican parties — Social Democrats, German Democratic Party and the Catholic Centre — had the majority. But through the 1920s the parliamentary parties and popular forces which were more or less hostile to a democratic state went from strength to strength. The Weimar Republic was a "republic without republicans," rabidly fought by its opponents and only half-heartedly defended by its supporters. Especially the postwar economic misery and the oppressive terms of the peace of Versailles Germany had to sign in 1919 bred deep scepticism towards the republic. Growing domestic instability was the result.

In 1923 the confusion of the postwar era reached its peak (inflation, Ruhr occupation by France, Hitler coup, communist overthrow attempts). This was followed by economic recovery and with it some political pacification. The foreign policy of Gustav Stresemann regained political equality for defeated Germany through the Pact of Locarno (1925) and accession to the League of Nations (1926). The art and sciences experienced a brief, intensive flowering in the "golden 20s." After the death of the first Reich President, the Social Democrat Friedrich Ebert, the former Field Marshal Hindenburg was elected head of state in 1925 as the candidate of the Right. Although abiding strictly by the constitution, he never developed a personal commitment to the republican state.

The ultimate collapse of the Weimar Republic began with the world economic crisis in 1929. Left and right-wing radicalism exploited unemployment and the general deprivation to their ends. No more majorities capable of government could be found in the Reichstag,

Gustav Stresemann addresses the League of Nations in Geneva 1926

the cabinet being dependent on the support of the constitutionally very strong Reich President. From 1930, the up to then insignificant National Socialist movement of Adolf Hitler which fused extreme anti-democratic tendencies and a raging anti-Semitism with pseudo-revolutionary propaganda gained strength in leaps and bounds and by 1932 had become the strongest party. On January 30, 1933, Hitler became Reich Chancellor. Apart from members of his own party his cabinet included politicians of the right and non-partisan specialist ministers, so that it was hoped that sole rule by the National Socialists could be prevented.

The Hitler dictatorship. Hitler soon rid himself of his allies. An Enabling Act, approved by all the middle-class parties, gave him practically limitless power. He banned all parties but his own. The trade unions were smashed, basic rights virtually removed and press freedom abolished. The regime exercised ruthless terror and violence against anyone who stood in its way. Thousands disappeared without trial in hastily constructed concentration camps. Parliamentary institutions at all levels were abolished or made powerless. The "Führer" (Leader) principle advanced everywhere. When Hindenburg died in 1934, Hitler united in his person the offices of president and chancellor. By this he gained control as commander in chief of the armed forces which up to then had still had a certain inner life of their own.

In the few years of the turbulent Weimar Republic the majority of Germans had not acquired any deep-rooted affinity to freedom and democracy. More than anything else, years of political turmoil, violence between the various camps – including bloody street battles – and the mass unemployment engendered by the world economic crisis had shattered confidence in government. Hitler, on the other hand, succeeded with job-creation and armament production programmes to reinvigorate the economy and quickly reduce unemployment. He was favoured in this by the world depression coming to an end. His position was also bolstered by foreign policy successes.

In 1935 the Saar region, until then administered by the League of Nations, returned to Germany and the same year the Reich regained its defence sovereignty. In 1936 German troops moved into the up to then demilitarised Rhineland. In 1938 Austria was joined to the Reich and the Western powers allowed Hitler to annex the Sudetenland. All this helped him quickly to achieve his political ends, although in all classes of society there were people who courageously resisted the dictatorship.

Immediately after taking power, the regime began to carry out its anti-Semitic programme. Step by step the Jews were stripped of all human and civic rights. Those who could tried to escape the persecution by fleeing abroad. The persecution of political opponents and the suppression of freedom of opinion also drove thousands out of the country. Many of the best German writers, artists and scientists fled the country – an irredeemable loss to German culture.

World War II and its consequences. Hitler was not to be satisfied. From the outset he prepared for a war he was willing to wage to subjugate Europe. With his attack on Poland on September 1, 1939, he unleashed World War II, which lasted five and a half years, devastated much of Europe and killed 55 million people.

The German armies defeated Poland, Denmark, Norway, Holland, Belgium, France, Yugoslavia and Greece. In the Soviet Union they advanced to a position just short of Moscow and in North Africa they threatened the Suez Canal. Harsh occupation regimes were set up in the conquered countries. They were fought by resistance movements. In 1942 the regime began the "Final Solution of the Jewish Question": all the Jews the regime could lay its hands on were taken to concentration camps in occupied Poland and murdered. The total number of victims is estimated at six million. The year this inconceivable crime began brought the turning point in the war. From then on Germany and its allies, Italy and Japan, suffered setbacks in all theatres.

The terror of the regime and the military setbacks strengthened resistance against Hitler in all classes of society. A coup attempt on July 20, 1944, carried out mainly by officers, failed. Hitler survived a bomb planted in his headquarters and took terrible revenge. Outstanding among the many victims were Col. Gen. Ludwig Beck, Col. Graf Stauffenberg, and Carl Goerdeler, former chief mayor of Leipzig.

The war continued, Hitler pursuing it with enormous losses, until the entire Reich area was occupied by enemies. Then, on April 30, 1945,

Berlin 1945

he killed himself. Eight days later the successor he had willed by testament, Grand Admiral Dönitz, carried out the unconditional capitulation and was arrested shortly afterwards by the victors.

Germany had suffered the greatest defeat in its history. Most towns lay in ruins, a quarter of all houses were destroyed or heavily damaged. The economy and transportation networks were smashed. The most urgent things to sustain life were lacking. Millions of Germans were captives, millions homeless, millions in flight. Germany appeared to have no future.

From division to unity

Reorientation after 1945. Following the unconditional surrender of the German forces on 8/9 May 1945, the last government of the German Reich, headed by Admiral Karl Dönitz, remained in power for another 23 days. Its members were then arrested and, together with other nazi leaders, tried by the Nuremberg Tribunal for crimes against peace and humanity.

On 5 June the victorious powers - the United States, the United Kingdom, the Soviet Union and France - assumed supreme authority in the territory of the Reich. Their basic objective, according to the London Protocol (12 September 1944) and follow-up agreements, was to exercise total control over Germany. They divided the country into three occupation zones, and Berlin, the capital, into three sectors. There was an Allied Control Council composed of the three commanders in chief. Once and for all Germany was to be prevented from again aspiring to world domination as she had done in 1914 and 1939. The allies wanted to curb her appetite for conquest, to destroy Prussia as a stronghold of militarism, to punish the Germans for genocide and war crimes, and to reeducate them in the democratic spirit.

At the conference of Yalta (Crimea) held in February 1945, France was coopted as the fourth controlling power and allocated its own occupation zone. In Yalta the only allied intention which remained valid was that of terminating Germany's existence as an independent state but keeping the country intact. Stalin especially was keen to preserve Germany's economic unity. He demanded such huge reparations for the Soviet Union's terrible sacrifices as a result of Germany's invasion that they could not possibly have been made by one occupation zone alone. Moscow wanted 20 billion dollars and control over 80 per cent of all of Germany's factories.

In contrast to the original plans, the British and Americans, too, wanted to preserve a viable rump Germany, not out of greed for reparations but because, as from about the autumn of 1944, US President Roosevelt was aiming to establish a stable Central Europe as part of a system of global balances. Germany's economic stability was indispensable to this plan. He had therefore quickly discarded the notorious Morgenthau Plan (September 1944), which would have reduced Germany to an agricultural country.

Germany after World War II

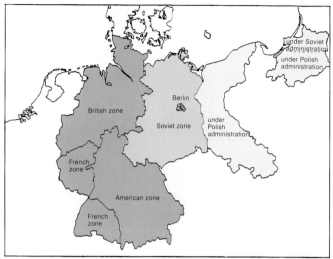

—— German within the borders of 1937

Western zones and Western sectors of Berlin (Federal Republic of Germany from 1949)

Soviet zone and Eastern sector of Berlin (German Democratic Republic from 1949)

German eastern territories under Polish or Soviet administration

Soon the only common aim remaining to the victorious powers was that of disarming and demilitarizing Germany. The original idea of partitioning the country quickly became no more than "lip-service to a dying idea" (Charles Bohlen) when the western powers watched with dismay as Stalin, immediately upon liberating, that is to say conquering, Poland and south-eastern Europe, launched a massive operation to sovietize those regions.

On 12 May 1945 Churchill cabled President Truman that an "iron curtain" had come down in front of the Soviet troops and that no one knew what was going on behind it. But the western powers carefully weighed up the possible consequences of letting Stalin have a say in reparations on the Rhine and the Ruhr. The result was that at the Potsdam Conference (17 July to 2 August 1945), the original aim of which was to create a new European order, agreements were

Potsdam Conference 1945. From the left: Attlee, Truman and Stalin

reached which consolidated rather than eased the tensions. The four powers agreed on the matter of denazification, demilitarization, economic decentralization and the reeducation of the Germans along democratic lines. The western powers also agreed to the expulsion of Germans from Poland, Hungary and Czechoslovakia. The west had insisted that the transfer be carried out in a "humane" fashion, but in the following years some 6.75 million Germans were brutally deported. They were made to suffer for Germany's war crimes, but also for the shift in Poland's western boundary as a result of the Soviet Union's occupation of Königsberg and eastern Poland. Practically the only point on which East and West agreed was that the four occupation zones should be preserved as economic and political units. At first, each power was to draw its reparations from its own zone. As was to be seen later, however, this set a precedent in that not only the reparations arrangement but also the attachment of the four zones to different political and economic systems made Germany the country where the Cold War manifested itself most of all. This came about in stages.

Meanwhile the task of establishing German political parties and administrative authorities had begun in the occupation zones. This happened very quickly in the Soviet zone under rigid control, with the result that even before the end of 1945 parties and several central administrative bodies had been formed.

In the three western zones the development of a political system was a bottom-to-top process, that is to say, political parties were permitted only at local level at first, then at state level after the Länder had been created. Only later were they allowed to form associations at zonal level. Zonal administrative structures were materializing very slowly, and as the destroyed country's material want could only be overcome by means of generous planning across state and zonal borders, and as quadripartite administration was not functioning, the United States and the United Kingdom decided in 1947 to merge their zones economically into what was known as the bizone.

The conflicting systems of government in East and West and the different approach to reparations in the occupation zones were an obstacle to the introduction of uniform financial, taxation, raw materials and production policy throughout Germany, and led to considerable regional disparities. France was not interested in a common economic administration (bizone/trizone) at first. Stalin wanted to have a say in the management of the Ruhr but at the same time sealed his own zone off to the others. He would not have any western interference with the appointment of pro-communist officials in the Soviet-occupied zone. The western powers were powerless to prevent such arbitrary measures as the compulsory merger of the KPD (East German Communist Party) and the SPD (Social Democratic Party) to form the SED (Socialist Unity Party) in April 1946.

In view of this development the British and Americans, too, began safeguarding their own interests in their respective zones. The military commanders, most of whom were from the conservative mould, detested socialism. Consequently, the old social structure and system of property ownership were retained in the western zones. Moreover, the state of the economy made it necessary for the authorities, rather than continue the denazification process, to engage efficient, hard-working German specialists to help rebuild the western zones so that they could be protected from Soviet encroachments.

Thus attitudes on both sides hardened into a cold war. Each accused the other side of being responsible for Germany's division, but these mutual charges hardly concealed the fact that both blocs had gone over to defending their bastions.

An enemy becomes a partner. With his famous speech in Stuttgart on 6 September 1949, US Secretary of State Byrnes had indicated the changed approach. Stalin's occupation of Poland and the redrawing of that country's borders were described as merely temporary measures. As Byrnes saw it, the military role of the western allies in

West Germany changed from one of occupation and control to that of protecting powers. And he said that a "soft" reparations policy was intended to deter the Germans from any nationalist thoughts of revenge and encourage their cooperation.

Finally, on the initiative of the United Kingdom and the United States, a trizone was established as a unified western economic area, after initial French resistance. The threat of another Soviet advance westwards following the coup d'état in Prague on 25 February 1948 induced the French to fall into line. Byrnes' views were reflected first in the Brussels Pact of 17 March 1948 and ultimately in the North Atlantic Treaty of 4 April 1949.

For such an organization to work West Germany had to have a coherent political and economic system. Thus at the Six-Power Conference in London (23 February to 3 March and 20 April to 1 June 1948), which was attended for the first time by the Benelux countries, France, Britain and the United States agreed that the western occupation zones should have a common political structure.

At the 82nd meeting of the Control Council on 20 March 1948, the Soviet representative, Marshall Sokolovski, asked for information on the London Conference. When his western colleagues answered evasively Sokolovski walked out, never to return.

While the western powers were still finalizing their recommendations for a constituent assembly to be convened by West Germany's minister presidents (regional premiers), Stalin used the introduction of the deutschmark in the West (currency reform of 20 June 1948) as a pretext for imposing a blockade on West Berlin with the aim of annexing it to the Soviet-occupied zone. During the night of 23 June 1948 all land routes between the western zones and West Berlin were closed. Supplies of energy and food from the eastern sector of Berlin and the Soviet zone stopped.

On 3 August 1948 Stalin demanded that Berlin be recognized as the capital of the GDR (German Democratic Republic), which on 7 October 1949 was given a government of its own. But US President Harry Truman refused to budge, having declared on 20 July that the western allies could not forgo West Berlin nor the creation of a west German state ("no Munich of 1948"). Until 12 May 1949 West Berlin was kept supplied by an allied airlift. This visible solidarity with Berlin as a western outpost, together with America's demonstration of strength, evoked a spirit of cooperation in West Germany, with the result that former enemies became partners.

The founding of the Federal Republic of Germany. West Germany had already begun receiving American foreign aid in 1946 (under the

GARIOA Programme), but it was George C. Marshall's programme to combat "hunger, poverty, despair and chaos" (the Marshall Plan) that provided the crucial boost for the country's economic recovery (1.4 billion dollars between 1948 and 1952). While in the Soviet-occupied zone the process of transferring industry to public ownership continued, the "social market economy" system (Alfred Müller-Armack 1947) continued to gain ground in the West after the currency reform. The new economic order was intended to prevent, on the one hand, the "stagnation of capitalism" (Walter Eucken) and, on the other, a centrally, planned economy which would be a hindrance to creativity and initiative.

This concept was supplemented by the rule-of-law and the welfare-state principle embodied in the Basic Law and by the country's federal structure. The constitution was deliberately termed the "Basic Law" in order to emphasize its provisional character. The idea was that a definitive constitution should only be adopted after Germany's reunification.

The Basic Law naturally included many of the intentions of the western occupying powers, who, with the Frankfurt Documents presented on 1 July 1948, authorized West Germany's minister presidents (i.e. the heads of government of the Länder) to draw up a constitution. But that document also reflects much of Germany's experience with the Weimar Republic and the "legal" installation of the nazi dictatorship. The constitutional convention held at Herrenchiemsee (10-23 August 1948) and the Parliamentary Council which met in Bonn on 1 September 1948 (65 delegates of the state parliaments) incorporated in the Basic Law (adopted on 8 May 1949) provisions requiring future governments, parties and other political groupings to protect the democratic system. Ever since, all attempts to do away with the liberal, democratic system, or to replace it with a right-wing or left-wing dictatorship, have been treated as criminal offences and the organizations concerned can be banned. The Federal Constitutional Court, the guardian of the constitution, is the authority which decides whether a party is legal or not.

Whereas the authors of the Weimar constitution, naively believing in the uprightness of parliament, had, through article 76, made it possible for enemies of the constitution to destroy what in those days was the most liberal constitution in the world, article 79 of the Basic Law prohibited any change in its article 1 (which ties the use of all public authority to protection of human rights), and any attempt to do away with the country's democratic, social and federal system (article 20 (4)).

These requirements were an immediate reaction to what had happened under the nazi dictatorship, at whose hands most of the "poli-

ticians of the Federal Republic's first hour" had suffered, those men
and women who were now rebuilding Germany on the democratic
traditions of 1848 and 1919 and in the spirit of the "revolt of the conscience" of 20 July 1944. All of them personified in the eyes of the
world the "other Germany" and won the respect of the occupying powers. They included the first Federal President Theodor Heuss (FDP),
the first Federal Chancellor Konrad Adenauer (CDU), and Economics
Minister Ludwig Erhard (CDU), the "locomotive" of the "economic miracle", but also the outstanding leaders of the SPD opposition such
as Kurt Schumacher and Erich Ollenhauer, as well as the cosmopolitan Carlo Schmid. It was they who gave the new party system in West
Germany its unmistakable character. Gradually, Germany's involvement and political influence increased (Occupation Statute, Peters-
berg Agreements, membership of GATT, accession to the European
Coal and Steel Community). In July 1951 the United Kingdom, France

Paris Treaties 1954. From the left:
Mendès-France, Adenauer, Eden, Dulles

and the United States declared that Germany was no longer a war enemy. The Soviet Union did the same on 25 January 1955.

Security through integration with the west and European reconciliation. To Chancellor Konrad Adenauer, who until 1963 had largely held the reigns of foreign and domestic policy himself ("Chancellor democracy"), Germany's reunification in peace and freedom was the foremost political objective. To achieve this it was necessary for West Germany to be integrated in the Atlantic Alliance. Accordingly, the restoration of the Federal Republic's sovereignty on 5 May 1945 coincided with its accession to NATO. This alliance was to be the main protective shield, the proposed European Defence Community having proved abortive due to French resistance.

At the same time the European Communities (Treaty of Rome, 1957) were developed into an anti-communist bastion. Adenauer's distrust of Moscow was so deep rooted that in 1952 he, together with the other western powers, rejected Stalin's offer of reuniting Germany as a neutral country as far as the Oder-Neisse line. To the Chancellor the protection of American troops in Germany was indispensable. His suspicion seemed only too justified when, on 17 June 1953, the people's uprising in East Germany in protest against their life of bondage and against the excessive productivity norms imposed by the regime, was savagely put down by Soviet tanks. This showed once again that without Moscow little progress could be made on the German question. Thus for sober political reasons it was expedient to establish diplomatic relations with the Soviet Union as the largest power in Europe. This was accomplished during Adenauer's visit to Moscow in September 1955, on which occasion he also secured the release of the last 10,000 German prisoners-of-war and about 20,000 civilians.

The crushing of the popular revolt in Hungary by Soviet troops in November 1956, as well as the "Sputnik shock" (4 October 1957), signalled a considerable growth of Soviet power, which manifested itself in the establishment of a socialist system in East Germany, but above all in the Berlin ultimatum issued by Stalin's successor, Nikita Khrushchev, who demanded that the western allies leave West Berlin within six months.

Their adamant refusal caused Khrushchev to try a softer approach on Berlin. His visit to the United States in 1959 did indeed considerably improve the atmosphere ("spirit of Camp David"), and the American President, Dwight D. Eisenhower, to the great concern of the Bonn government, felt that the Russian transgressions of internation-

John F. Kennedy in Berlin, 1963

al agreements regarding Berlin were not so serious as to warrant a military conflict outside Germany.

Bonn's disquiet with regard to Berlin's security increased when John F. Kennedy became President of the United States. This represented a change of generation in the American leadership which considerably reduced Adenauer's influence on US policy towards Europe. True, Kennedy guaranteed with his three "essentials" (25 July 1961) free access to Berlin, the presence of the western powers in the city, and its overall security, but when the Berlin wall was built on 13 August 1961 the allied reaction went little beyond diplomatic protests and symbolic threats. Once again Moscow was able to safeguard its protectorate. Barricades, death strips and repression prevented the people from "voting with their feet" against the East German regime. In July alone, the month before the wall was erected, over 30,000 people had fled from east Germany. The wall had staked out the claims of the superpowers. Although the German question had not been resolved it at least seemed regulated. Even after the Cuba crisis in 1962 the two superpowers continued to seek a better understanding – they had to on account of the nuclear stalemate.

Bonn therefore had no option but to look in other directions, and the temporary estrangement with Washington was in fact outwardly compensated for by the "summer of French friendship". With the Ely-

The Berlin Wall at Potsdam Square

sée Treaty which they signed in January 1963 Chancellor Adenauer and President de Gaulle laid special emphasis to Franco-German friendship. In order to stress the new quality of this relationship de Gaulle, during his triumphant state visit to Bonn a few months previously, had spoken of the "great German nation". In his view the Second World War had to be seen more in terms of tragedy than of guilt.

As the Federal Republic became increasingly integrated into the western community the atmosphere also began to improve in the relationship with eastern Europe. In December 1963 NATO, at a ministerial meeting in Athens, had signalled this change with its new strategy of flexible response in place of that of massive retaliation.

In an attempt to soften the rigid East-West relationship, the Federal Republic tried to improve contacts at least with the Soviet Union's satellite countries. Without officially abandoning the Hallstein Doctrine, that is to say Bonn's policy of severing relations with any country which recognized the GDR, Adenauer's successors, Ludwig Erhard and Kurt Georg Kiesinger, based their policy on the harsh realities prevailing in Central Europe. They were prompted to do so not least by the new approach adopted by the SPD opposition, which was manifest in Egon Bahr's formula of "change through rapprochement" (15 July 1963).

The establishment of German trade missions in Bucharest and Budapest was a promising start. In the west increasing efforts were being made to merge the European Coal and Steel Community, the European Atomic Energy Community (EURATOM) and the European Economic Community, into one European Community (8 April 1965). The establishment of diplomatic relations with Israel despite pan-Arab protests was a major step in the Federal Republic's policy of rapprochement. At the beginning of 1967 Bonn established diplomatic relations with Romania, and in June the Federal Republic and

German-French friendship: Adenauer and de Gaulle 1963

Schloss Bellevue, the Federal President's official residence in Berlin

Czechoslovakia opened trade missions in their respective capitals.

The Harmel Report of December 1967 at least prepared the way for further steps towards detente by laying down the western alliance's twofold aim of maintaining its military strength whilst at the same time being ready to talk to the eastern bloc. In that year Bonn and Belgrade resumed diplomatic relations, they having been broken off by the Federal Republic on account of Yugoslavia's recognition of the GDR. And from Poland came proposals for a non-aggression pact.

In addition to the policy of reconciliation with Germany's European neighbours and her integration into the western community, Adenauer too had attached special importance to restitution for the Jews. Six million Jews had been systematically exterminated by the nazis. It was not least the close personal relationship between the Federal Republic's first Chancellor and Israel's Prime Minister Ben Gurion which fostered the process of reconciliation between Jews and Germans. One outstanding event at that time was their meeting in New York's Waldorf Astoria Hotel on 14 March 1960. Addressing parliament in 1961, Adenauer stressed that the Federal Republic could only prove that the Germans had broken completely with their nazi past by making material restitution as well. As early as 1952 the first agreement had been signed in Luxembourg. It provided for assistance for the integration of Jewish refugees in Israel. Of the total sum of about 90 billion marks provided for restitution purposes, roughly one third went to Israel and Jewish organizations, and especially to the Jewish Claims Conference, a hardship fund which helped Jews all over the world who had been persecuted by the nazis. However, diplomatic relations between the two countries were not established until 1965.

German-German dialogue in spite of the GDR's self-detachment.
In spite of the GDR's continuing efforts to cut itself off completely from the west (e.g. by requiring passports and visas for persons in transit between the Federal Republic and West Berlin) and in spite of the Warsaw Pact's crushing of attempted reforms in Czechoslovakia (the "Prague Spring" of 1968), the "Brezhnev Doctrine" of the indivisibility of the socialist bloc did not have any serious repercussions on the process of detente. In April 1969 Bonn said it was ready to enter into agreements with the GDR below the level of international recognition.

Obviously, German-German agreements of this kind could hardly be achieved without some kind of prior understanding with Moscow. When the Soviet Union proposed a non-aggression pact, the "new eastern policy" adopted by the Social-Liberal coalition that had assumed power in Bonn on 21 October 1969 quickly began to take on substance. A few months previously (5 March 1969) Gustav Heinemann, who even in Adenauer's day had been a strong advocate of East-West rapprochement, had been elected Federal President. Willy Brandt, who had played an active part in the resistance against the Hitler dictatorship, was now head of a federal government which directed its energies to the construction of a peaceful order throughout Europe. The international constellation was favourable. Moscow and Washington were negotiating on the limitation of strategic arms (SALT), and NATO proposed negotiations on mutual balanced force reductions (MBFR). On 28 November 1969 the Federal Republic became a party to the treaty banning the proliferation of nuclear weapons (NPT). Following the turbulence experienced by its predecessor, the grand coalition government (Viet Nam conflict, emergency legislation, Auschwitz trials, Extra-Parliamentary Opposition, and student revolts), the new cabinet, by embarking on its "Ostpolitik", placed itself under considerable pressure to produce results.

While talks on a non-aggression agreement were being conducted in Moscow and Warsaw, Bonn and East Berlin, too, explored the possibilities of improving relations. On 19 March 1970 the heads of government of both German states, Willy Brandt and Willi Stoph, met for the first time in Erfurt. This was followed by another meeting on 21 May in Kassel. On 12 August 1970 a treaty on the renunciation of force and recognition of the status quo was signed in Moscow. Both sides proclaimed that they had no territorial claims against anyone. In a "letter on German unity" presented to the Soviet Government in Moscow, the Federal Republic stated that the treaty did not contradict its aim of working towards a state of peace in Europe "in which the German people will regain their unity in free self-determination".

On 7 December of that year the Treaty of Warsaw was signed which reaffirmed the inviolability of the existing border (the Oder-Neisse line). Warsaw and Bonn, too, gave an assurance that they had no territorial claims against one another and declared their intention of improving mutual cooperation. In an "information" document on humanitarian measures, Warsaw agreed to the transfer of ethnic Germans from Poland and the reunion of separated families by the Red Cross.

In order to pave the way for the ratification of those treaties, France, the United Kingdom, the United States and the Soviet Union signed an agreement on Berlin which stated that Berlin was not a constituent part of the Federal Republic but that Bonn was entitled to represent West Berlin. In addition, the "ties" between West Berlin and the Federal Republic were to be improved and relations between East Berlin/GDR and West Berlin developed (signing of the Transit Agreement on 17 December). Germany's efforts to foster peace and detente received worldwide recognition which culminated in the award of the Nobel Peace Prize to Willy Brandt (1971).

However, the CDU/CSU, who were in opposition for the first time, considered the results of the negotiations too meagre. Yet their constructive vote of no confidence against Brandt came to grief (247 for, 249 against) and the Bundestag (parliament) ratified the treaties with the Soviet Union and Poland on 17 May. Most CDU/CSU members of parliament abstained. The Bundestag, in an "interpretative resolution", declared that the treaties did not conflict with the aim of restorring German unity by peaceful means.

The series of treaties with Eastern Europe was rounded off by a Treaty on the Basis of Relations between the two Germanies which had been preceded by talks and negotiations since June 1972. After Willy Brandt's reelection as Chancellor on 14 December, the way was clear for the signing of the treaty on 21 December. Both sides undertook not to threaten or use force against one another and to respect each other's independence. The inviolability of the border between the two states was also endorsed. Furthermore, the two sides expressed their willingness to resolve humanitarian problems in a practical manner. It was agreed that, owing to the special nature of their relationship, they would establish "representations" in their respective capitals instead of the usual embassies.

At the signing ceremony the Federal Government again handed over a letter emphasizing its intention to pursue German unity. The government of the state of Bavaria asked the Federal Constitutional Court to confirm that the treaty did not run contrary to this objective. It also noted that the German Empire continued to exist in international law and was partially identical with the Federal Republic. The Court ruled that the GDR could not be regarded as a foreign country, only as domestic territory.

In 1973 the Treaty of Prague between Czechoslovakia and the Fedderal Republic was signed. It declared the Munich Agreement of 1938 to be null and void "in accordance with this Treaty". The two sides also agreed that their borders were inviolable and that they would not use force against one another.

Whilst negotiations were going on in Vienna on mutual balanced force reductions, the Soviet Union and the United States completed an agreement designed to prevent a nuclear war, and 35 countries attended a Conference on Security and Cooperation in Europe (CSCE) in Helsinki, little change came about in the relationship between the GDR and the Federal Republic. On the one hand, East Berlin benefited both materially and financially from the follow-up agreements to the Basic Treaty, but on the other the East German regime meticulously kept its ideological distance. The East German constitution was amended and the term "socialist state of the German nation" was replaced by "socialist state of workers and peasants". Also omitted was the passage "... fulfilling its responsibility to show the entire German nation the way into a future of peace and socialism".

Nonetheless, Helmut Schmidt, too, strived to continue the policy of developing a balanced relationship. On 16 May 1974 he had succeeded Willy Brandt, who had resigned from the chancellorship when one of his aides, Günther Guillaume, was unmasked as an East German spy. The "swing" arrangement, a facility which allowed the GDR to overdraw by as much as DM 850 million on its credit from the Federal Republic, was extended until 1981.

The GDR continued to profit handsomely from the various transit agreements which were financed by the West, without budging on the political issues. The Final Act of Helsinki (1975), which called for greater freedom of movement in transboundary traffic and more respect for human and civil rights, proved to be a disappointment, not only to the East Germans but to the people of other East European countries as well. There was no end to the chicanery at East Germany's borders. People were arbitrarily turned back, as were visitors to the Leipzig Fair. Western journalists who criticized the GDR were forced to leave the country.

The East German regime suffered a further loss of prestige around the world when it deprived Wolf Biermann, a well-known singer-songwriter, of his citizenship. In spite of all this, the Federal Republic decided for the sake of the people in East Germany to continue its efforts to improve relations. Thus in 1978 an agreement was reached to build an autobahn from Berlin to Hamburg and to repair the transit waterways to West Berlin, the greater proportion of the cost being borne by the Federal Republic. The Federal Government also continued to buy the release of political prisoners from the GDR. In the end Bonn had paid over DM 3.5 billion for the release of 33,755 people, and to have 250,000 families reunited.

Missiles versus detente. Whereas the process of European integration continued steadily in the West, the transition from the 70s, the decade of detente, to the 80s was marked by fresh conflicts in Eastern Europe. The Soviet invasion of Afghanistan and the imposition of martial law in Poland, as well as the emplacement of new intermediate-range nuclear weapons (SS 20) in East Germany and Czechoslovakia, worsened the climate of East-West relations.

NATO reacted to this serious upset of the balance of security by deciding that it, too, would introduce new missiles as from 1983. But at the same time it proposed arms control negotiations to the Soviet Union. This was the "two-track" decision. In protest at the invasion of Afghanistan, the United States, the United Kingdom, Canada, Norway and the Federal Republic refused to take part in the Moscow Summer Olympics (1980).

The Americans tried a new initiative, the "zero" solution, by which the Soviets would remove their intermediate-range missiles whilst NATO would promise not to deploy its Pershing II and the new Cruise missiles.

Chancellor Schmidt insisted on the missile modernization alternative so as not to leave any gaps in the Western security shield, but at the same time tried to keep the damage to the German-German relationship within limits. Although East German leader Erich Honekker proposed to introduce a separate East German citizenship, and although the East German regime drastically increased the daily amount of currency which visitors from the West had to exchange on entering the GDR, Schmidt visited East Germany, but without getting any substantial concessions from Honecker. The regime's hardening ideological stance was not least a reaction to the growing protest movements in neighbouring Poland, where the people were demanding economic reform, freedom and disarmament.

But the missile question was not only problematical in the East. In Bonn the FDP decided to change its tack on economic policy and began to drift out of the coalition. Grassroots SPD followers, largely because of pressure from the peace movement and some union factions, withdrew their support for Schmidt for adhering to the NATO two-track decision. As a result, Helmut Kohl replaced him as Chancellor at the head of a CDU/CSU/FDP coalition. He continued Bonn's security policy and close cooperation with Paris and Washington with a view to uniting Europe within a stable and secure framework. In the face of massive protest from the peace movement, sections of the SPD and the Greens (who had polled 5.6% of the votes in the 1983 election for the Bundestag and thus were represented in parliament for the first time), the German parliament approved in November 1983 the deployment of intermediate-range missiles because of "the Warsaw Pact's conventional superiority" (Chancellor Kohl).

Whereas the growing peace movement had been one of the causes of a change in government in West Germany, protest groups in East Germany, which through the initiative of the Church ("swords into ploughshares") had become more and more vociferous since the beginning of 1982, led ultimately to the disintegration of the entire socialist system.

From the GDR's decline to German unity. The German Democratic Republic, which had been founded on 7 October 1949, was a product of the Soviet Union. Nonetheless, many Germans, their experience with the nazi dictatorship still fresh in their memories, were at first willing to help develop this anti-fascist model. But the command economy, secret police, the all-powerful SED (the East German communist party), as well as strict censorship, increasingly alienated the people and the regime. In spite of this, very cheap housing, health care and social services gave this self-contained system a certain amount of flexibility which enabled the people to eke out an existence in many different ways. East Germany's great success in international sport was a sort of compensation, just as the "workers" gained satisfaction from the fact that they soon had the highest rate of industrial production and the highest standard of living in the Eastern bloc, despite having to make huge reparations to the Soviet Union. The people's reaction to state control and tutelage was to withdraw into their private sphere.

In spite of all the propaganda about annual production targets having been more than achieved, and behind the facade of anti-imperialist hatred spread in the schools, factories and the armed forces, it became increasingly clear that East Germany's original intention of overtaking the Federal Republic economically would remain a dream. Depleted resources, industry's vicious destruction of the environment, coupled with dwindling productivity as a result of central planning, forced the East German regime to go easy on its promises. It had to raise increasingly large loans in the West. Improvisation became the order of the day with regard to consumer goods. The quality of life and infrastructure (housing, transport, environmental protection) thus deteriorated. All the assurances of socialism's ultimate victory turned out to be nothing more than a caricature. The image of the capitalist class enemy in the West which had been propagated by the regime was thoroughly spent by the early 80s at the latest. There was a Big-Brother spy network which kept watch on everybody, and the system's indoctrination and strained appeals for solidarity made the claim about the leadership role of "the working class and their Marxist-Leninist party" (article 1 of East Germany's constitution) sound like hollow rhetoric, especially to the young generation. The people began to demand a bigger say in running their own lives, more individual freedom and more and better consumer goods. These wishes were often coupled with the hope that the socialist system, ossified by bureaucratic constraints and anti-Western ideology, would prove capable of reforming itself.

As the atmosphere of diplomatic relations deteriorated as a result of the quarrel over the deployment of medium-range missiles, the proposed Strategic Defence Initiative, a space-based defensive umbrella proposed by the Americans, and East Germany's continued aggravation of the West (for instance, by building a second wall at the Brandenburg Gate and impeding traffic in the air corridor to Berlin), the East Germans themselves put pressure on their own leadership. Some had entered the Federal Republic's representation in East Berlin and refused to leave until they had been given a definite assurance that they could move to the West.

In order to make life easier for the Germans in the east, the Federal Government arranged various large bank credits for the GDR. Moscow's fear that this would soften the socialist system was allayed by Erich Honecker, who wrote in "Neues Deutschland", the regime's mouthpiece, in 1984: "Merging socialism and capitalism is just as impossible as merging fire and water." But this self-assurance on the surface could hardly conceal the fact that the reform movements in Eastern Europe had thrown the whole socialist bloc onto the defen-

Midnight on October 3, 1990 in front of the old Reichstag in Berlin:

the people celebrate unification

sive. Honecker's rejection of the accusation made at the CSCE conference in Ottawa (1985) that the people in Eastern bloc countries were denied free speech and freedom of movement was a propagandistic lie.

From the beginning of 1985 more and more people sought admission to the Federal Republic's permanent representation in East Berlin and the German Embassy in Prague. Soon the new General Secretary of the Soviet Communist Party, Mikhail Gorbachev, who had succeeded Konstantin Chernenko (who had died in March), became the main standard bearer for the East German people, who were longing to gain their freedom, but also for international cooperation on security matters.

Meetings and conferences. In 1986, Gorbachev declared that his main political objective was to eliminate nuclear weapons by the end of the century. His meetings with US President Ronald Reagan in Geneva and Reykjavik, the Conference on Confidence and Security-Building Measures and Disarmament in Europe held in Stockholm, as well as the preparations for negotiations on the reduction of conventional forces in Europe, showed that the East was ready for dialogue. This new approach was conducive to agreements between the two German states on cultural, educational and scientific cooperation. A skeleton agreement providding for cooperation in the field of environmental protection was also signed. That same year Saarlouis and Eisenhüttenstadt made a twinning arrangement, the first of its kind between cities in East and West Germany.

But the East German regime did not want to be infected by Gorbachev's perestroika and glasnost. They didn't want the process of democratic reform in the Soviet Union to spread to the GDR. Kurt Hager, a member of the politburo and the SED's principal ideologue, stubbornly argued that there was "no need to redecorate one's home just because the neighbour is doing so".

The extent to which the East German leaders ignored the expectations of their own people was shown by the protest demonstrations in East Berlin on 13 August, the anniversary of the wall. Chancellor Helmut Kohl spoke against the continuation of Germany's division when, during Honecker's working visit to Bonn (1987), he said: "We respect the present borders but we want to overcome the country's division by peaceful means through a process of mutual understanding. We have a joint responsibility for preserving the vital foundations of our nation."

A step towards safeguarding those vital foundations was the INF Treaty signed by Reagan and Gorbachev. Under that accord, all US and Soviet missiles with a range of 500 to 5,000 km deployed in Europe had to be withdrawn and destroyed. The Federal Republic for its part pledged to destroy its 72 Pershing IA missiles.

The general climate of détente led to increasing demands for greater freedom and reform in East Germany. During demonstrations in East Berlin in early 1988, 120 supporters of the peace movement known as "Church from the Grassroots" were arrested. Prayers were said for them in the Gethsemane Church. Over 2,000 people attended the service, and a fortnight later their number had swollen to 4,000. In Dresden the police broke up a demonstration for human rights, free speech and freedom of the press. In May Honecker used the occasion of a visit by the Soviet Defence Minister Yasov to warn about the danger of imperialism and to call for a stronger Warsaw Pact.

Although Chancellor Kohl, in his state of the nation address to parliament in December 1988, welcomed the lifting of some travel restrictions, he had to denounce the suppression of the reform movement in the GDR. To Erich Honecker, however, the new civil rights movements were merely examples of "extremist intemperance". In response to appeals to remove the wall, he replied on 19 January 1989: "The wall protecting us from fascism will stay there until such time as the conditions which led to its erection are changed. It will still be in existence in 50, 100 years' time."

The population of East Germany protests: demonstration on East Berlin's Alexander Square 1989

The stubborn rigidity of the East German leaders at a time when Gorbachev saw a "common European home" taking shape and Helmut Kohl was speaking optimistically about "the disintegration of ossified structures in Europe", aroused even more discontent among the population. At times the Federal Republic's permanent representation in East Berlin had to be closed because of the surge of people wanting to move west. In September 1989 Hungary opened its border, thus permitting thousands of people from the GDR to pass through to Austria and from there into West Germany. This breach of Warsaw Pact discipline encouraged ever more people in the GDR to take to the streets in protest, including growing numbers outside the church. And when the regime, in October 1989, celebrated the 40th anniversary of the founding of the GDR with great pomp and ceremony, mass demonstrations were held, primarily in Leipzig ("We are the people").

Honecker finally realized that his only chance of preserving the essence of the SED regime was for him to resign. He was succeeded as SED secretary general and GDR head of state by Egon Krenz, but his promise of "change" was drowned by the protests of the people, who did not trust him. Under the pressure of events the Council of Ministers and the SED politburo resigned en bloc. The peaceful revolution seemed to paralyze the authorities. As a result, a mistaken announcement by Günter Schabowski, party secretary in the district of Berlin, that travel restrictions were to be eased prompted thousands of people to cross the border on the evening of 9 November 1989. The authorities could only watch numbly. The wall was open. Soon it was to be broken down and tiny pieces were offered as souvenirs all over the world.

News of the breach in the wall reached Chancellor Kohl whilst he was on a visit to Warsaw. He suspended his engagements for a day and hurried to Berlin where he addressed a crowd of 20,000 from the balcony of Schöneberg town-hall. He asked them to remain calm in that joyous hour, and thanked Mr Gorbachev and Germany's friends in the West for their support. He said the spirit of freedom had gripped the whole of Europe. Upon his return to Warsaw he signed a declaration in which Germany and Poland promised to intensify their cooperation in the cause of peace, security and stability in Europe.

The revolution in East Germany opened up the opportunity for the country's reunification after a wait of decades. But caution was required. Paris and London did not have German unity on the agenda. Mr Gorbachev, during talks with US President Ronald Reagan off the coast of Malta (December 1989), warned against any attempt to force the German issue. And in the GDR itself the new government under

Hans Modrow, though demanding rapid reform, also wanted the GDR to keep its statehood. Helmut Kohl therefore proposed a ten-point programme for achieving national unity. It envisaged a "contractual arrangement" based on a confederal system leading to fundamental political and economic change in the GDR. The Chancellor proposed that the direct negotiations with the GDR should take place within a pan-European setting under the aegis of the European Community and the CSCE. He avoided specifying a time-frame for the negotiations so as not to spark any further comment abroad about Germany seeking superpower status. The road to unity still seemed long to both sides, especially when Mr Gorbachev, addressing the Communist Party Central Committee, said as late as 9 December 1989 that Moscow would not leave East Germany "in the lurch", that it was Moscow's strategic ally in the Warsaw Pact and that one still had to start from the assumption of two German states, though there was no reason why they should not develop a relationship of peaceful cooperation.

Chancellor Kohl said the people in East Germany themselves should be the ones to decide on the speed and the substance of unification. But the government saw events rapidly slipping from their control. The people in East Germany distrusted their new government. They became increasingly attracted to the West and the process of destabilization increased rapidly. But still Mr Gorbachev held back, particularly as Poland and Hungary were escaping Moscow's grasp, Ceausescu's overthrow in Romania was in the offing, and therefore East Germany's departure from the Warsaw Pact would upset the balance of power. From western quarters, too, came exhortations to the Germans to "take account of the legitimate concerns of neighbouring countries" (US Secretary of State Baker speaking in Berlin) as they pursued national unity.

And finally, the unification process could only be continued after Bonn had given an assurance that there would be no shifting of the present borders, that, in the event of unification, NATO's "structures" would not be extended to the territory of the former GDR, and that Germany would reduce its armed forces to offset its strategic advantage. President Bush was in favour of German unification provided the Federal Republic remained a member of NATO.

The Unification Treaty. In order that the GDR could be represente in the negotiations people with a democratic mandate, free elections were held there on 18 March 1990, the first in 40 years. The result was a CDU/CSU/FDP coalition headed by Lothar de Maizière. With him the

Bonn government agreed on a time-table for economic, monetary and social union with effect from 1 July 1990, it having become palpably clear that the GDR had no economic basis on which to continue alone, and that the majority of the people in the GDR wanted accession to the Federal Republic.

In August the Volkskammer (East German parliament) voted in favour of accession as soon as possible, and on 31 August GDR State Secretary Günter Krause and Wolfgang Schäuble, Federal Minister of the Interior, were able to sign the "Unification Treaty". Thus on 3 October 1990 the German Democratic Republic officially acceded to the Federal Republic in accordance with article 23 of the Basic Law. The East German states of Brandenburg, Mecklenburg-Western Pomerania, Saxony, Saxony-Anhalt and Thuringia became states (Länder) of the Federal Republic of Germany. Berlin was made the capital and the Basic Law, after appropriate amendments, applied to the former GDR as well.

The road to unity had been opened by Mikhail Gorbachev, who had given his approval after talks with Chancellor Kohl in Moscow and the Caucasian town of Stavropol in July 1990. He did so on condition that the Federal Republic would forgo NBC weapons and reduce its

Green light for German unification:
Federal Chancellor Kohl (right) in the Caucasus talking
to Gorbachev (middle) and Genscher (left)

After signing the German Unification Treaty:
interior ministers Schäuble (West) and Krause (East)

In 1990, the Two plus Four Treaty is signed in Moscow

The first session of the Pan-German Federal Parliament in the Berlin Reichstag, 1990

forces to 370,000, and that NATO's military organization would not be extended to GDR territory so long as Soviet forces remained stationed there. The two leaders also agreed that the Soviet troops would be withdrawn from East Germany by the end of 1994, and that the Federal Republic would provide financial support for their repatriation. Mr Gorbachev's agreement also meant that the so-called Two-plus-Four Treaty could also be signed. Within that framework the Soviet Union, the United States, France and the United Kingdom, as well as the representatives of the two German states, confirmed the unification of Germany consisting of the territories of the former GDR, the Federal Republic and Berlin. Germany's external borders were recognized as definitive. Bonn and Warsaw concluded a separate treaty to take account of Poland's special security needs in the light of history. The two sides agreed to respect each other's territorial integrity and sovereignty.

The ratification of the Unification Treaty and the Two-plus-Four Treaty marked the termination of the rights and responsibilities of the four victorious powers "with respect to Berlin and Germany as a whole". Germany thus regained complete sovereignty over her internal and external affairs which she had lost 45 years previously with the fall of the nazi dictatorship.

The Basic Law

The Basic Law for the Federal Republic of Germany was adopted in 1949. Its authors intended it as a "temporary" framework for a new democratic system, not as a definitive constitution. The Basic Law called upon the people "to achieve in free self-determination the unity and freedom of Germany". As time passed by the Basic Law proved to be a solid foundation for democracy. Its requirement of national reunification was fulfilled in 1990.

The preamble and concluding article of the Basic Law have been amended in accordance with the Unification Treaty, which formed the basis for the accession of the German Democratic Republic (GDR) to the Federal Republic. They now state that, by virtue of the GDR's accession, the German people have achieved their unity. Since 3 October 1990 the Basic Law has applied to the whole German nation.

Unification has given rise to the question whether the Basic Law should be replaced by a new constitution. There is little doubt that at least constitutional changes are necessary and a joint committee of the Bundestag and the Bundesrat are considering possible amendments to strengthen the country's federal structure and incorporate specific national objectives on such matters as environmental protection.

On the occasion of the Federal Republic's 40th anniversary in 1989 the Basic Law was acknowledged to be the best and most liberal constitution Germany had ever had. As manifest in the life of the community, its principles have largely been put into practice, its requirements by and large fulfilled. More than any previous German constitution, the Basic Law is understood and accepted by the people. It created a state and society which so far has been spared any serious constitutional crises.

The Basic Law's content was greatly influenced by the personal experience of its authors under the Nazi dictatorship. In many parts it clearly indicates that they were trying to avoid the mistakes that had been partly responsible for the demise of the Weimar democracy. Those who drafted the constitution in 1948 were the Ministers President (with roughly the functions of a premier or governor) of the states that had been formed in the western occupation zones, and the

Signing of the Basic Law in the Parliamentary Council in 1949

Parliamentary Council elected by the state parliaments. This Council formally adopted the Basic Law, which was promulgated on 23 May 1949.

The basic rights. Pride of place in the constitution is given to a charter of basic rights, the first of which obliges the state to respect and protect the dignity of man. This guarantee is supplemented by the right of every individual to develop his personality as he sees fit. It affords comprehensive protection from unlawful interference by the state. Both Germans and non-Germans can invoke these constitutional rights. The classical freedoms embodied in the Basic Law include freedom of religion, free speech (including freedom of the press) and the guarantee of property. There are also freedom of art and scholarship, the right to form coalitions, the right to privacy of mail and telecommunications, protection from forced labour, privacy of the home, and the right of conscientious objection.

The so-called civil rights, which apply only to German nationals, relate for the most part to their involvement in the political process and their free choice of occupation or profession. Basically, they include the right of assembly, the right to form associations and societies, freedom of movement within (including the right to enter) the country, the ban on extradition, and the franchise.

These freedoms are accompanied by rights which guarantee equality. The Basic Law expresses the general principle that all people are equal before the law by providing that no one may be discriminated against or privileged on account of his origin, race, language, convictions, religion or political views. It expressly states that men and women must be treated as equals, and it guarantees equal access to public office for all Germans.

The basic rights in the social sphere concern the individual's position with regard to marriage, family, church, school, but also the state, especially in its capacity as a body politic based on social justice. These rights entitle the citizen to certain means of support by the state, for instance in the form of social services, some of which can be claimed direct.

One basic right, which by its very nature can only apply to foreigners, is the right of political asylum. The Basic Law is the first German constitutional instrument to provide refuge in Germany for foreigners persecuted on political grounds.

The scope of some basic rights may be restricted by other laws, but these may never encroach upon the essence of those rights. The basic rights are directly applicable law. This was a crucial innovation compared with previous constitutions, whose basic rights were largely non-binding declarations of intent. Nowadays, parliament is just as strictly bound by the basic rights as the government, the courts, the authorities, the police and the armed forces. Thus every citizen has the right to complain to the Federal Constitutional Court that his or her basic rights have been violated by the state.

By acceding to the European Convention for the Protection of Human Rights and Fundamental Freedoms in 1952, the Federal Repu-

Federal Coat of Arms

Federal flag

blic of Germany subjected itself to international control. Under article 25 the citizens of signatory states have the right to complain to the European Commission of Human Rights and the European Court of Justice, even if this means taking their own government to task.

Fundamental characteristics of the state. The principles on which the state as shaped by the Basic Law is founded can be summarized in the following sentence: Germany is a republic and a democracy; it is a federal state based on the rule of law and social justice. Its republican system is constitutionally manifest in the name "Federal Republic of Germany", and in the fact that the head of state is the elected Federal President. A democracy is based on the sovereignty of the people. The constitution says that all state authority emanates from the people. Thus it opted for indirect, representative democracy, in other words state authority must be recognized and approved by the people but they have no direct say in the exercise of that authority. This responsibility is entrusted to the organs specially established by the constitution for this purpose: the legislature, the executive, and the judiciary. The people exercise their constitutional authority primary by periodically electing a new parliament. In contrast to some countries, provision for other forms of direct democracy, such as referendums, has been made only with regard to modifications of state boundaries.

The authors of the Basic Law opted for an "adversarial" democracy, they having seen the Weimar Republic undermined by radical parties which were hostile to the constitution. In this context "adversarial" means that the free play of political forces must stop where any party or faction attempts to remove democracy with democratic means. This explains why the Basic Law makes it possible to ban political parties who seek to damage or do away with the country's democratic system.

The constitutional decision in favour of a federal state implies that not only the country as a whole but its 16 constituent parts, the Länder, have some of the features of a state. Each has its own powers, though they are restricted to certain spheres, which it exercises through its own legislature, executive and judiciary. Public responsibility has been apportioned in such a way that law-making is largely in the hands of the central state, the Federation, whereas the constituent states have the task of administering legislation. This division of responsibilities is an essential element of the power-sharing system provided for in the Basic Law. It helps prevent the emergence of a single, all-powerful central authority.

This power-sharing principle is the very foundation of the rule of law. The exercise of state authority has been entrusted to parliament, government, and the judiciary, each independent of the others. The significance of this division of authority is that the power of the state is moderated through mutual checks and balances. It thus protects the individual's freedom. Another major feature of the rule of law principle is that all state activity is governed by law. This means in particular that parliament is strictly bound by the constitution and the authorities (e.g. the police) by the law. Any action by the state may be examined by independent judges as to their consistency with the law if the person or persons affected take the matter to court.

The social state is a modern extension of the traditional rule of law concept. Under this system the state is required to protect the weaker members of society and to strive for social justice. Numerous laws and court rulings have ensured the application of this principle, which

Ei · nig · keit und Recht und Frei · heit
Da · nach laßt uns al · le stre · ben

für das deut · sche Va · ter · land!
brü · der · lich mit Herz und Hand!

Ei · nig · keit und Recht und Frei · heit

sind des Glük · kes Un · ter · pfand.

Blüh im Glan · ze die · ses Glük · kes,

blü · he, deut · sches Va · ter · land!

*The national anthem of the Federal Republic of Germany is the
"Song of Germany". The text of the three-stanza song was written
by August Heinrich Hoffmann von Fallersleben (1798–1874); the melody
is that of the "Imperial Anthem" by Joseph Haydn (1732–1809).
The third stanza is sung on official state occasions.*

manifests itself in the provision of old-age, invalidity, health and unemployment insurance, social assistance for needy people, rent allowances, child benefit, laws on industrial safety and working hours, etc. The Basic Law does not, however, state specifically how the country's economy should be run. Where economic policy is concerned it remains for the most part neutral.

Amendments to the Basic Law. The Basic Law may only be amended with a majority of two thirds of the members of the Bundestag (Federal Parliament) and two thirds of the votes cast in the Bundesrat (Federal Council). Since one single party or coalition rarely has such a majority in both the Bundestag and the Bundesrat, amendments to the Basic Law require a very broad consensus. This can only be achieved with the support of members of the opposition.

Some provisions of the Basic Law may not be changed at all, not even with a two-thirds majority. Those are the parts relating to the federal system, power-sharing, democracy, rule of law, and the social state. Likewise untouchable are the commitment to protect the dignity of man and the basic rights and freedoms.

The constitutional bodies

"All state authority emanates from the people" - this underlying principle of democracy is codified in the constitution. The people exercise that authority directly in elections, indirectly through bodies instituted by the constitution: the legislature, the executive and the judiciary. The constitutional bodies with primarily legislative functions are the Bundestag and the Bundesrat. Executive responsibilities lie principally with the Federal Government, headed by the Federal Chancellor, and the Federal President. Judicial functions in connection with the constitution are performed by the Federal Constitutional Court.

The Federal President. The head of state of the Federal Republic of Germany is the Federal President. He is elected by the Federal Convention, a constitutional body which convenes only for this purpose. It consists of the members of the Bundestag and an equal number of members elected by the state parliaments. Sometimes eminent persons who are not members of a state parliament are nominated for the Federal Convention. The Federal President is elected for a term of five years with the majority of votes in the Federal Convention. He may only be reelected once.

The Federal President represents the Federal Republic in its international relations and concludes agreements with foreign states in its name. He also accredits and receives ambassadors, although foreign policy itself is the responsibility of the Federal Government. He appoints and dismisses federal civil judges, federal civil servants, officers and non-commissioned officers of the armed forces. The President can pardon convicted criminals. He checks whether laws have come about by the proper constitutional procedure and publishes them in the Federal Law Gazette.

He proposes to the Bundestag a candidate for the office of Federal Chancellor (taking account of the majority situation in parliament) and, in response to proposals from the Chancellor, appoints and dismisses cabinet ministers. If the Chancellor seeks but fails to gain a vote of confidence the Federal President may, on the Chancellor's proposal, dissolve the Bundestag. Premature elections were brought about in this way in 1972 and 1983.

Theodor Heuss

Heinrich Lübke

Gustav Heinemann

Walter Scheel

Karl Carstens

Richard von Weizsäcker

The Federal Presidents:

Theodor Heuss (FDP)	1st term of office	1949-1954
	2nd term of office	1954-1959
Heinrich Lübke (CDU)	1st term of office	1959-1964
	2nd term of office	1964-1969
Gustav Heinemann (SPD)		1969-1974
Walter Scheel (FDP)		1974-1979
KarlCarstens (CDU)		1979-1984
Richard von Weizsäcker (CDU)	1st term of office	1984-1989
	2nd term of office	1989

Konrad Adenauer   *Ludwig Erhard*   *Kurt Georg Kiesinger*

Willy Brandt   *Helmut Schmidt*   *Helmut Kohl*

The Federal Chancellors:

Konrad Adenauer (CDU)	1st Cabinet	1949-1953
	2nd Cabinet	1953-1957
	3rd Cabinet	1957-1961
	4th Cabinet	1961-1963
Ludwig Erhard (CDU)	1st Cabinet	1963-1965
	2nd Cabinet	1965-1966
Kurt Georg Kiesinger (CDU)		1966-1969
Willy Brandt (SPD)	1st Cabinet	1969-1972
	2nd Cabinet	1972-1974
Helmut Schmidt (SPD)	1st Cabinet	1974-1976
	2nd Cabinet	1976-1980
	3rd Cabinet	1980-1982
Helmut Kohl (CDU)	1st Cabinet	1982-1983
	2nd Cabinet	1983-1987
	3rd Cabinet	1987-1990
	4th Cabinet	1990

The Federal President personifies the country's political unity in a special way. He is the link between all elements in society regardless of party distinctions. Although his tasks are mainly of a representational nature he can exercise considerable personal authority through his neutral, mediating function. By commenting on the fundamental aspects of current issues he can rise above general party-political controversy and set standards for the public's political and moral guidance.

The Bundestag. The German Bundestag is the parliamentary assembly representing the people of the Federal Republic of Germany. It is elected by the people every four years. It may only be dissolved prematurely under exceptional circumstances, the final decision lying with the Federal President. The Bundestag's main functions are to pass laws, to elect the Federal Chancellor, and to keep check on the government.

The Bundestag is the forum for major parliamentary debates on foreign policy and domestic issues. It is in the parliamentary committees, which are not usually public, that the extensive preparatory work for legislation is done. Here it is a question of harmonizing political intentions with the detailed knowledge provided by the experts. It is likewise in the committees that parliament scrutinizes and controls government activity. Otherwise it would not be possible to cope with the multitude of technical questions. The Bundestag's committees correspond to the Federal Government's departments and range from the foreign relations committee via the social affairs committee to the budget committee, the latter having special significance in that it represents parliament's control of the budget. The petitions committee is open to requests and complaints from any member of the public.

From 1949 until the end of the last legislative term in 1990 about 6,700 bills were introduced in parliament and 4,400 of them passed. Most of them are initiated by the Federal Government, the others coming from the floor of the house or the Bundesrat. They receive three readings in the Bundestag and are usually referred to the appropriate committee once.

The final vote is taken after the third reading. A bill (providing it is not intended to amend the constitution) is passed if it receives a majority of the votes cast. In some cases, however, it still requires the approval of the Bundesrat to become law. Members of the Bundestag are returned in general elections, which are direct, free, equal, and secret. They represent the people as a whole, are not bound by instructions and

Federal structure

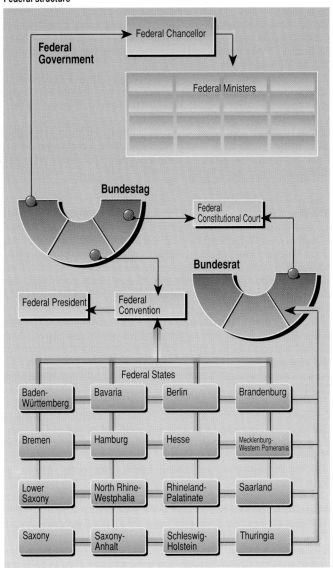

must obey only their conscience. In line with their party allegiances they form parliamentary groups. Freedom of conscience and the requirements of party solidarity sometimes collide, but even if in such a situation a member feels obliged to leave his party he keeps his seat in the Bundestag. This is the clearest indication that members of the Bundestag are independent.

The relative strengths of the party groups determine the composition of the committees. The President (Speaker) of the Bundestag is elected from the ranks of the strongest parliamentary group, in keeping with German constitutional tradition.

Members are paid "compensation" corresponding to the importance of their status as MPs. Anyone who has been a member of parliament for at least six years receives a pension upon reaching retirement age.

The Bundesrat. The Bundesrat represents the sixteen federal states and participates in the shaping and administering of federal legislation. In contrast to the senatorial system of federal states like America or Switzerland, the Bundesrat does not consist of elected representatives of the people but of members of the state governments or their representatives. Depending on the size of their population, the states have three, four, five or six votes which may only be cast as a block.

More than half of all bills require the formal approval of the Bundesrat, which means that they cannot pass into law against its will. This applies especially to bills that concern vital interests of the states, for instance their financial affairs or their administrative powers. No proposed amendments to the constitution can be adopted without the Bundesrat's blessing.

In all other cases the Bundesrat only has a right of objection, but this can be overruled by the Bundestag. If the two houses of parliament cannot reach agreement a Mediation Committee composed of members of both chambers must be convened which, in most cases, is able to work out a compromise.

In the Bundesrat state interests often override party interests. In such cases the voting may not reflect party strengths in the council. This points to an active federalism. The Federal Government cannot always rely on a state government under with the same party to follow its lead in every respect, for each state takes its own special interests into consideration and sometimes takes sides with other states who pursue the same aim, irrespective of the party it is governed by. This produces fluctuating majorities, and compromises have to be found

The Reichstag in Berlin

where the parties forming the Federal Government do not have a majority in the Bundesrat.

The Bundesrat elects its president from among the Ministers President of the federal states for a period of twelve months according to a fixed rota. The President of the Bundesrat exercises the powers of the Federal President in the event of his indisposition.

The Federal Government. The Federal Government, the cabinet, consists of the Federal Chancellor, the chairman and head of government, and the federal ministers. The Chancellor alone nominates the ministers, who are formally appointed by the Federal President. He also determines the size of his cabinet.

The Chancellor is in a strong position mainly owing to the fact that he lays down the guidelines of government policy. The federal ministers run their departments independently and on their own responsibility but within the framework of those guidelines. In a coalition government the Chancellor must of course take account of agreements reached with the other party in the coalition.

This explains why the German system of government is often referred to as a "Chancellor democracy". The Chancellor is the only member of the government elected by parliament and he alone is responsible to it. This responsibility may manifest itself in a "constructive vote of no confidence", which was introduced by the authors of the Basic Law in deliberate contrast to the Weimar constitution. Its

Meeting of the German Parliament in Bonn

purpose is to ensure that opposition groups who are agreed only in their rejection of the government but not as regards an alternative programme are not able to overthrow the government. A Bundestag vote of no confidence in the Chancellor must at the same time be a majority vote in favour of his successor.

Of the two attempts to bring down a Chancellor with the help of a constructive vote of no confidence, only one has succeeded. That was in 1982, when a no-confidence motion removed Helmut Schmidt from office and put Chancellor Kohl in his place. The Basic Law makes no provision for motions of no confidence in individual federal ministers.

The Federal Constitutional Court. The Federal Constitutional Court in Karlsruhe is the guardian of the Basic Law. It rules, for instance, on disputes between the Federal Government and the federal states or between individual federal institutions. Only this court has the power to declare that a party constitutes a threat to freedom and democracy and is therefore unconstitutional, in which case it orders that party's dissolution. It scrutinizes federal and state laws as to their conformity with the Basic Law. If it rules that a law is unconstitutional it may no longer be applied. The court acts in such cases only if called upon by certain authorities, such as the Federal Government, the state governments, parliament, lower courts, etc.

In addition, every citizen has the right to file a complaint with the Federal Constitutional Court if he feels his basic rights have been violated by the state. Before doing so, however, he must have exhausted all other legal remedies.

So far the Federal Constitutional Court has passed judgment in more than 80,000 cases. Some 76,000 of them dealt with constitutional complaints, although only just under 2,000 of them were successful. Often matters of great domestic or international significance are dealt with. Recently, for instance, the court ruled on the electoral law relating to the first general election in the whole of Germany in 1990. Another issue put before it concerned the treaty establishing German unity. Federal Governments of all political hues have had to submit to decisions of the judges in Karlsruhe. The Court has repeatedly stressed, however, that it does not see its task as prescribing a certain course of political action by institutions of the state.

The Federal Constitutional Court has played a large part in ensuring the practical application of the Basic Law. In particular it gives substance to the basic rights. For instance, it ruled in a case brought before it that article 6 of the Basic Law, which says that children born in and outside marriage must be treated as equals, be made applicable law.

Meeting of the Federal Cabinet

The Federal Constitutional Court consists of two senates (panels), each with eight judges, half of whom are elected by the Bundestag, the other half by the Bundesrat. The judges serve for twelve years and may not be reelected.

Federalism and self-government

The name "Federal Republic of Germany" itself denotes the country's federal structure. The Federal Republic consists of sixteen states. After 1945 the eleven states of the original Federal Republic were reestablished or newly founded. Following the peaceful revolution in the GDR, the states of former times were restored there too. Since 3 October 1990, when the nation was reunited, they have been part of the Federal Republic.

The states are not mere provinces but have been endowed with their own powers. Each has a constitution which must be consistent with the republican, democratic and social principles embodied in the Basic Law. Subject to these conditions they can shape their constitution as they like.

Federalism is one of the constitutional principles that may not be tampered with. But this is not to say that the constituent states may not be altered. Provision for boundary adjustments has been made in the Basic Law. In fact, now that there are 16 states the question of redefining boundaries with a view to creating larger, economically more efficient units is now under discussion.

The federal system has a long tradition in Germany, which was only disrupted by the Nazi unitary state of 1933-45. Germany is one of the classical federal states. With such a structure it is much easier to take account of regional characteristics and problems.

Benefits of a federal system. German federalism, much as in the United States and Switzerland, binds the country's external unity with its internal diversity. Preserving that regional diversity is the traditional task of the federal system. This function today acquires new substance in the form of "local" responsibilities such as landscape management, nature conservation, the protection of monuments and historical sites, the preservation of architectural traditions, and the promotion of regional culture.

But the main purpose of federalism is to safeguard the nation's freedom. The distribution of responsibilities as between the Federal Government and the states is an essential element of the power-sharing arrangement, the checks and balances, as provided for in the

Basic Law. This also embraces the participation of the states in the legislative process at federal level through the Bundesrat.

The federal structure also enhances the democratic principle. It enables the citizen to engage in the political process in his own region. This gives democracy greater vitality.

There are other benefits as well. The federal system leaves room for experiments on a smaller scale and for competition among the states. For instance, a single state may try out innovative methods in, say, education which may later serve as a model for reform throughout the country.

Furthermore, parties which are in opposition at national level may be in government in some of the states. Thus all parties have the chance to prove their ability to govern.

The powers of the federal states. The Basic Law determined the powers of the Federation in terms of whether laws should be the same for all states or whether the regions should be allowed to make their own laws. This is illustrated by the fact that the Federation's law-making powers fall into three different categories: exclusive, concurrent or framework legislation.

Areas of legislation which fall into the exclusive sphere of competence of the Federation are foreign affairs, defence, monetary matters, railways, air traffic, and some elements of taxation. In the case of concurrent legislation, the states may only pass laws whereon matters not covered by federal law. The Federation may only legislate in such cases where it is necessary to have a uniform law for the whole country.

The areas which fall into this category are commercial law, nuclear energy, labour and land law, housing, shipping, road transport, refuse disposal, air pollution, and noise abatement. Since it has proved necessary to have standard laws for these matters, the states have practically no authority in this respect.

Where the Federation has the power to adopt framework laws, the states have a certain amount of legislative latitude. This applies, for instance, in the fields of education, nature conservation, landscape management, regional planning and water management. There are also a number of other supraregional tasks which, though not mentioned in the Basic Law, are today jointly planned, regulated and financed by the Federation and the states. They were incorporated in the Basic Law in 1969 as "joint responsibilities". They cover university building, improvement of regional industrial and agricultural structures, as well as coastal preservation.

Direct federal administration is more or less limited to the Foreign Service, the federal railways, posts and telecommunications, labour placement, customs, federal border protection, and the Federal Armed Forces. Most administrative responsibilities are carried out by the states independently.

The Federation's jurisdiction is confined to the Federal Constitutional Court and the supreme courts, which ensure the uniform interpretation of the law. All other courts fall within the ambit of state jurisdiction.

As mentioned above, the states can fill in any gaps left by federal legislation or in areas not specified in the Basic Law. Thus they are responsible for education and culture almost in their entirety as a manifestation of their "cultural sovereignty". They are also responsible for local government law and the police.

The real strength of the states lies in their participation in the legislative process at federal level through the Bundesrat. All internal administration lies in their hands and their bureaucracy implements most federal laws and regulations. Thus state administration is threefold: it handles matters that are exclusively the responsibility of the federal state (e.g. schools, police, town and country planning); it implements federal law on its own responsibility (planning for building projects, trade and industry, environmental protection); and it applies federal law on behalf of the Federation (e.g. national highways, promotion of vocational training).

Thus in the course of its development the Federal Republic has become a country in which most laws are enacted centrally while the bulk of legislation is administered by the federal states.

Local government. Local government, as an expression of civic freedom, has a long tradition in Germany. It can be traced back to the privileges of the free towns in the Middle Ages, when civic rights freed people from the bonds of feudal serfdom. (As they said in those days, "town air makes people free".) In modern times local government has primarily been linked, however, to the great reforms of the Prussian Minister Freiherr vom Stein, in particular the Local Government Code of 1808.

This tradition of civic liberty is manifest in the self-government of towns and counties expressly guaranteed by the Basic Law. The constitution grants them the right to regulate local affairs within the framework of the law. All municipalities and counties must have a democratic structure. Municipal law falls within the sphere of competence of the federal states. For historical reasons the munici-

The town hall in Mainz

pal constitutions vary greatly from state to state, but in practice the administrative system is by and large the same everywhere.

Self-government embraces in particular local transport, road construction, electricity, water and gas supply, and town planning, as well as the building and maintenance of schools, theatres and museums, hospitals, sportsfacilities and public baths. Other local responsibilities are adult education and youth welfare. The expediency and cost-benefit aspects of programmes in these fields are the responsibility of the local council. Many such measures are beyond the means of smaller communities but these matters can be taken over by the next higher level of local government, the county (Kreis). The county, too, is part of the system of local government through its own democratically elected bodies. The larger cities do not form part of a county.

Local government and independence are bound to suffer if the municipalities are unable to finance their programmes. Their financial situation is frequently a subject of public debate. Local autho-

Town hall Stolberg (Saxony-Anhalt)

rities raise their own taxes and levies, which include land tax and trade tax. They are also entitled to raise local taxes on certain luxury goods. This revenue does not suffice to cover their financial needs, however. They therefore receive from the federal and state governments a share of the nation's income tax. They also receive allocations under the financial equalization arrangement which applies in every state.

Local self-government gives the citizen an opportunity to play his part and have a controlling influence. He can discuss such matters as new building projects with elected councillors at town meetings and inspect budget estimates. The municipalities are the smallest cells in the political system. They must always be able to thrive and develop as the basic source of freedom and democracy.

Parties and elections

In a modern democracy competing political parties are of fundamental importance. They are elected for a specific term during which they assume the powers of government and keep check on the activities of the current administration. They therefore play a major role in the shaping of public policy.

These functions are taken into account in the Basic Law, which devotes a separate article (article 21) to the parties, which defines their task as participating "in the forming of the political will of the people". The parties must be democratically structured and are required to disclose their sources of income and their assets.

Parties in the Bundestag. Since the first general election to be held in the whole of Germany (1990), there have been six parties in the Bundestag: the Christian Democratic Union of Germany (CDU), the Social Democratic Party of Germany (SPD), the Free Democratic Party (FDP), the Christian Social Union (CSU), the Party of Democratic Socialism (PDS) and the group known as Alliance 90/Greens. The

CDU Chairman Helmut Kohl and his deputy
Angela Merkel

CSU Chairman Theodor Waigel

CDU has no party association in Bavaria, while the CSU puts up candidates for election in Bavaria only. In the Bundestag, however, CDU and CSU have a joint parliamentary group.

The SPD, CDU, CSU and FDP were formed in the western states between 1945 and 1947. The SPD was a recreation of the former mainly labour-oriented party of the same name which had been out-

FDP Chairman Otto Graf Lambsdorff (2nd from left)
with his deputies

SPD Chairman Björn Engholm (centre)
with his deputies

lawed by the Hitler regime in 1933. The other parties were completely new. The Christian parties, CDU and CSU, in contrast to the Catholic Centre Party of Weimar days, drew their support from both of Germany's two major Christian creeds, Roman Catholicism and Protestantism. The FDP laid claim to the heritage of German liberalism.

In the four decades since their establishment these four parties have undergone significant changes. At federal level they have all formed coalitions with one another or been in opposition. Today they all see themselves as "popular" parties representing all sections of the population. They have distinct right and left wing factions which reflect the various elements of a people's party.

From 1983 to 1990 the Greens, too, had its own group in the Bundestag. It had been established at national level in 1979 and was gradually voted into some of the state parliaments as well. Its roots lie in a radical ecologist movement which embraces factions opposed to nuclear energy as well as pacifist protest groups. In the 1990 general election, however, the Greens failed to clear the five per cent hurdle, but they are nonetheless represented in the Bundestag, sharing a list with Alliance 90, a product of the civil rights movement which in 1989-90 brought about the peaceful revolution in the former GDR.

The PDS is the successor to the former Socialist Unity Party of Germany (SED), the communist party which ruled in the GDR. It was not able to establish itself as a major political force in united Germany but it is represented in the Bundestag by virtue of an exception allowing the five per cent clause to be applied separately in the new federal states and the existing ones in the west for the benefit of the parties in the eastern part of the country. This rule also applied to the Alliance 90/Greens group.

The five per cent clause. Of the 36 parties which sought election to the first Bundestag in 1949, only four remained in the parliament elected in 1990. This is the result of a "five per cent debarring clause" which was introduced in 1953 and made stricter still in 1957. This clause stipulates that only parties gaining at least five per cent of the votes or at least three constituency seats can be represented in parliament. This arrangement was explicitly accepted by the Federal Constitutional Court since its purpose was to prevent tiny splinter parties from entering the Bundestag (which is what happened in the days of the Weimar Republic) and thus enable the larger parties to obtain majorities that would enable them to govern.

This five per cent hurdle is waived in the case of national minorities. Thus the South-Schleswig Voters' Association, which represents the Danish minority, has a representative in the state parliament of Schleswig-Holstein even though he obtained fewer than five per cent of the votes.

Local government elections sometimes produce results that differ greatly from those of federal and state elections. Here the "town

Election poster of Alliance 90/Greens for the 1990 General Election

hall parties", independent voters' associations, often play an important role.

The electoral system. Elections for all parliaments in Germany are general, direct, free, equal and secret. Every German aged 18 or over may vote. There are no primary elections. Candidates are nominated by their parties. Elections for the German Bundestag are based on a system of "personalized" proportional representation. Electors have two votes, the first of which is given to a candidate in their constituency, who is elected on a first-past-the-post basis. The second vote is given to a list of candidates put up by the parties. The votes from the constituencies and those for the state lists are offset in such a way that the composition of the Bundestag almost identically reflects the distribution of votes among the parties. If a party has won more direct seats in the constituencies than its proportion of the votes would justify (they being known as "overhang" seats), it is allowed to keep them. Whenever this happens the Bundestag has more than its present 662 members. The object of having the electorate vote for state lists is to ensure that the strengths of all parties in parliament

Shares of votes at federal elections

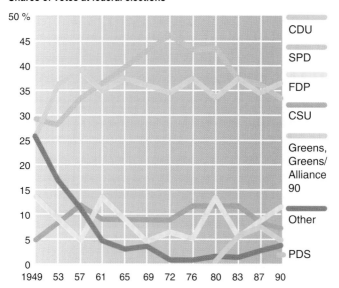

1990 General Election

Party	Valid se-cond votes	Percent	M.P.s
CDU	17,055,116	36.7	268
SPD	15,545,366	33.5	239
F.D.P.	5,123,233	11.0	79
CSU	3,302,980	7.1	51
Greens	1,788,200	3.8	--
PDS	1,129,578	2.4	17
Alliance90/Greens	559,207	1.2	8
Other	1,952,062	4.3	--
Total	46,455,772	100	662

*(Turnout was 77.8%. Party strengths including overhang seats, as at 1990)

Distribution of seats in the German Parliament *

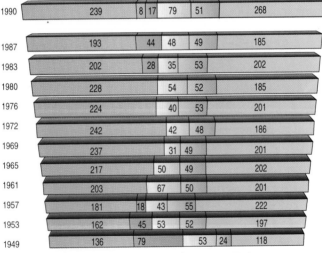

* at beginning of each legislative period; until 1987 including members from Berlin (West)

CDU   SPD   Alliance 90 / Greens
CSU   FDP   PDS   Other

represent their shares of the votes obtained. On the other hand, the constituency vote, the first vote, gives them the chance to choose a particular candidate.

Normally the people take a keen interest in elections. The turnout for the Bundestag election of 1990 was 77.8 per cent. It tends to fluctuate at state and local elections, but it is nearly always around 70 per cent.

Membership and finances. The memberships of the parties represented in the Bundestag in 1991 were as follows: SPD 935,000, CDU 790,000, CSU 180,000, FDP 162,000, PDS 180,000. All parties require their members to pay contributions, which, however, cover only a portion of their expenses. Nor do the donations received by the parties suffice. Moreover, there is a danger of donors influencing them for their own ends. The Parties Act therefore stipulates that donations of more than DM 20,000 must be made public. In addition to their own funds the parties receive public grants towards their election campaign costs. All parties who poll at least 0.5 per cent of the votes receive five marks per head on the basis of second votes in the electoral area. The Federal Constitutional Court has banned any public financial support for the parties beyond this amount.

Social Democratic Party of Germany
Ollenhauerstr. 1, 5300 Bonn 1

Christian Democratic Union of Germany
Friedrich-Ebert-Allee 73-75, 5300 Bonn 1

Christian Social Union in Bavaria
Nymphenburgerstr. 64, 8000 München 2

Free Democratic Party
Baunscheidtstr. 15, 5300 Bonn 1

Party of Democratic Socialism
Kleine Alexanderstr. 28, 1020 Berlin

Alliance 90
Friedrichstr. 16, 1080 Berlin

The Greens
Colmantstr. 36, 5300 Bonn 1

The legal system

The law of the Federal Republic of Germany is predominantly written law, most of it federal and comprising more than 4,000 acts and statutory instruments. The states, too, pass laws, mainly on such matters as the police, local government, schools and universities as well as the press, radio and television. In accordance with the Unification Treaty of 31 August 1990, all federal laws apply in principle in the former German Democratic Republic with effect from 3 October 1990.

During the forty-odd years when the country was divided the legal systems of the Federal Republic and the GDR became totally different. The GDR's "socialist legislation" was a political instrument used to impose Marxist-Leninist ideology. The crucial decision was taken in 1990 to merge the two legal systems as soon as possible after the GDR's accession to the Federal Republic. This was also of fundamental importance for the process of economic recovery in the new federal states. Extensive adjustments were made in nearly all fields of law in order to take account of the special situation in the GDR and the existing system.

A state based on the rule of law. Historically, federal legislation goes back partly to Roman law and partly to numerous legal sources in the German regions. In the 19th century a uniform system of private law was created for the first time. It applied to the entire German empire. The Civil Code and Commercial Code to this day preserve the liberal spirit of those times. Their underlying principle is freedom of contract. The guarantees afforded by a democratic state are manifest above all in substantive and procedural law. Criminal law starts from the constitutional premise that no act or omission may lead to the offender's punishment unless it has been declared punishable by law before it was committed (nulla poena sine lege). This means that judges may not make up for gaps in penal law by applying legal provisions which apply to similar cases, nor may they apply laws retroactively. Another principle embedded in the constitution is that no one may be punished more than once for the same offence under general criminal law.

Personal liberty may not be restricted except on the basis of a formal law. Only a judge may determine whether a person's imprisonment is justified and only he can decide for how long. Whenever a person is detained without a judicial warrant the matter must be brought before a judge for decision without delay. Although the police may hold someone in temporary custody, they may not detain him any longer than the end of the day following the arrest. Everyone has a right to a court hearing - that, too, is guaranteed by the constitution and is a fundamental democratic principle.

The administration of justice is entrusted to judges who are independent and answerable to the law only. They may not be dismissed from office nor transferred against their will. Special tribunals are banned.

Nearly all of these fundamental principles had already been established by the judiciary laws of the 19th century. They include the Judicature Act, which governs the structure, organization and jurisdiction of the courts, the Code of Civil Procedure and the Code of Criminal Procedure. The Civil Code, which entered into force in 1900, and the Code of Civil and Criminal Procedure were wrested by liberal and democratic forces from the imperial government towards the end of the last century after a long drawn out struggle in parliament. Some German codified laws have found their way into foreign legal systems. The Civil Code, for instance, was the model for its Japanese and Greek counterparts.

The citizen and public administration. After an evolutionary period of more than 100 years, the Basic Law set the seal on a comprehensive system of legal protection against the actions of public authorities. It enabled the citizen to challenge any measure that affected him on the ground that it violated his rights. This applies to all administrative acts, be they tax assessment notices or the decision whether or not to promote a school pupil to the next grade, be it the withdrawal of a driving licence or the refusal of a building permit.

Administrative courts were unknown in the GDR. Now administration in the new federal states will be subject to comprehensive control by the courts. The legal protection afforded by the specialized courts is complemented by a right of complaint to the Federal Constitutional Court. This "constitutional complaint" is open to every citizen and is an extra form of legal redress against any violations of basic rights by a public authority. The plaintiff must show that one of his basic rights has been infringed by a public act, for instance a court decision or an administrative measure. Normally, such com-

Federal Court of Justice, Karlsruhe

plaints may only be lodged after all other legal remedies have been exhausted.

Social justice. The Basic Law prescribes the development of the welfare system, hence much greater consideration is now given to the people's social needs than in former times. In the years since the creation of the Federal Republic a whole range of special labour and welfare legislation has been enacted to provide the citizen with various financial benefits in the event of sickness, accident, invalidity, and unemployment, and after retirement.

Labour law is a good example of how these welfare-state principles have been put into effect. Originally, these matters were only briefly dealt with under the heading of "service contract" in the Civil Code. Today, labour legislation embraces an abundance of laws and collective agreements. They include in particular the Collective Agreements Act, the Protection against Dismissal Act, the Works Constitution Act, and the various laws on codetermination.

Court structure and the legal profession. The Federal Republic's courts are largely specialized and provide full legal protection. They fall into five categories:

— The "ordinary courts" are responsible for criminal matters, civil cases (e.g. disputes arising from contracts of sale or lease agreements, family affairs and inheritance) and voluntary jurisdiction, — which includes conveyancing, probate and wardship matters. There are four levels: local court (Amtsgericht), regional court (Landgericht), higher regional court (Oberlandesgericht) and Federal Court of Justice (Bundesgerichtshof). In criminal cases, depending on their nature, each of the first three courts can have jurisdiction, whereas in civil proceedings it will be either the local court or the regional court. One or two other courts may be appealed to on points of fact or law.

— The labour courts (three levels, local, state and federal) handle disputes between employers and unions, and concerning works constitution matters, which are covered by the Works Constitution Act. The labour courts have to decide, for instance, whether an employee has been fairly or unfairly dismissed.

— The administrative courts (local, higher - i.e. state – and federal) handle all proceedings under administrative law that do not fall within the jurisdiction of the social and fiscal courts or, in exceptional cases, the ordinary courts, or disputes which fall under constitutional law.

— The social courts (local, state, federal) rule on all disputes concerned with social security matters.

— The fiscal courts (state and federal) deal with taxation and related matters.

In the five new federal states the old court structure has been retained for the time being. In those regions, therefore, the county and district courts deal with all matters which, in the western regions, are the responsibility of five different types of courts. Some of the new states have already established independent labour courts.

Separate from the five branches of jurisdiction is the Federal Constitutional Court, which is not only the country's supreme court but a constitutional body.

There is a complex system of appeals which provides numerous possibilities for judicial review. There are two stages in the appeal procedure. In the first, the case can be reviewed both as regards the facts and points of law, i.e. its merits. Thus at this level new evidence can still be introduced. In the second stage, however, the court will only consider whether the law has been properly applied and the essential procedural formalities observed.

In the Federal Republic of Germany there are approximately 20,000 professional judges, more than three quarters of whom are assigned to the ordinary courts. Most judges are appointed for life and in exercising their profession are bound only by the spirit and letter of the law. At local court level most proceedings of non-contentious litigation are handled by judicial officers, who are not judges but intermediate-level civil servants. In several types of court lay judges sit with the professional judges. Their experience and specialized knowledge in certain fields, such as labour and welfare matters, enable them to help the courts make realistic decisions. They also reflect part of the citizen's direct responsibility for the administration of justice.

The public prosecutors, of whom there are over 4,000, are for the most part concerned with criminal proceedings. It is their responsibility to establish the facts where a person is suspected of a crime. They have to decide whether to discontinue the proceedings or to indict the person concerned. In court proceedings they are the prosecuting council. Unlike judges, public prosecutors are public servants and therefore under orders from their superiors - though within very narrow limits. More than 60,000 lawyers act as independent counsel and representatives in all legal matters. Through representing their clients in court they are involved in the administration of justice. They must adhere to their professional code and any violations are dealt with by disciplinary tribunals.

All professional judges, public prosecutors and attorneys at law must have the qualifications to be a judge, in other words they must have graduated in law from a university and completed the compulsory course of practical training, each of which ends with a state examination.

Data protection. The advance of electronic data processing in the modern industrial society has created new problems for the judicial system. These days computers are used to maintain bank accounts, to book seats on aircraft, to issue tax notices or to collect crime data at police headquarters. EDP has become indispensable in nearly all fields of administration, making it possible to store and retrieve huge quantities of data. Modern technology has greatly eased the workload of many companies and public authorities and is increasingly finding its way into even small offices and private homes. There are hazards as well, however. Stored data can be put to improper use and fall into the hands of unauthorized persons. Anyone with sufficient quantities of data has information on the citizen's private life, which must remain inviolable.

In 1977 federal and state legislation was introduced to safeguard the community against such dangers. The law specifies those cases

Simplified overview of court structure in the Federal Republic of Germany

Federal Constitutional Court — 2 Senates

Constitutional Courts of Federal States

Ordinary jurisdiction	Administrative jurisdiction	Fiscal jurisdiction	Labour jurisdiction	Social Insurance jurisdiction
Federal Court of Justice Grand Senate for civil matters | Grand Senate for criminal matters Civil senates | Criminal senates	**Federal Administrative Court** Grand Senate Senates	**Federal Fiscal Court** Grand Senate Senates	**Federal Labour Court** Grand Senate Senates	**Federal Social Insurance Court** Grand Senate Senates
Higher Regional Court Civil senates | Senates for family matters | Criminal senates Criminal senates for serious criminal offences against the state	**Higher Administrative Court** Senates	**Fiscal Court** Senates	**Regional Labour Court** Senates	**Regional Social Insurance Court** Senates
Regional Court Civil divisions | Commercial divisions | Lower criminal divisions | Higher criminal divisions (1st level) | Higher criminal divisions (2nd level) | Juvenile divisions (1st level) | Juvenile divisions (2nd level)	**Administrative Court**		**Labour Court**	**Social Insurance Court**
District Court Single judge | Family court | Criminal judge | Lay assessors | Judge in juvenile matters | Lay assessors in juvenile matters				
Civil | Criminal jurisdiction				

where the authorities and industrial enterprises may store personal data. In other instances it is forbidden. Staff involved in data processing are bound to secrecy. The citizen is legally entitled to know what data concerning his or her person is held by any agency. He can demand the correction of wrong data and have others removed which are either disputed or have been improperly obtained.

On the recommendation of the Federal Government, the Federal President appoints a Federal Commissioner for Data Protection who is independent of any other authority. He is a kind of ombudsman to whom any person who feels that his personal data have not been adequately protected may complain. He submits an annual report to the Bundestag. Each of the federal states, too, has a data protection ombudsman. And enterprises who process data must likewise have someone in charge of data protection. The authorities check whether they observe the legal requirements with regard to data protection.

The constitutional significance of data protection emerged in a ruling of the Federal Constitutional Court in 1983. It said that under article 2 of the Basic Law the citizen has the right to determine himself whether data regarding his person may be disclosed and how it may be used. In 1990 the Federal Data Protection Act was updated to take account of the Federal Constitutional Court's ruling and the advancement of data processing. The rights of persons affected have been strengthened and the Federal Commissioner for Data Protection given wider powers.

Germany has some of the most up-to-date and comprehensive legislation in this field which has helped increase public awareness of the need for data protection. Parliament will continue to respond to rapid technological change in the field of data processing.

Public finance

In recent decades the public sector has assumed responsibility for an increasing number of tasks that were previously of a private character. And new public tasks have emerged as well. The scope and significance of public finance has grown accordingly. The overall budget of the Federal Republic of Germany consists not only of the federal budget but those of the federal states and local authorities, and several special budgets.

Distribution of responsibility. The lowest level of public service is that of the municipality, which is concerned with all aspects of local government. The local authority is responsible for water, gas and electricity supply, refuse disposal and roads. And it is jointly responsible with the state government for schools and other matters.

The responsibilities of the states fall mainly into the category of cultural affairs, primarily school education. The police and public health also fall within their sphere of confidence.

The greatest responsibility is borne by the Federal Government, its tasks covering social security, education and vocational training, transport and communications, defence, science and research. It is also responsible for energy and the promotion of industry, agriculture, housing and urban development, public health, the environment, internal security and development assistance.

There are in addition various responsibilities which the federal and state governments plan, carry out and finance jointly. These include the building of universities, improving regional economic structures, agricultural structure and coastal preservation, as well as cooperation in educational planning and the promotion of research.

Financial planning. A 1967 Law for the Promotion of Economic Stability an Growth requires the Federal and state governments to orientate their budgets to the main economic policy objectives. These are stability of prices, high employment, balanced foreign trade and steady, commensurate growth. The Federal Government and the states must draw up financial plans for their areas of responsability in which incomes and expediture are projected for a period of five years. The main purpose of this pluri-annual financial planning is, above all, to harmonize public revenue and expenditure with national economic resources and requirements. The municipalities, too, must draw up medium-term financial plans.

The great importance of the public budgets requires close coordination through all administrative levels. The most important body of this voluntary cooperation is the Financial Planning Council set up in 1968, in which Federal Government, states, municipalities and the Federal Bank participate. The Economic Policy Council also has a coordinating and advisory function.

Distribution of revenues. The major source of revenue for the Federal and state governments, as well as local authorities, is taxes. There are more than two dozen different types, but five of them – income, corporation, turnover, mineral oil and trade taxes – account for more than four fifths of all tax revenue. Today the Federal Government controls just under half of it.

The distribution of tax revenues among the three levels of government is complicated. Income, corporation and turnover taxes are "joint taxes". They are shared between the Federal Government and states according to a fixed, in the case of sales tax a periodically re-negotiated, distribution scale. The local authorities also receive a part of the income tax revenue. In exchange they have to surrender to the

Tax revenues 1991
(in millions of DM, estimated)

Federal Government	317,791
States	227,848
Local communities	83,667
EC funds	31,494
Total	660,800

Important taxes:

Wage tax	214,177
Assessed income tax	41,532
Turnover tax, import turnover tax	179,646
Oil tax	47,266
Tobacco tax	19,591

A public-sector project: the Klinikum in Aachen

Federal Government and the states part of the trade tax they raise, which used to be a purely local government tax. Another part of the sales tax, VAT, goes to the EC.

Other taxes apply to only one level of government. Federal Government sources are the customs and excise duties, monopolies (e.g. spirits monopoly) and various consumer and traffic taxes (e.g. mineral oil, tobacco and capital transfer taxes). The states receive the motor vehicle, property, inheritance and beer taxes as well as a number of smaller taxes. The municipalities receive the revenue from trade tax, less the proportion taken by the Federal and state governments, real estate and local consumption and expenditure taxes.

Most revenue comes from income tax. This is the one which affects the average person most of all. Dependently employed, i.e. wage-earning or salaried workers and public servants, have it deducted from wages or salary by the employer who remits it to the tax office (the "pay-as-you-earn" principle). The rate of taxation rises with income. After deduction of certain non-taxable amounts it comprises at present at least 19% and at most 53%.

Apart from tax revenues a major source of public finance is government borrowing. The Federal Republic's budgets in 1991 were DM 1,203 billion in debt, which broke down to just under DM 15,000 per inhabitant. This was a high level of public debt. In recent years new borrowing at the three national budget levels was cut by means of a consistent retrenchment policy.

Financial equalization. The tax-raising capability of the states varies considerably because their natural conditions and economic structures are also very different. Thus there are financially strong states like Baden-Württemberg, Hamburg and Hesse and financially weak states like Lower Saxony, Saarland, Schleswig-Holstein and Bremen. These differences in tax-raising potential are large balanced out by a "horizontal financial equalization". This is achieved in part by a differential sharing of the states' turnover tax income, partly by equalization payments by the financially stronger to the weaker states.

A "vertical financial equalization" takes place between states and local authorities. The tax and other revenues of the municipalities are inadequate for their tasks. They therefore depend on subsidies from the states. Some of them are tied to specific purposes but others are freely disposable. This equalization aims at reducing the differences between local authorities with high tax revenues and those with low tax revenues.

Financial problems in connection with German unity. Germany's unification in 1990 raised special problems with regard to economic and financial assimilation. The Unification Treaty provided that the new federal states should be incorporated in the financial system established by the Basic Law as far as possible from the very beginning. Thus since 1991 the new states are basically subject to the same regulations with regard to budgetary management and tax distribution as the western states. A "German Unity Fund" was set up to provide financial support for the new states and their municipalities. It is fed jointly by the Federal Government and the western states, most of the money being raised in the capital market.

This fund will be a substitute for a nation-wide financial equalization arrangement among the federal states until the end of 1994. As from 1995, the financial relations between the Federal Government and all sixteen states are to be completely readjusted. In addition to untied assistance via the German Unity Fund, the states and local authorities in the former GDR receive untied aid from the central government. In order to finance structural reform in the new federal states it was necessary to increase public borrowing, and especially the borrowing of the Federal Government. A consolidation process over the next few years is intended to reduce the government's public sector borrowing requirement considerably.

Federal Budget 1992

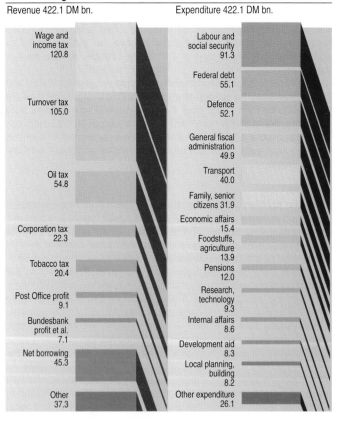

Revenue 422.1 DM bn.	Expenditure 422.1 DM bn.
Wage and income tax 120.8	Labour and social security 91.3
	Federal debt 55.1
Turnover tax 105.0	Defence 52.1
	General fiscal administration 49.9
Oil tax 54.8	Transport 40.0
	Family, senior citizens 31.9
Corporation tax 22.3	Economic affairs 15.4
	Foodstuffs, agriculture 13.9
Tobacco tax 20.4	Pensions 12.0
Post Office profit 9.1	Research, technology 9.3
Bundesbank profit et al. 7.1	Internal affairs 8.6
Net borrowing 45.3	Development aid 8.3
	Local planning, building 8.2
Other 37.3	Other expenditure 26.1

Public service

For the average citizen the state as such is an abstract concept. It takes shape, however, in the person of public servants who provide the vast range of services for which the Federal and state governments and local authorities are responsible. In the western states of the Federal Republic, i.e. those which existed prior to unification, public servants number more than 4.6 million, not counting the armed services. They will increase when the process of reorganizing the public service in the former GDR has been concluded. Public servants include various occupations, for instance departmental civil servants and dustmen, swimming baths supervisors and professors, judges and nurses, policemen, teachers and engine drivers.

Over the years the public service has assumed many new functions. Today they range beyond the purely administrative functions and cover education and a variety of public institutions, as well as environmental protection. And the number of civil servants is increasing accordingly: In 1950, 9% of all gainfully employed persons were public servants, now the proportion is about 17%. Some 40% of all public servants are civil servants, the remainder workers and salaried employees.

Professional civil servants. The professional civil service has been part of the German system that has developed since the 18th century. The Basic Law has guaranteed this proven institution and allows only civil servants to carry out "sovereign responsibilities". Such functions are performed, for instance, by the police, the inland revenue offices and the ministerial departments, and also by those who order the demolition of a dangerously dilapidated house, impose fines or go in armed pursuit of criminals.

The civil servant has a special obligation of loyalty to his employer and the constitution. This is prescribed by law. Although civil servants, like all citizens, have the right to participate in political activities, they are obliged to exercise moderation and restraint. They also have the right of association, i.e. to form professional groups, but they are not allowed to strike. But as well as special duties they also have special rights. As a rule they are appointed for life. For the period of their active employment and in retirement they and their families receive welfare benefits from the state. If they become incapacitated, or upon reaching retirement age, they receive a civil service pension. Salary scales are related to four service grades: ordinary, intermediate, higher intermediate and higher. Access depends on educational achievement and professional qualifications. Generally, members of the higher grades have a university degree.

Judges and members of the armed services are not, in the legal sense, civil servants, but they are subject to regulations similar to those for civil servants. Their special status derives from the independence enjoyed by judges and the requirements of military discipline.

Wage earners and salaried employees. Wage earners and salaried staff in the public service correspond in many respects to employees in the private sector. They pay social insurance contributions and are not appointed for life. Only after fifteen years' service and having reached the age of at least 40 does their status become permanent. Upon appointment they sign an employment contract which is largely determined by collective wage agreements. They have a right to strike, otherwise their responsibilities and conditions of work have been brought more and more into line with the rights and duties of civil servants. For instance, they are required to maintain official secrecy; they must be incorruptible and loyal to the constitution. In the 19th century there were very few wage earners in the public service, but their number has increased in the meantime corresponding to the importance of services for the local community.

Internal security

The maintenance of public security and order is one of the most important tasks of government. In the Federal Republic of Germany it is carried out by the federal states and the central government. The police are for the most part under the jurisdiction of the states. Only in certain fields does the Basic Law assign responsibility to the Federal Government.

The police in the federal states. There are the general police forces, the criminal police, river police, and the alert forces. The general police forces are mainly concerned with the prevention and prosecution of petty crime. They also include traffic police, with whom the citizen has most contact.

The criminal police are chiefly concerned with serious offences (organized, industrial and serial crimes, including sexual offences, robbery, blackmail, serious theft, homicide, drug trafficking and the passing of counterfeit money). It sometimes forms special units, in some cases jointly with the general forces, to combat terrorism and hostage-taking, and they are used for observation and detection.

The river police, as the name implies, controls all river traffic and is especially concerned with the transport of dangerous goods.

The alert forces are responsible for the training of new recruits and provide support for the general and criminal forces during state visits, demonstrations, major sporting events, international fairs, and in the event of a disaster. The alert forces are trained and deployed as units and are accommodated in garrisons. They number about 25,000 at present in the western states. New forces are gradually being built up in the new states (in 1991 they numbered about 3,000).

The Federal Border Guard. The Federal Border Guard is a federal police force responsible to the Federal Ministry of the Interior. Its overall strength is about 30,000. Its main task is to control the Federal Republic's borders, which includes combating international terrorism and drug trafficking and checks to prevent the illegal entry of foreigners. The Federal Border Guard also protects key public buildings,

Policewoman on duty

such as the Federal President's and the Federal Chancellor's office, the ministries and the Federal Constitutional Court in Karlsruhe. In the new federal states it is responsible for railway and airport security as well. Similar functions are performed on major occasions such as state visits. A special border police guard, the GSG 9, formed in 1973, won worldwide recognition through its success in combating international terrorism.

The Federal Criminal Police Office. The Federal Criminal Police Office (BKA), which is based in Wiesbaden with a central department near Bonn, is the focal point of cooperation between the federal and state law enforcement agencies. It is concerned with international crime. It collects and evaluates information and documentation. The BKA is the main body for criminological research and serves as the national centre for INTERPOL, the international criminal police organization. The BKA handles serious crimes itself, e.g. international drug trafficking, weapons transactions and terrorist activities. In large-scale operations it supports the police of the federal states. The BKA's security group in Bonn protects the Federal President, the Chancellor, ministers, etc. The BKA numbers about 4,000 and comes under the authority of the Federal Ministry of the Interior.

Protection of the constitution. Protection of the free, democratic, basic order is defined in the Basic Law as "protection of the constitution". In order to be able to provide effective protection the federal and state authorities collect information on extremist activities and on other developments which constitute a threat to national security and evaluate it for the central and state governments, ministries and courts. Another major field of responsibility is counter-espionage. The federal authority charged with these tasks is the Federal Office for the Protection of the Constitution in Cologne. It is accountable to the Federal Ministry of the Interior and cooperates with the corresponding state agencies. This agency merely gathers information; it has no executive police powers, i.e. it may not arrest or interrogate anyone. A law enacted in 1990 has defined the legal basis for its activities more precisely and thus provided greater protection for personal rights.

The federal and state agencies for the protection of the constitution are under the supervision of the competent ministers, parliaments and commissioners for data protection. Further control is exercised by the courts.

Foreign policy

In 1990 the German people were reunited in free self-determination. They achieved this goal by peaceful means and with the support of their friends and partners in East and West. The signing of the Treaty on the Final Settlement with respect to Germany (the Two-plus-Four Treaty) in Moscow on 12 September 1990 marked the ending of the post-war era. That accord confirmed that Germany, after the restoration of its unity on 3 October 1990, had regained its sovereignty and was no longer burdened by status and security problems in relation to other countries. Its ten articles regulate the external aspects of unification.

Thus, 45 years after the Second World War, the division of Germany, but also the division of Europe, was overcome. The united Germany has a greater responsibility to bear: for Europe's further integration as it remains allied to North America, the development of Central and Eastern Europe, and the Third World. German policy will remain above all a policy for peace. To the Germans, nation-state attitudes are a thing of the past.

As before, German foreign policy will be based on the Federal Republic's lasting membership of the community of free democracies, the European Community and the Atlantic Alliance. This translates into four major objectives: continued progress towards European integration, the further development of NATO, the stabilization of the reform processes in Central and Eastern Europe together with the necessary support, and partnership with the nations of the Third World.

The Federal Republic of Germany will continue to contribute to peaceful progress in the world. As one of the largest industrial and trading nations it is also dependent upon a stable and well-functioning world economic system. Its main aim is to establish a fair balance of interests between north and south, between the industrial and the developing countries, on the basis of a fruitful dialogue.

Currently, the Federal Republic of Germany maintains diplomatic relations with nearly all countries. It has more than 230 embassies and consular posts. In addition it has nine missions at international organizations as well as two offices protecting its interests in other countries.

European integration. Ever since it was founded the Federal Republic of Germany has been one of the main advocates of European unification. Together with Belgium, France, Italy, Luxembourg and the Netherlands it formed in 1952 the European Coal and Steel Community, and in 1957 the European Economic Community and the European Atomic Energy Community (EURATOM). In 1967 these three institutions were merged to form the European Community (EC). The EC developed into a supranational organization with its own institutions, some of whose decisions become directly applicable law in member states.

These institutions include especially

— the European Parliament, which since 1979 has been elected direct by the people and has acquired increasing powers;

— the Council of Heads of State and Government, which decides on fundamental European issues;

— the Council of Ministers, which as the EC's legislative body decides Community policy;

— the European Commission, the Community's executive body. It is independent of national governments, ensures that Community regulations are applied, and draws up proposals for the further development of Community policy, and

— the European Court of Justice, which ensures that Community laws and treaties are properly interpreted and applied. The Court's decisions have played a large part in further developing Community law.

The EC has acquired considerable influence not only as an economic community but as a political force and as a champion of democratic values. By 1986 the six founder members of the Community had been joined by the United Kingdom, Denmark, Ireland, Greece, Portugal and Spain. As a result of German unification the European Community now has a total population of about 340 million.

From the very outset the aim was to develop the European Community into a political union. The results of the European Council meeting held in Maastricht, Holland, on 9/10 December 1991 mark a major step towards this goal. The Community will be known as the European Union.

One of its basic elements will be the common foreign and security policy which has emerged from European Political Cooperation which, after a modest inception 20 years ago, has become a major instrument of European foreign policy and a second pillar in the process of unification. The common foreign and security policy will adopt the basic features of EPC as established in the Single European Act of 1986. New important elements will be added to it, including the principle of majority decision-making, the addition of a security and defence policy dimension to the integration process.

This represents a true breakthrough since the Single Act. It will significantly strengthen the European identity in terms of foreign and security policy. It will at the same time broaden the basis of the Alliance and of transatlantic partnership. Furthermore, it will enable the Community and its member states to render a crucial contribution to the stabilization of the pan-European security system.

The Maastricht meeting of December 1991 marked the successful conclusion of the intergovernmental conferences on political as well as economic and monetary union and the beginning of the decisive phase leading to the completion of European integration. The course has been charted for the introduction of a common currency before the end of this decade. This will make the Community the world's most important economic area. The political signposts are:
— the merging of the Community treaties into a "Treaty on Political Union",
— the common foreign and security policy,
— wider powers for the European Parliament,
— the inclusion of domestic and judicial policy in the treaty, and
— the start towards social union.

Nearly all customs and trade barriers between EC member states have disappeared. 31 December 1992 will mark the completion of the European internal market. There will be a huge market allowing free movement of persons, goods, services and capital, and it will be much the same size as the north American market. The single market's growth stimulus is already being felt in Germany's export-led economy.

The European Community has impressively demonstrated its attractiveness as a model community of free nations. But Europe is much larger than the present Community. Numerous important European countries have already applied for or are considering membership. The Community is open to any democratic European country – that is the letter and spirit of the Treaties of Rome. By further developing its structures it is preparing itself for the forthcoming negotiations with the new democracies of Central and Eastern Europe leading to their association and eventual accession. Already in 1993 the members of the European Free Trade Association, EFTA (Austria, Switzerland, Sweden, Norway, Finland, Iceland and Liechtenstein), will form the European Economic Area together with the EC and thus be linked up with the internal market.

In the course of its development the European Community has helped strengthen Europe's freedom and democracy. As the member

1991: The European Council sets the pointers in Maastricht

with the most powerful economy, Germany makes substantial financial contributions to the Community's expansion. It will continue to make every effort to further the Community's integration. Germany wants the European Community to progress to a European Union and, one day, the United States of Europe.

The European Community pursues an outward-looking trade policy. It advocates a market-oriented world economic order and is opposed to protectionism. It develops its economic relations with third countries within a close network of trade cooperation and association agreements. A typical example is the Lome Convention, which is the basis for cooperation in partnership with 69 African, Caribbean and Pacific developing countries, known as the ACP states.

The CSCE summit conference held in Paris in November 1990 ushered in a new era of pan-European cooperation. It produced the Charter of Paris for a New Europe which ended the East-West confrontation once and for all and formed the basis for a united Europe with a common perception of human rights, democracy and the rule of law.

Absolute respect for human rights, freedom and self-determination, to which all CSCE participating states have committed themselves, is the foundation on which the new Europe must be built. Thus one of the aims of German foreign policy is to increase not only the EC's but also the CSCE's scope for action.

For Germany's cooperation with her eastern neighbours it was important to conclude treaties as the framework for a proper relationship. Such accords have meanwhile been signed with Russia, Poland, the Czech and Slovak Federal Republic and other nations of Central and Eastern Europe. Germany's relationship with the successor states of the former Soviet Union is of crucial importance to the whole of Europe. To her it is particularly important to create the material foundations for European unity and to establish the fundamental values of democracy and rule of law. In order to develop a free market economy the nations of eastern, central and south-eastern Europe need the support of the west as a whole.

Germany has strongly backed the reforms in these countries from the very beginning, as shown in particular by the financial assistance in excess of DM 90 billion she provided in the period 1989 to 1991 alone. This makes Germany the principal donor. The help provided will ultimately benefit the whole of Europe. The desire for self-determination in eastern Europe will grow the more it coincides with the development of pan-European structures and pan-European solidarity.

The Atlantic Alliance. The Atlantic Alliance (NATO) has always been the indispensable foundation of the security of its members in Europe and North America. The Federal Republic of Germany joined NATO in 1955. That ensured peace and freedom. From the very outset all operative formations of the Bundeswehr (Federal Armed Forces) were under NATO's supreme command. The defence preparedness and capability of all NATO member states has, over the decades, safeguarded the free democracies, starting from the dual strategy of defence and dialogue in relation to the Warsaw Pact countries, as pronounced in the Harmel Report of 1967. It was not least the Atlantic Alliance which paved the way for the transformation in Europe and Germany.

Meanwhile the political change in Europe has removed the confrontation between East and West. The security situation, although there are some residual risks, has improved considerably. Nevertheless, NATO has not become superfluous.

Relations with the western states. Germany's and Europe's close ties with the democracies of North America remain unchanged. Transatlantic partnership is based on vital mutual interests and values. Europe, the United States and Canada have manifold historical,

*Federal Chancellor Kohl and U.S. President Bush
in front of the White House, 1991*

human, cultural and political ties. Thus America's and Canada's involvement in Europe continues to be of vital importance to the continent's, and hence Germany's, peace and security. NATO remains an indispensable security bond between Europe and North America.

Biannual summit meetings and various bilateral consultations provide renewed stimulus for the special relationship between Germany and France established by Chancellor Konrad Adenauer and President Charles de Gaulle through the treaty signed in the Elysee Palace, Paris, in 1963. In recent years attention has focused on the question of European Union, progress towards which has been considerably helped by the joint initiatives of Chancellor Kohl and President Mitterrand. Following German unification, France has also become economically and culturally involved in the development of the new federal states.

The stability of Franco-German friendship is guaranteed by the existing contacts between the citizens of both countries (there being more than 1,400 town twinnings, 2,000 school twinnings, as well as cooperation between the regions) and by the close economic relations between the two countries, who are each other's principal trading partner.

Germany's cooperation with other western countries has also been continuously intensified. Semi-annual summit meetings are held with the United Kingdom, and a close network of agreement, consultations and mutual visits makes for a similarly close relationship with Germany's other western partners.

There is also a close bilateral relationship between Germany and Israel. Relations are intensive and good at all levels and in most spheres. Since the establishment of diplomatic relations in 1965 they have in many respects developed into a genuine friendship.

Policy towards the Third World. In spite of the heavy financial burden of German unification, economic cooperation with the nations of Africa, Asia and Latin America remain an important element of German foreign policy. This is of vital importance to Germany.

The Federal Republic of Germany has for many years maintained relations with Third World countries on the basis of equal partnership. It supports their claim to independence and autonomous development. In this connection the Federal Government would like to see all nations decide for themselves what kind of political, economic and cultural system they want and to follow their chosen way of life in partnership with others.

The biggest task facing the international community is to reduce the prosperity gap between the industrial and developing countries. Germany intends to make its contribution, principally in the form of aid to the least developed countries. Together with her partners in the European Community, it is engaged in the dialogue between industrial and developing countries and actively involved in the fight against hunger and misery and in efforts to improve living conditions.

The Federal Republic of Germany has steadily increased its development aid contributions, conscious of the fact that it itself received foreign aid after the devastation of the Second World War. Between 1950 and 1990 total official and private development assistance provided by the Federal Republic amounted to nearly DM 355 billion.

Membership of the United Nations. The day of German unity is also a landmark in Germany's relationship with the United Nations, for since 3 October 1990 the interests of all Germans are represented by one single mission to the world organization. And the termination of four-power reservations means that Germany no longer has a special status in the United Nations. Today it has the same rights and responsibilities as any other member state.

A major aim of German foreign policy is to strengthen the role of the United Nations as the principal institution of the community of nations. Only this will enable the world organization to respond adequately to such global challenges as conflict prevention, the population explosion and environmental protection. This applies especially to the UN Secretary-General, who should be placed in a stronger position to mediate in preventing conflicts.

By dint of its own history Germany is particularly committed to freedom, democracy and human rights. All over the world, therefore, German policy is based on respect for human rights and human dignity.

Cultural relations. Cultural policy is one of the main elements of German foreign policy. It consists of
— giving other countries a comprehensive and self-critical picture of the Federal Republic of Germany and its cultural achievements, a picture which reflects the country's pluralist democracy and embraces the whole nation's spiritual and intellectual values;
— promoting the German language all over the world;
— promoting cultural exchange with other countries in a spirit of partnership.
The aim of this policy is to remove prejudices and strengthen mutual respect. In this way it helps to promote political and economic cooperation. In the development of cultural relations the Federal Foreign Office cooperates with the state governments, the churches, unions, sporting associations, political foundations and many other organizations.

Germany has concluded cultural agreements with 68 countries which form the framework for cultural cooperation. But there are also intensive cultural exchanges with most other countries. The practical implementation of Germany's cultural policy is largely the responsibility of intermediate organizations acting on behalf of the Federal Government. Such organizations include
— the Goethe Institute, which has 147 branches abroad and 16 in Germany. Its main tasks are to cultivate the German language abroad and to promote international cultural cooperation;
— the German Academic Exchange Service (DAAD), which organizes exchanges of academic staff and students;
— Inter Nationes, which hosts foreign guests of the government and

provides a wide range of information on the Federal Republic of Germany through films, tapes and printed material; and
— the Institute for Foreign Relations, which organizes German exhibitions abroad and foreign exhibitions in Germany.

External security

The principal of the Federal Republic's security policy is to maintain peace and safeguard the country's freedom and independence. "Maintaining peace with fewer weapons" was the Federal Republic's motto in helping to end the East-West confrontation. Germany is playing a constructive part in shaping Europe's new security relationship. Disarmament and restructuring of the armed forces are major elements of this process. Prior to unification Germany undertook by treaty to reduce the size of its armed forces significantly by 1994. With 370,000 servicemen the Bundeswehr of united Germany will be smaller than it was prior to unification. Up to 1990 the Bundeswehr had a personnel strength of 490,000, while the GDR's National People's Army (NVA) had 170,000. The Federal Republic of Germany is a member of NATO and still provides the largest contingent of conventional forces for the Alliance in Europe.

In the Treaty on Conventional Forces in Europe signed in 1990, the Federal Republic also agreed to sizeable disarmament measures. As in the past, the Bundeswehr remains a purely defensive army. It has no weapons of mass destruction and does not wish to have any at its disposal. However, security precautions are still necessary because only a country prepared to defend itself can exercise sovereign powers and thus be in a position to conduct negotiations and form alliances.

The Bundeswehr. The Bundeswehr consists of modern armed services based on conscription for men. The basic period of military service is at present twelve months. There are also career servicemen and others on engagements for up to 15 years. For women there are careers available in the medical and music corps. The civilian staff of the armed forces number about 186,000 men and women.

The Bundeswehr consists of the army, the navy and the air force. In all services considerable disarmament measures are to be put into effect. Hundreds of tanks and aircraft are to be scrapped and ships decommissioned. The defence budget is dwindling. In the mid-90s new plans for the armed forces will come into effect. Combat forces and the territorial army will be merged. Only a few mobile units of

Federal Chancellor Kohl talks to soldiers

10,000 to 15,000 men with a large proportion of career servicemen will have a full complement in peacetime.

On 3 October 1990, the day of German unity, the armed forces of the former GDR, the National People's Army (NVA), were disbanded. NVA servicemen with different periods of service are being incorporated in the Bundeswehr.

In 1991 the Soviet Union began withdrawing its approximately 340,000 troops as well as 210,000 dependents and civilian personnel from the territory of the former GDR. This process is being partly financed by the Federal Republic and is due to be completed in 1994. At the same time, the United States is likewise reducing its forces stationed in Germany. The other NATO countries with troops stationed in Germany are also reducing their military presence.

The Bundeswehr's mission. According to article 87 a of the Basic Law, the Bundeswehr's mission is
— to maintain the security of the Federal Republic of Germany together with its NATO partners,
— to maintain the country's scope for political action,
— to defend Germany and the territory of the North Atlantic Alliance against any attack from outside, and
— in the event that a state of defence is declared, to secure or restore Germany's territorial integrity.

Manpower of German armed forces

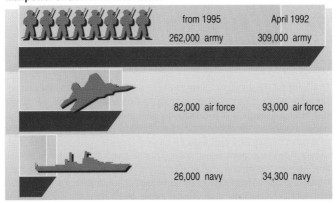

	from 1995	April 1992
	262,000 army	309,000 army
	82,000 air force	93,000 air force
	26,000 navy	34,300 navy

The Bundeswehr and the community. The Bundeswehr is responsible to the political leadership. In peacetime supreme command of the armed forces lies with the Federal Minister of Defence, and in the event of war with the Federal Chancellor. Parliamentary control of the Bundeswehr is exercised by the Bundestag committees, especially the Defence Committee.

An important control function is also exercised by the Defence Commissioner of the Bundestag, who is elected by parliament for a five-year term. His task is to protect the constitutional rights of servicemen. Every serviceman has the right to turn to him directly with complaints without going through his superiors. The Defence Commissioner is authorized to demand information and access to files from military units and to visit any Bundeswehr installation unannounced. He submits an annual report to the Bundestag on the complaints he has received.

General conscription (12 months) indicates a country's intention to defend itself and at the same time serves to integrate the armed forces in the community as a whole.

Apart from having the civic duty to serve in the armed forces, the individual has a basic right to refuse on grounds of conscience. Under article 4 of the Basic Law, no one may be assigned to armed combat against his conscience. Anyone recognized as a conscientious objector is no longer under obligation to serve in the armed forces. Instead, he must do 20 months of alternative civilian service (in hospitals, old people's homes, etc.).

Cooperation with developing countries

The Federal Republic of Germany is one of the biggest donors of development aid. It has economic cooperation arrangements with over 150 countries which are based on partnership. As early as 1961 a Federal Ministry for Economic Cooperation was created – the first time any country had appointed a cabinet minister with sole responsibility for development assistance. This showed the determination of the German parliament, government and people to help other nations in need in the light of Germany's own experience after the war, when her economic recovery would not have been possible without help from outside.

Even after unification and the fundamental changes in Central and Eastern Europe, Germany has broadened her relations with the developing countries in awareness of its increased global responsibility. All leading members of the government and the opposition want the united Germany to honour her commitments to the developing countries and to increase her development assistance further still.

In a period of more than 30 years the Federal Government, together with non-governmental organizations and private institutions, has gathered valuable experience and created a broad range of instruments for the promotion of overseas development. Through close cooperation with recipient countries it has been possible to adapt assistance measures to the differing economic and social conditions in Africa, Asia and Latin America.

Despite all efforts to reduce the prosperity gap between industrial and developing countries and despite their partial success, the task of removing hunger and poverty has still not been accomplished in many parts of the world. Consequently, combating mass poverty and removing its structural causes is still the foremost objective of German development policy. The world of tomorrow will only be able to live in peace if it proves possible to solve these problems and at the same time ensure respect for human rights.

It is now generally recognized that the people in North and South, in East and West, in poor and rich countries, are interdependent. This is clearly illustrated by the alarming extent of environmental destruction and its repercussions on relations between industrial and developing countries. The Federal Government, apart from pursuing a progressive environmental policy in Germany, also supports Third World countries in their efforts to promote environment-friendly development. It does so partly by linking debt relief with environmental protection measures.

Being a leading export nation, the Federal Republic of Germany has an interest in healthy economic progress in the developing countries. It considers itself to have a special responsibility to help liberalize international trade. The more efficient the economy of the developing countries, the more attractive they becomes as partners for trade and investment.

There is also another motive for promoting development. Improved living conditions in the Third World open up better economic and social prospects for millions of people who otherwise would leave their native countries in quest of a new life in the industrial countries.

Aims of development policy. It is the developing countries themselves who must decide what they want from development policy because effective aid can only be a way of helping them help themselves. But such assistance will only be effective if the countries concerned create conditions which will enable the people to participate through the democratic process in the task of building the country's economicand social system and to employ their skills in a meaningful and worthwhile manner.

Experience has shown that such conditions are most likely to be found in a country that has a law-based system with market elements which offer incentives to the people. The governments of developing countries themselves are alone responsible for creating such conditions that are conducive to development.

In the autumn of 1991 the German government laid down new political criteria for official development aid, viz:
— respect for human dignity and human rights,
— a democratic, pluralistic form of government based on the rule of law,
— a market-oriented economic system and a well-functioning administration, and
— domestic policies which serve the economic and social interests of the majority (this includes cuts in excessive arms expenditure).

Of course, not all developing countries will be able to meet these conditions entirely, but the German government will even then continue to look for ways and means of helping the people direct, of alleviating their poverty, and of preserving the natural foundations of life.

Overhauling an Artesian well in Egypt

Development cooperation takes the form of direct bilateral assistance from government to government, multilateral assistance via international organizations, principally the United Nations and its specialized agencies, and through the European Community. It also takes the form of private sector cooperation and the promotional activities of non-governmental organizations, who have long experience with cooperative measures in the Third World.

In 1990 the German Government spent nearly DM 10.3 billion on development cooperation. That is equivalent to 0.42% of the Gross National Product and above the average for all industrial countries.

Financial and technical cooperation, personnel. Financial cooperation, or capital aid, is the main instrument in terms of volume. Capital aid mainly takes the form of concessional loans to finance social infrastructure and environmental protection projects, as well as non-repayable grants. The money provided is used to finance individual projects (e.g. road construction) or comprehensive programmes, in the field of health, for instance, or to provide credits for small-scale farmers. Capital assistance is also granted to developing countries with few foreign exchange resources to enable them to import the machinery, spare parts and raw materials they need to maintain or improve production, as well as equipment for scientific, technical and medical facilities. Since 1987 the German Government has also been providing what is known as "structural aid", that is to say currency to enable recipients to speedily import commodities and services in the context of structural adjustment programmes. German structural aid is not tied to German supplies and services. The Federal Government attaches considerable importance to mitigating the social repercussions of structural adjustment measures.

The terms on which capital aid is granted depend on the economic situation of the recipient. Since 1978 the poorest countries have only been receiving non-repayable grants (financial contributions). The other developing countries receive loans with ten years of grace, long periods to maturity, and minimum interest rates.

Assistance within the framework of technical cooperation is generally provided free of charge. It is made available in cooperation with existing institutions or by those newly established by the recipient countries. The aim of all such technical cooperation arrangements is that joint projects or programmes are taken over as soon as possible by local staff. Specialists, advisers and instructors are seconded to developing countries and paid by the German Government, and equipment and material for the promoted institutions are either dispatched or financed, and training is provided for local specialists and managerial personnel who later assume the responsibilities of the German experts.

Under personnel training cooperation specialist and managerial personnel from developing countries attend courses, mostly in Ger-

On the Philippines: how do you protect tobacco plants?

In Senegal: farmers plant new cashews

many. So far 160,000 persons from developing countries have benefited from such programmes. The object of this cooperation is to give
people from developing countries suitable opportunities to develop
their knowledge and skills on their own responsibility. Thus they
are helped to start up in business or employed on development cooperation projects. In 1990, 3,006 local experts worked alongside 1,412
German experts on technical cooperation projects financed by Germany. Of the 2,000 or so working on financial cooperation projects,
approximately 900 were experts from developing countries.

Where personnel training is concerned, distinctions are made. The
experts seconded by the German Government are employed as advisers on various technical cooperation projects and programmes.
They are under contract to a German organization. Integrated experts, on the other hand, are under contract to an institution in the
developing country concerned, from which they receive the usual local salary. Germany also funds social security arrangements and
temporary assistance. German development volunteers have a special status within the framework of non-governmental assistance projects. They differ from other specialists in that they work in closest
possible contact with the population in return for a small allowance.

Areas of development cooperation. Decisions as to which sectors
of the economy require priority German assistance are made on the

basis of proposals and data submitted by the developing country concerned. Cooperation projects range from meeting basic needs via help towards self-help, protection of the environment and natural resources, rural development, education and science, industry, crafts and mining, transfer of technology, and the development of administrative infrastructures, to combating drug crime.

In all sectors women are included in development measures as key figures in the development process. Even in the planning stage their interests must be taken into consideration. This applies especially to areas where women bear the main burden, as in agriculture, water and fuel supply, and where they are particularly affected by poor conditions, for instance health and housing, food production and training.

The main areas of concentration are food production and rural development. The aim is to help the developing countries to maintain food supplies through their own efforts. This is why efforts are being made to increase agricultural production by promoting small farmers, by providing agricultural equipment, developing efficient marketing systems and promoting agricultural research. These are major contributions towards improving the general supply situation in rapidly growing, densely populated urban areas.

Food aid is only intended as a means of removing supply bottlenecks as a result of natural disasters, harvest failures or flows of refugees as a result of armed conflict. The German Government tries to buy an increasing proportion of its food aid supplies, i.e. grain, in regions or localities of developing countries that have surplus production. In this way it is able to supply the kind of food which the people affected normally eat. At the same time support is provided for food production in surplus countries.

Measures to preserve and restore the natural sources of life constitute an important part of development assistance. Consequently, every project is examined as to its compatibility with the environment. The Federal Government also supports national environmental protection programmes, which include land-use planning, afforestation, forest management and measures to prevent soil erosion. Priority is given to measures for the preservation of tropical rainforests and the prevention of desertification.

Other sectoral priorities are energy supply and education, especially educational infrastructure. Increasing support is being provided for the reform of general education. Improvement is also being sought in the provision of educational opportunities for rural populations and for girls and women. Germany has helped considerably to raise international standards of vocational training. With regard to population control, the German government promotes family planning programmes in agreement with the governments concerned.

Development aid projects sponsored by the former German Democratic Republic have been continued since unification provided they were still appropriate. As a result, the Federal Ministry for Economic Cooperation has taken over 64 new projects in twelve countries which are supported by grants totalling approximately DM 120 million.

The economic system

The Federal Republic of Germany is one of the major industrial countries. In terms of overall economic performance it is the fourth largest, and with regard to world trade holds second place. Since 1975 it has been participating in the world economic summit meetings of the seven leading western industrial countries (the G 7 countries), at which every year they coordinate their economic and financial policies.

The country's gross national product, that is to say the value of all goods and services produced in the course of a year after price adjustment, increased by more than two and a half times in the old (western) federal states between 1960 and 1991. Expressed in 1985 prices, that is an increase from DM 860 billion to DM 2,207 billion. Taking the respective market prices as a basis, the GNP increased from DM 303 to DM 2,614 billion since 1961.

The Federal Republic owes its recovery from the devastation of the Second World War to become one of the world leading industrial nations not to its natural resources but to its skilled manpower. The crucial factors which account for the country's economic efficiency are the training and industry of the labour force, managerial ability, and the broad scope which the social market economy has afforded hard working people.

After the Second World War people often spoke of the German "economic miracle". Ludwig Erhard, the Federal Republic's first Minister of Economics, didn't like this term. He said it wasn't a miracle, "merely the result of honest endeavour on the part of a whole nation who were given the opportunity and freedom to make the best of human initiative, freedom and energy".

The social market economy. The Federal Republic's economic system has developed since the war into a socially responsible market economy coupled with macroeconomic management. This system rejects equally the old-style laissez-faire and government interventionism. It combines the free initiative of the individual with the principles of social progress. The Basic Law, which guarantees freedom of private enterprise and private property, stipulates that these basic rights be exercised for the public good. Under the tenet of "as little

Gross domestic product of major industrial nations 1991
(Federal Republic of Germany:"old" federal states)

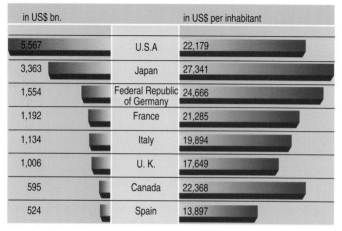

in US$ bn.		in US$ per inhabitant
5,567	U.S.A	22,179
3,363	Japan	27,341
1,554	Federal Republic of Germany	24,666
1,192	France	21,285
1,134	Italy	19,894
1,006	U. K.	17,649
595	Canada	22,368
524	Spain	13,897

government as possible, as much government as necessary" the state has a mainly regulatory function in the market economy. It sets the general conditions for market processes. The question as to which and how many goods are produced and who gets how much of what is decided above all in the marketplace. In the Federal Republic there is almost no state intervention in price and wage fixing.

Market economy. The prerequisite for the functioning of the market mechanism is competition. Without it there can be no market economy. But competition demands effort, so it is understandable that entrepreneurs time and time again try to neutralize competition, be it by agreements between competitors or by mergers of firms. Preventing this is the purpose of a Law against Restraints on Competition (Cartel Act), first enacted in 1957 and substantially improved meanwhile. It forbids concerted practices and agreements which influence market conditions by restricting competition. Enforcement of the law is the function of the Federal Cartel Office in Berlin and the state anti-trust departments.

The driving force of the market economy is profit. This is why it is bound to fail wherever no profit can be made or overriding public interests have precedence. For this reason a number of sectors of the

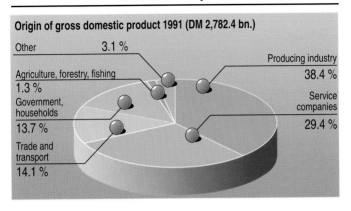

Origin of gross domestic product 1991 (DM 2,782.4 bn.)

Other 3.1 %

Agriculture, forestry, fishing 1.3 %

Government, households 13.7 %

Trade and transport 14.1 %

Producing industry 38.4 %

Service companies 29.4 %

German economy were never completely subject to the market economy system, for example agriculture, parts of the transportation system and hardcoal mining. A current example are the former state enterprises of the former GDR, now the new federal states. They are being run by the public Treuhandanstalt (Trust Agency) without profit with the intention of gradually incorporating them in the market system. Once this has been achieved the government will revert to its proper role. Mainly for social reasons, agriculture cannot be completely exposed to free market competition. Moreover, it is subject to European Community regulations. The German Federal Railways, the Reichsbahn of the former GDR, and the German Federal Post Office are publicly owned. They cannot orientate their activities purely to profit but have to serve the general public. The railways must, for example, offer socially acceptable fares and the post office cannot exclude remote villages from its services.

The shortage of housing resulting from the war initially led to the market being state-controlled. In the meantime it has by and large become free again. The state does, however, ensure that competition does not result in socially intolerable conditions. The most important measures to this end are laws protecting tenancy, the payment of rent supplements to low-income households, the promotion of building projects and the modernization of housing. In several sectors where, in principle, there is free competition, lawmakers have made entry into the market subject to conditions. Thus craftsmen and retail traders, for instance, must prove they have the necessary professional qualifications before they can set up in business. For other occupa-

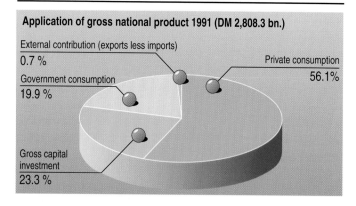

Application of gross national product 1991 (DM 2,808.3 bn.)

External contribution (exports less imports)
0.7 %

Private consumption
56.1%

Government consumption
19.9 %

Gross capital investment
23.3 %

tions the state requires special training and a minimum age, for example in the fields of health, legal practice, accountancy and tax consultancy.

Industrial relations. In the labour market, too, the free play of forces applies. There is free collective bargaining, that is to say, that labour-employer agreements on pay, working hours, vacation entitlements and general working conditions are freely negotiated. The organizations of the two parties to the agreements, the trade unions and the employers' associations – often called "social partners" in Germany – thus play an important role in economic life. Although their main task is to represent their members' interests with determination and sometimes toughness, they at the same time bear a large measure of responsibility for the economy as a whole. The way they bargain can greatly influence the functioning of the economic system.

Labour and employers in the Federal Republic have always been aware of this responsibility. The stability of the economic system is due largely to them. Here the specific form of trade unionism which has grown in West Germany since the war shows its value. The trade unions in the Federal Republic of Germany are "unitary unions" in a double sense: each represents all the workers in an entire branch of industry (i.e. not only the members of a certain trade), and they are party-politically and denominationally neutral (i.e. not split into various allegiances). This unity gives them their strength, spares them rivalries and makes them pillars of social stability.

Social welfare. One major reason why it has been easier to avoid social unrest in the Federal Republic than in other countries is that its inhabitants are protected by a dense social security network. Social protection is considerable, especially for employees. Whether an employee is old or sick, injured by accident or jobless, affected by the bankruptcy of his employer or retraining in a more promising occupation - most of the financial problems are solved by the welfare system.

This support is not charity. It is based on a system of solidarity. Those in employment pay contributions to the various branches of the social insurance system and are thus assured of getting what they need when they need it.

However, the social system extends far beyond the employees' contributions. It includes child benefit, rent supplements, social benefits for the needy and compensation for war victims. Total public and

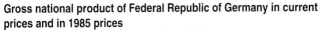

Gross national product of Federal Republic of Germany in current prices and in 1985 prices

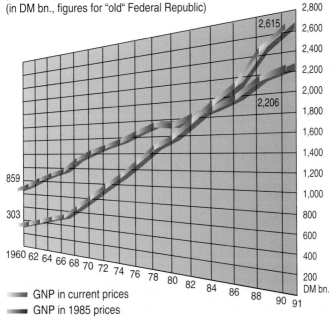

(in DM bn., figures for "old" Federal Republic)

GNP in current prices
GNP in 1985 prices

private expenditure on social security amounts to about a third of GNP.

Macroeconomic development. Undesirable developments can also happen in a market economy. The state must try to counter them by means of budgetary, taxation, welfare and competition policies. Since 1967 the Federal Repubic has had an instrument for management of the economy in the shape of the Economic Stability Act. It prescribes stable prices, a high level of employment and external economic balance under conditions of steady and adequate growth, although they can rarely be achieved simultaneously. However, it is not only the state which is required to pursue these aims. The independent Federal Bank, which is responsible for money supply, as well as the trade unions and employers' associations also bear a large part of the responsibility for the economy. The following bodies participate in the coordination of economic and fiscal policy:

— The Economic Policy Council, consisting of the federal ministers of economics and finance, one member from each state government and representatives of the local authorities. The Federal Bank can also take part in the consultations which take place at least twice a year. The council seeks a coordinated approach to economic policy.

— The similarly composed Financial Planning Council, which has the task of coordinating financial planning at all levels of government. The Federal and state Governments have to draw up multi-year plans so that public revenues and expenditure can be harmonized with the needs and capacity of the national economy.

— The Board of Experts for the Assessment of Overall Economic Trends, which was set up in 1963. This panel of five independent economic experts (popularly known as the "five wise men") evaluates overall economic developments every autumn as a basis for government decision-making.

Every January the Federal Government presents to the Bundestag and the Bundesrat an annual economic report, which contains a response to the annual assessment of the Board of Experts as well as an outline of economic and financial policy objectives for the current and subsequent years.

Restructuring of the economy. The Federal Republic is a country that has high wages and a correspondingly high level of prosperity. But the level of achievement has to be constantly maintained. Adaptation to innovations in the fields of science and technology and on

1991: Federal Chancellor Kohl receives the annual economic report

world markets is a continuous process. This has not always been easy, as shown by the disruptions caused by the oil crises of 1973/74 and 1979/80. During that period the country not only had to cope with a price explosion but also with the revolutionary impact of microtechnology in industry, commerce and public administration. During that restructuring phase economic growth, as in most other western industrial countries, slowed down. But in spite of this, real output increased by almost 24% between 1973 and 1985, this period having been interrupted by two recessions.

Growth picked up again in 1983 following the realignment of economic and financial policy. In comparison with other countries prices have risen only moderately since then. Employment figures have improved. In the West German states the number of people in employment increased by some three million, comparing the 1991 average with 1983. Nonetheless, a continuing high level of unemployment remains a serious problem. It is compounded by the heavy financial burden of rebuilding the economy in the new federal states.

Reducing unemployment is a central task of government policy. The key to more employment lies in higher investment. To ensure adequate profitability for investments the Federal Government is trying to strengthen the market's own forces, especially through incentives for individual performance. State influence on the economy is being reduced, regulations that obstruct market activity are being eliminated. This makes for freer competition and adaptation to new developments. Considerable impetus came from a major tax reform programme, the final stage of which became effective in 1990.

The Federal Republic of Germany favours free world trade and rejects all forms of protectionism. Because it exports a third of its GNP it depends on open markets. Its economy therefore needs a growing European internal market. But outside the European Community as well Germany must hold on to old markets and develop new ones. This constant pursuit of open markets and free world trade corresponds with the country's internal market economy.

The new federal states:
an economy in the making

Rebuilding eastern Germany is a pioneering task and one that is unique in legal and economic history. For within the space of a few years a whole economy, including its judicial and administrative system, must be reshaped in accordance with the principles of a social market economy.

The socialist command economy had deprived the people in the former GDR of any private initiative or responsibility. Creativity and enterprise were for the most part paralyzed and productivity was similarly low. For a modest output the regime ruthlessly exploited natural resources and caused tremendous environmental damage. Housing, transport and communications, too, are urgently in need of modernization.

The restructuring process is now in top gear. The new federal states have made a good start towards adopting the social market economy. Over half a million new business have been started up. Massive funds are being provided – one quarter of the Federal Republic's 1992 budget is earmarked for economic aid in Eastern Germany, infrastructure being the main priority. Since 1990 at least DM 100 billion a year flows to East Germany, either from the Federal Government or through joint federal and state facilities such as the "German Unity Fund". Another source of federal funds is the joint project "Recovery East", which is used to promote investment. It is costing DM 24 billion for 1991 and 1992. The private sector, too, has launched considerable investment. In 1992 alone, West German companies intend to invest DM 44 billion – two thirds more than in the previous year.

It is not possible to rebuild the economy without efficient regional and local administrations and a properly functioning legal system. That is why the Federal Government has sent, for instance, 2,300 judges, public prosecutors and court clerks to east Germany at its expense. Experienced administrative staff from the west are also helping in the restructuring process.

The Trust Agency (Treuhandanstalt): a key factor in the recovery process. A key factor in the process of economic recovery in Eastern Germany is the Trust Agency which has the task, on behalf of the Federal Goverment, to privatize, rehabilitate, or if necessary close down the former collectives and combines from the days when the economy was centrally controlled. This process is to be completed by 1994.

When the agency began operations in 1990 it assumed control of 8,000 combines and "peoples' enterprises", which embraced some 45,000 factories and thus nearly the entire economy of the former German Democratic Republic, where 90% of companies were controlled by the state. Already in the first year, the agency was able to privatize about 5,000 of 11,000 establishments. In so doing it provided for investment in excess of DM 100 billion and the creation of over 900,000 jobs. When this task is completed the government will withdraw and let private initiative take over within the framework of the social market economy.

Good prospects. The standard of living in the new federal states is lower and the number of jobless higher than in the western states, but the initial financial support provided by the west is having an effect. Everywhere in the new states there is a mood of renewal. There are signs of progress everywhere — in the building, transport, telecommunications and administrative sectors. New, modern industries are emerging, agriculture is being modernized, and more and more suc-

New tram lines in the eastern part of Berlin

Leipzig: Post Office instals new technology

cessful marketing strategies are being developed for local products. There is also a stronger entrepreneurial spirit. In 1990 alone, 280,000 new firms were established between Rostock and Dresden, between Leipzig and Frankfurt on the Oder.

Since the Economic and Monetary Union was established on 1 July 1990, incomes (and thus purchasing power) have increased considerably. A wide range of training programmes offers new prospects for young people. And government-sponsored measures, including retraining programmes or courses providing vocational qualifications, are helping create new jobs.

Annual growth rates of 10% are already being forecast for the next few years. East Germany is on the best way to becoming an attractive place for industry, with state-of-the-art production facilities and a lively market which should prove particularly interesting to East European countries.

The labour market

In past decades developments on the German labour market have been influenced by different factors. In the early years the Federal Republic was preoccupied with finding jobs for millions of expellees from Germany's former eastern territories and for resettlers from East Germany.

These people contributed greatly to the Federal Republic's economic upswing. From the mid-50s to the early 70s the country enjoyed a phase of full employment, but afterwards the number of unemployed began to rise.

Germany's regained unity has also had an impact on the labour market. Although the ranks of the jobless decreased in the western states on account of the favourable economic situation, their numbers swelled in the new states. This is primarily due to the transition from socialist central planning to a social market economy.

Employment. The labour force in the old federal states increased from 20.4 million in 1950 to over 29 million in 1991. In the new federal states the number of persons in employment in 1991 was about 7.3 million. From about 1960 onwards the increase of the workforce was due mainly to ever larger numbers of foreign workers streaming into the Federal Republic. In 1965 the number of "guest workers" had risen above a million and in 1973, at the peak of foreign-worker employment, it was more than 2.6 million. Since then, recruitment of foreign workers has been cut, with the exception of those from European Community member countries. In 1991 there were 1.85 million foreign workers in the Federal Republic. The biggest contingent are the Turks, followed by Yugoslavs, Italians, Greeks, Austrians and Spaniards.

Full employment in the Federal Republic reached its peak in 1970, when only 150,000 were out of work. At the same time there were almost 800,000 job vacancies. Thereafter the labour force diminished gradually and the number of unemployed increased. It rose above one million in 1975, and in 1982 there were more than two million jobless. Meanwhile the number of unemployed in the western part of the Federal Republic has fallen well below this figure. In 1991 some 1.7 million were registered as unemployed.

Work promotion also includes vocational counselling

Government policy in the western part of the country since 1982 has improved the conditions for economic growth and considerably reduced the obstacles to employment. As a result some three million new jobs were created between 1984 and 1990.

In the former GDR there was always full employment – at least that was the official version as presented by the communist regime. In actual fact, however, there was much concealed unemployment, estimated at about three million.

The policy adopted by the Federal Institute for Employment has prevented a further growth of unemployment in the new federal states. On the other hand, old, unproductive jobs are being abandoned faster than new ones can be created. For a transitional period, therefore, the institute is employing considerable government funds to finance job creation, retraining and further training programmes in order to ease the strain on the labour market, to give workers better prospects, and to accelerate the modernization process. As economic activity picks up the employment situation, too, will improve considerably.

Some groups are especially hard hit by unemployment, such as those with inadequate vocational qualifications and older people, as well as those who have been out of work for long periods of time. The government and industry are making great efforts to help them. Because of the increasing use of modern technology, vocational skills are very important. But it is also important that those affected by unemployment should receive adequate social security.

Unemployment insurance. Since 1927 there has been a statutory unemployment insurance scheme in Germany. It is covered today by the Work Promotion Act of 1969. The authority administering the scheme is the Federal Institute for Employment in Nuremberg and the 150 or so local labour exchanges and many sub-branches.

All employees (except professional civil servants), are subject to obligatory insurance (i.e. payment of contributions into the scheme). Contributions are paid half by the employee and half by the employer. Any unemployed person whose previous employment was subject to insurance contributions and who is ready to accept "tolerable" employment offered by the labour exchange is entitled to draw unemployment benefit. The "unemployment benefit" can be as much as 68% of the last net pay. As a rule it is paid for a maximum period of one year, in the case of older unemployed people at most for 32 months. Thereafter anyone who is still unemployed can apply for "unemployment support", which can be up to 58% of the net wage or salary, other sources of income, including those of family members, being taken into account. The Institute also pays benefits to employees on short time or those unable to work during the cold winter months (e.g. construction workers).

Labour promotion. The Institute for Employment is also responsible for job placement and vocational guidance. A particularly important function is the promotion of vocational training. The Institute gives juveniles and adults subsidies and loans for vocational training if they cannot raise the funds themselves. In 1991 it launched a major retraining programme for some 900,000 people in the new federal states. It also promotes vocational advancement by granting loans and covering costs during training.

Labour market and vocational research is another of the Institute's functions. The research findings are submitted to the Federal Minister for Labour and Social Affairs as an aid to decision-making.

The Federal Institute for Employment:
Bundesanstalt für Arbeit
Regensburger Str. 104
8500 Nuremberg

Incomes and prices

Incomes. Incomes in Germany are from a wide range of sources. The major one by far is dependent employment, i.e. wages and salaries. In addition there are shareholders' dividends, property and assets and state transfer payments such as child benefit, unemployment benefits and pensions of various kinds. If from the sum of these incomes one substracts the public levies, such as taxes and social insurance contributions, one arrives at the disposable income of private households.

In the Federal Republic of Germany this rose from DM 188,000 million in 1960 to DM 1,509,000 million in 1990. 91% was used for private consumption and 9% saved, as compared with 13,9% in 1991. The increases enabled people to spend more on "consumer durables" and services, i.e. motor cars, household appliances, furniture, leisure pursuits, recreation and holidays.

In 1964 the average monthly income of a four-person household was DM 904. Of this, DM 823 was spent on private consumption; nearly two thirds of this outlay went for food, clothing and housing. In 1990 the same type of household in West Germany disposed of a monthly income of DM 4,380 of which only about half went on food, clothing and housing. This means that the ordinary family's financial scope has widened. However, other items of expenditure have increased substantially, e.g. transport, telephone and postal charges. The average disposable income in the new federal states in 1990/91 was about DM 2,300. However, the gap between east and west should close rapidly as a result of eastern Germany's economic integration.

Assets. At the end of 1990 private assets in the old federal states stood at approximately DM 2,970 billion. It includes cash, savings, bonds, life insurance and other forms of property. The per-capita average in western Germany is about DM 47,000. In the new federal states, however, private assets were worth only about DM 137 billion, or DM 8,500 per inhabitant. Assets and available monthly incomes are distributed unevenly throughout Germany. At the top of the incomes pyramid are the self-employed, followed by farmers, public employees and civil servants as well as wage earners. The pattern is much the same in the western and eastern parts of the country.

Whereas the social structure in the new federal states is only just beginning to take shape, a process has taken place within the old states which has led to the approximation of most social groups. Beneath a top layer of about 2% of the population, there has emerged a very broad middle class. About four fifths of all Germans live entirely or predominantly from the fruits of their labour, while only a small minority can live on their assets.

As a result of over 40 years of the social market economy, about half of the labour force have their own house or flat. Most households also have a car, in former times a status symbol of the wealthy class. The same applies to expensive consumer goods such as refrigerators, washing machines, television sets and video recorders. However, many households can only maintain this high standard of living because both man and wife have a job.

Since the 50s the government has promoted private capital formation by means of various bonuses, tax and other allowances. Tax incentives are provided for people saving with building societies or through insurance policies. People contributing to house-building schemes also receive other bonuses. The bonuses for the various types of savings are payable up to certain annual limits. The house-building bonus is also tied to income limits.

In addition to the general incentives for all citizens, the government has provided special bonuses for employees since the 1960s. Since 1991 they have also been applicable in the new federal states. Under the Capital Formation Act employees receive a bonus on limited amounts which they instruct their employers to transfer direct to their building society accounts, other capital formation accounts with banks (which also include investment certificates and shares), or to the employer's capital formation scheme.

Savings of up to DM 936 a year qualify for this bonus. It can only be claimed by people whose earnings do not exceed a particular limit. In the western part of Germany capital formation savings arrangements are made for most employees, primarily within the scope of collective wage agreements, in addition to their normal wage. Employees can also obtain bonuses for parts of their wages which they save. In 1991 about 13 million employees in western Germany received bonuses totalling some one billion marks for capital formation savings. They also receive tax concessions on limited amounts which they invest with their employer.

Shopping centre in Remscheid

Prices. The standard of living depends not only on income but also on prices. In the Federal Republic consumer prices are therefore a major domestic issue. Opinion polls have consistently shown that for many people the chief consideration is stable prices. This is mainly because Germans have personally experienced what devaluation of money means. They have suffered two enormous inflations this century, each resulting in collapse of the currency and huge losses of financial assets.

Although the Federal Republic has not been able to evade world-wide inflation entirely, it has managed to keep prices under control better than many other countries. The cost of living in the Federal Republic has at times rose by more than 6% annually since the 1970s. Meanwhile, however, the inflation rate has tended to flatten out, and in December 1986 the cost of living fell for the first time in almost 30 years, down 1.1% on December 1985. This was due mainly to the drastic fall in the price of petroleum. In the whole of 1986 the cost of living was 0.1% lower than in the previous year. In later years, too, the Federal Republic managed quite well by comparison, its inflation rates not rising above 3%. Since mid-1990, however, the impact of the Gulf War, but also taxation and increased demand in the new federal states, have accelerated prices, with the result that the inflation rate in 1991, compared with 1990 was about 3.5%.

Price policy. In the Federal Government's view successful price policy can be pursued only with measures which do not tamper with the

Cost of living index in various countries
(1985=100)

Country	1989	1990	1991
Federal Republic of Germany (old)	104.2	107.0	110.7
Belgium	107.3	111.0	114.6
Denmark	118.1	121.2	124.1
France	112.7	116.5	120.2
Great Britain	121.8	133.3	141.1
Ireland	113.9	117.6	121.4
Italy	123.8	131.8	140.2
Netherlands	101.7	104.3	108.4
Austria	107.8	111.4	115.0
Switzerland	107.4	113.2	119.7
Spain	128.2	136.8	144.9
Canada	118.7	124.5	131.5
USA	115.2	121.5	126.6
Japan	103.7	107.0	112.3
Australia	136.5	146.4	151.1

A rich selection: the Small Market Hall in Frankfurt/Main

Working time required to pay for certain household goods *

To purchase the specified goods an industrial worker had to work the stated number of hours and minutes:

	1950 hrs.	1950 mins.	1960 hrs.	1960 mins.	1985 hrs.	1985 mins.	1990 hrs.	1990 mins.
1 kilo sugar	0	56	0	30	0	10	0	6
1 kilo bread	0	20	0	17	0	11	0	10
1 kilo meat	2	40	2	9	1	5	0	54
1 kilo coffee	22	19	6	34	1	29	0	48
Men's shoes	18	53	11	25	8	22	7	25
Men's bicycle	117	19	63	48	21	47	21	46

* "Old" federal states

market mechanism. Interventionist measures would greatly disturb the system of self-regulation. Apart from a small number of fields in which state intervention does take place (notably transportation and agriculture), prices are formed by market forces. The government relies mainly on credit, fiscal and competition policy.

Housing and urban development

Living accommodation in Germany can be anything from a single room, a self-contained flat, a single family house or a mansion. There are about 33 million dwellings, over 26 million of them in the old (western) states. Roughly 40% of these are occupied by the owners themselves, the rest being rented. Flats in apartment buildings are traditionally rented, hence most of those inhabited by their owners are in houses for one or two families. Owner-occupied housing has increased steadily since the late 70s.

20% of dwellings in the western states have been subsidized by the government. This "social" accommodation is intended for large families, the disabled, old people and those with low incomes.

Statistically, there is a flat available for every household, but since the late 80s demand has exceeded supply. Germany had a real housing crisis after the Second World War, when many towns and cities lay in ruins. In the early 50s there were only 10 million dwellings available for 17 million households. Gradually, however, the crisis was overcome by means of a housing programme under which as many as 700,000 dwellings a year were built.

Today the main problems are in the metropolitan areas. Young couples, large families and foreigners have difficulty finding flats which meet their needs or which they can afford. There are many reasons for the housing shortage. Accommodation is being sought by people in the high-birthrate age groups and by the many resettlers from eastern Europe. High interest rates and the cost of land are major obstacles to house building. As a result of the generally increasing affluence, everyone is demanding more individual living space. There is also a growing trend towards single-person households. In 1991 there was a shortage of about 1.5 million dwellings in the western part of Germany, while in the new federal states about a million were considered not worth renovating. But after years of declining building activity, the pendulum has swung the other way. In 1990 about 320,000 new dwellings were built in the entire Federal Republic, due to considerably increased government subsidies. And in 1991 the Federal Government introduced another social housing scheme which provided a further boost.

Housing quality. There are still large differences in quality between accommodation in the old and the new federal states, and in the amount of living space available. In western Germany the average living space available for each individual is 36 sq m, which is more than twice as much as in 1950. 95% of all flats have a bath and 75% central heating. The housing stock in the west is on the whole much younger than accommodation in the new federal states, where two thirds of the houses were built before the war. Many of them are in

A renovated house in Hamburg dating from the 19th century

a poor state. They lack modern sanitary facilities and the heating systems are outmoded. The communist regime in the former GDR kept rents extremely low. As a result, the authorities and private owners had hardly any funds for maintenance and modernization. In the western states, on the other hand, quality has its price. Rents account for about 20% of an average household's net income, apart from the incidental expenses. In some cities the rents are even higher, in the countryside lower.

There remains a tremendous housing problem to be solved. In eastern Germany not only must new dwellings be built but millions of old ones renovated. Many houses are owned by local authorities and are to be privatized. Private investors will receive tax relief and grants for this purpose. But greater efforts are required in the western part of the country as well.

Housing allowance and tenants' rights. Dwelling space is a basic human need, which is why in Germany everyone whose income is insufficient to meet the cost of adequate accommodation has a statutory right to housing allowance. It is paid as a grant towards the rent or as a subsidy towards the cost of home ownership, though subject to income limits. In 1990 the Federal Government and the states paid housing allowances to about 1.8 million households. Since 1991 they have also been paid in the new federal states. The number of new applicants for allowances is estimated at three million. These allowances help to offset rent increases resulting from the economic situation. On the whole, housing allowance has proved to be an effective social measure. Tenancy law, which is based on freedom of contract, is aimed at establishing a fair balance of interests between landlords and tenants. No tenant need fear unjust and arbitrary eviction or excessive rent increases. Thus a landlord can only give notice to a tenant who has met the requirements of his contract only if he can prove "justified interest" (that is to say if he can show that he needs the accommodation for his own purposes). He may demand more rent provided he does not go beyond what is charged for comparable accommodation in the same area. Tenants in the new federal states receive special protection against rent increases for a transitional period.

Home ownership. 90% of all German families dream of owning a house or flat. This coincides with the Federal Government's aim of spreading assets as far as possible. People deciding to build or buy

Home-building receives government support

A residential complex dating from the '80s in Berlin

their own home can thus count on many state benefits such as grants, loans and tax concessions.

Urban development. The Federal Republic is one of the most densely populated countries in the world. Most people today live in cities, towns or sizeable communities which were rebuilt after the war. Little consideration was given to traditional structures. Rapid motorization led to a boom in road construction, even in residential areas. For a time the "car-suited town" was the ideal of urban planners. The price of land in urban areas shot up and it became more and more difficult to insist on sensible building for the good of society as a whole. Many people moved to the countryside and commuted to work. The towns became deserted in the evening.

This trend has meanwhile been reversed, however. Since 1970 there has been a growing tendency to modernize old buildings and whole districts. More and more people are returning to the towns. Efforts are now made to preserve the structures of towns as they have evolved and to fill the centres with life again. Motor traffic is no longer given unconditional priority. In many places pedestrian zones have been established in the busiest shopping areas. New laws have given local authorities better instruments for planning and implementing building projects. Citizens are sooner and more intensively brought into the planning process, the aim being the "humane town".

Consumer protection

The range of products and services is growing. Every year more than 1,000 new products come onto the market in Germany alone. When Europe has a single market with effect from 1 January 1993, the range will be even greater and even more confusing. Products made in Germany compete with goods imported from all over the world. But so great a variety is a problem for the consumer, too. Hardly anyone is able properly to assess quality and value for money. Although advertising does provide some information to help people decide, its main aim is to persuade people to buy.

Consumer protection is intended to offset these disadvantages. This is done both by information and counselling and by legislation. Thus in 1964 the Federal Government set up a foundation in Berlin known as "Stiftung Warentest" which tests goods of all kinds from the ballpoint pen to the prefabricated house as to quality, value for money and compatibility with the environment. To date it has screened more than 30,000 products and services. The foundation only calls on independent experts and test organizations. The fact that there have been few court cases vouches for its good standing. In fact, manufacturers are glad to advertize the fact that their products have been approved by "Stiftung Warentest".

The foundation's main publication is "test", which appears monthly and has a circulation in excess of one million. Furthermore, the test results are regularly publicized in some 160 newspapers and periodicals, and on radio and television.

The public can also seek advice from a number of other organizations, particularly the Consumers' Association (AGV) and the 250 advice centres in the states. They provide free information on the quality and prices of goods and services and receive financial support from the government. Before parliament introduces new consumer protection legislation it consults the associations.

Consumer protection has been considerably improved by legislation. For instance, foodstuffs must be labelled, i.e. every product must bear information on composition and substances, durability and manufacturer. The rules governing pharmaceutical products are particularly strict. Goods in shop windows or salesrooms must indicate the price. This also applies to services (hair

The "Stiftung Warentest" tests all kinds of goods

stylists, for instance). General conditions of sale must not be to the customer's disadvantage. There are many other laws to protect consumers. This legislation is being increasingly switched to the European Community, however. The Community issues directives that must be converted into national law in member states. Not until 1989 did the European Council of Ministers adopt guidelines for determining priorities with regard to European consumer policy.

Consumers' Association:
Arbeitsgemeinschaft der Verbraucherverbände
Heilsbachstr. 20
5300 Bonn 1

Consumer goods testing organization:
Stiftung Warentest
Lützowplatz 11-13
1000 Berlin 30

Industry

The mainstay of the German economy is industry. In the old federal states alone there are 46,700 enterprises. Only about two percent of them are large companies with more than 1,000 employees, whereas roughly a half are small firms with less than 50 on the payroll. Thus the great majority of businesses are of medium size.

Industry is easily the biggest employer in Germany, although its importance has declined considerably as a result of structural change. Its contribution to West Germany's gross national product fell from 48.7% in 1973 to 40.6% in 1990. In the same period the public and private service sectors increased their share from 48.3% to almost 58%. By comparison, agriculture, forestry and fisheries declined from a mere 3% in 1973 to as little as 1.7% in 1990. In the industrial sector rapidly expanding branches like data processing or the aerospace industry have failed to compensate for the decline of such traditional branches as textiles or steel production.

The importance of large companies as a source of employment is in inverse proportion to their percentage of all enterprises. In the old federal states about half of the 7.4 million people in industry are employed by large companies, who also account for about 50% of total industrial turnover. Many of these firms have international names and branches or research facilities overseas. They include Siemens the electronics firm, Volkswagen, BMW and Daimler Benz, the carmakers, Hoechst, Bayer and BASF the chemical corporations, Ruhrkohle AG, VEBA the energy group, and the Bosch group. Nearly all of them are corporations and are extremely important for a large variety of small and medium-sized suppliers.

After the Second World War industry played a crucial part in Germany's economic recovery. A decisive factor in this process was the transition from a controlled economy to a market economy in 1948. One of the basic principles of the social market economy is entrepreneurial responsibility. The businessman must himself see to his company's growth and ensure that it can adapt to changing circumstances. Government policy is mainly confined to creating favourable conditions for industry. In the Federal Government's view competition is the best way to keep German industry technologically and structurally competitive on world markets. It ensures the largest possible number of small and medium-sized firms and this is the reason why the government tries to improve conditions for the smaller industries. The following is an outline of the main branches.

Vehicle manufacture. One of the biggest branches of industry in Germany in terms of turnover is vehicle manufacture, mostly cars.

The biggest industrial firms in the Federal Republic of Germany (1991)

Company, domicile	Sector	Turnover (DM m.)	Work force
1. Daimler-Benz AG, Stuttgart	automotive, electrical engineering, aerospace	94,660	375,300
2. Volkswagen AG, Wolfsburg	automotive	77,000	266,000
3. Siemens AG, Munich	electrical engineering	73,000	402,000
4. Veba AG, Düsseldorf	energy, chemicals	60,000	116,500
5. RWE AG, Essen	energy, building	49,900	102,200
6. Hoechst AG, Frankfurt	chemicals, pharmaceuticals	47,200	179,300
7. BASF AG, Ludwigshafen	chemicals, energy	46,600	129,400
8. Bundespost Telekom, Bonn	telecommunications	43,200	250,000
9. Bayer AG, Leverkusen	chemicals, pharmaceuticals	42,400	164,200
10. Thyssen AG, Duisburg	steel, machinery	36,600	148,400
11. Bosch GmbH, Stuttgart	electrical engineering	33,600	148,600
12. Bayerische Motorenwerke Munich	automotive	29,800	74,200

The Federal Republic is the largest producer of automobiles in the world after Japan and the United States. In 1991 the West German **automotive industry,** with a workforce of some 800,000, registered a turnover in the region of DM 217 billion. Car production was again high at 4,680,000. Just under 2.2 million were exported.

The car industry in the new federal states has a long tradition, but the models produced under the old communist regime had no chance when faced with international competition after the country was united. Their production has been phased out and several large West German companies have opened plants in Saxony, Brandenburg and Thuringia. West Germany's car makers intend to invest about 10 billion marks in the eastern part of the country by 1994. Once production is in full swing in the mid-90s as many as 500,000 cars a year will leave the production lines - twice as many as in the former GDR.

Mechanical engineering embraces over 3,600 companies in West Germany and some 930 in the new federal states and is thus Germany's largest branch of industry. Small firms have always predominated, and it is thanks to their flexibility and technological efficiency that Germany is among the world's leaders in this field. Only three per cent of companies have more than 1,000 employees. These are mainly firms who mass-produce or design and

Car-building is a pillar of German industry

manufacture large, complex facilities. Over 90% of companies in this branch are small or medium-sized with less than 300 employees. They are specialists who play a key role as suppliers of high-quality plant and production equipment for industry. Hardly any country has a wider range - 17,000 products, from consoles via printing machines and agricultural machinery to machine tools. In 1991 this branch of industry, with a total workforce of just under 1.2 million, produced a turnover of DM 240 billion. Some 60% of the goods produced were sold abroad. This means that the Federal Republic accounted for one fifth of total exports of machinery among the western industrial countries.

The chemical industry is the most important branch of the basic materials and production goods industry in the Federal Republic. Its state-of-the-art technology has put it among the world's leaders in this branch. This applies especially to its three principal corporations. There is also a large number of medium-sized companies. The total workforce is about 594,000, and turnover in West Germany in 1990 was DM 165.9 billion. Roughly 50% of the industry's output was exported. The chemical industry is making considerable efforts to improve environmental protection and has in some areas assumed a pioneering role. Although chemical production has a long tradition in the new federal states, it is in many fields unable to compete. The aim is to retain the core of the main chemical regions there. This will require fast privatization and the establishment of new companies. The prospects are good.

The electrical engineering industry, with a turnover of DM 207 billion (1991 in the western states) and more than a million employees, is likewise one of the main branches. The new federal states, too, have an electrical industry, and although production and turnover fell considerably after unification, the situation has been improving since 1991.

Other important branches of industry are food, where in 1991 a workforce of around 493,000 produced a turnover of DM 197.2 billion (in the western states), and the **textile and clothing industry** (204,000 employees, turnover DM 70 billion, likewise in the western part of the country). In 1991 the **steel industry** in western Germany had a turnover of DM 43.6 billion (workforce 149,000). **Mining** had a turnover of DM 31.4 billion (workforce 173,000). In the case of the precision engineering, **optics and watch and clock-making industry,**

Molecular design: the computer helps chemical research

Technical ceramics are an important material for tomorrow's industry

which has many small and medium-sized firms employing some 135,000 people, had a turnover of more than DM 19 billion. Many of these companies feature prominently in international trade. The **aerospace industry** is comparatively small but from the technology point of view is of great importance. It demands the highest standards from suppliers and co-manufacturers and is thus in many fields a pioneer of modern technology. Its turnover in 1990 was DM 17 billion (workforce 78,000). The development of civil aircraft has been subsidized by the Federal Government since 1963. This applies in particular to the Airbus models, which are an example of fruitful cooperation between European firms.

Federation of German Industries:
Bundesverband der Deutschen Industrie (BDI)
Gustav-Heinemann-Ufer 84-88
5000 Köln 51

Technology

Whether automobiles or pharmaceutical products, optical instruments, machine tools or complete power stations - the Federal Republic of Germany supplies the world market with high-quality products. She is one of the leading industrial nations in many branches of industry. In 1988 four German companies were among the world's top ten innovative enterprises. In the case of research-intensive products, Germany exported twice as much as she imported. In bilateral trade she has a negative balance with Japan only.

Competition. It is crucial for German firms to keep abreast of international competition, which is increasingly becoming a high-tech race. Structural change is forcing many enterprises to concentrate on areas of technological and industrial growth. As a country with few natural resources, Germany has always had to rely on exports of top-quality, advanced products. Thus production methods have to be efficient and economical and based on state-of-the-art technology. This is the only way to achieve a high "exchangeable value" in international trade and thus safeguard jobs and incomes in Germany.

Technological development and innovation are primarily the responsibility of companies themselves. The government only comes to their assistance if it is considered necessary in the national interest. It promotes cooperation between industry and research. This cooperation helps small and medium-sized enterprises cope with the challenges of new technology and creates favourable conditions for innovation.

In 1991 the Federal Ministry for Research and Technology invested some DM 500 million in projects implemented by small companies. This enabled them to improve their production methods. They are also helped as regards technology transfer, that is to say, the practical application of research findings. Small companies can obtain information about the latest technological developments, for instance with regard to the use of computers for production purposes, in "demonstration centres" established by the ministry.

Research and development in the former GDR concentrate on

Transrapid: a means of transport for the future

much the same areas as in the Federal Republic: steel, mechanical engineering, automobiles, electrical engineering and chemicals. These are the focal points for the current restructuring of East Germany's economy. Many West German companies are cooperating with firms or research establishments in the new federal states on projects concerned with communications technology, microelectronics, laser technology, environmental engineering and chemical technology.

Strengths and weaknesses. The significance of research-intensive products for Germany's international competitiveness is reflected in the industry's exports. In 1989 Germany accounted for 17.4% of world trade in manufactured industrial goods, the largest share among the OECD countries. Regarding advanced technology (14.4%) she comes third behind the United States and Japan, and regarding sophisticated technology (21.6%) second behind Japan. In the former category German industry has been successful in such fields as pharmaceutical products, new organic chemicals and synthetics, plant protection agents, electronic systems in the field of medicine, advanced optical and measuring instruments. It has been less

*Machine tools made in Germany have a good
reputation worldwide*

successful in the fields of electronic data processing, telecommunications and microchips.

One area where Germany dominates is environmental protection
technology. Here German companies are leading the way, having
filed more patents than any other country. German enterprises are
also actively engaged in biotechnology, which will be one of the key
technologies in the next few decades. The United States and Japan
hold the leading positions, however. Genetic engineering is not only
a challenge to science and technology but also raises many ethical
issues. The German Genetic Engineering Act ensures responsible
research which rules out manipulation, especially in respect of the
human genetic structure.

The advanced technology products include machinery, cars and
rolling stock, chemical and electrical products, as well as measuring
instruments. Germany has for decades played an outstanding role
in these fields despite all economic fluctuations. One of the main
reasons for this success is the high standard of training of German
engineers and skilled workers.

Crafts and trades

Although crafts and trades in the Federal Republic are smaller than the industrial sector, they have a much longer tradition. They flourished particularly in the Middle Ages, as proved by the mighty cathedrals and elaborately ornamented guild houses throughout the country. But today still they are a considerable economic factor. In 1991 over 4.5 million people were employed in this branch, which accounted for about 9% of the gross national product.

Crafts in the industrial society. Industry requires the small craft industries because they are very flexible suppliers of products and parts. But they are also the link between industry and the consumer since quality industrial products have to be serviced and repaired. Craftsmen are also producers themselves. Bakers, confectioners and

Meissner porcelain requires supreme craft skills

Electrical engineer does a final check

slaughterers provide a wide range of foodstuffs. Houses in Germany are still mostly produced by hand by builders, carpenters, glaziers and plumbers. And many trades, such as those of car mechanic, hair stylist, chimney sweep or contract cleaner, are indispensable.

But crafts and trades are of special importance for two other reasons. One is that they offer scope for a large number of self-employed people and are thus a school for young entrepreneurs. The other is that they provide some of the most important training centres. It is here that about 40% of all apprentices in the Federal Republic learn their trade. Although small craft industries cannot absorb all of the people they train, these skilled workers are highly valued in other branches of industry. In 1949 Germany had over 900,000 craft businesses. This number declined but the overall workforce increased. In 1991 there were some 660,000 such firms in the whole of Germany and 80,000 others in much the same category. On average each firm employs about eight people.

Crafts and trades are playing a very important role in the restructuring of East Germany's economy. They are providing the impetus for growth. Even in the days of communist central planning, some 82,000 small private firms were able to exist alongside the 2,700 production cooperatives. By the end of 1991, following the country's reunification, the number of small businesses in the new federal states had increased to about 130,000. Judging by the size of the workforce, the main trade is that of brick-layer or construction worker. The wide range of craft products is on display at the international craft trade fair held every spring in Munich.

State support. The Federal Government helps medium-sized and small enterprises to increase their competitiveness. Assistance covers tax relief, management consultancy and long-term, low-interest loans. In 1990 the Federal Government provided about DM 135 million and, together with the state governments, offers a wide range of promotional programmes to help new firms.

Organization. In the Federal Republic of Germany only persons listed in the Crafts Register are allowed to carry on a trade or provide apprenticeship training. The usual qualification is that of master craftsman, who must be at least 24 years old to employ and train apprentices.

Tradesmen are organized in guilds at town or county level which are responsible for vocational training and continuing education. They can also negotiate collective wage agreements and set up health insurance funds for their members. The craftsmen organize their own affairs and look after their interests through the chambers of handicrafts. The chambers maintain the Crafts Register and apprentices register and set examinations and supervise training. The guilds and chambers have an umbrella organization known as the Central Association of German Craft Industry and Trades.

Zentralverband des Deutschen Handwerks
Johanniterstr. 1
5300 Bonn

Agriculture, forestry and fisheries

Germany is not only a highly industrialized country but also has an efficient farming community who produce a broad range of high-quality foodstuffs. About half of Germany's total area of just under 36 million hectares is given over to farming. Agriculture also has responsibilities which assume increasing significance in a modern industrial society. It ensures that rural settlements can function efficiently and preserves farming landscapes that have developed over centuries. But like other sectors of the economy, agriculture has undergone radical changes in the past 40 years.

Agriculture. In West Germany the number of farms has decreased by about one million since 1950. Attracted by the prospect of better incomes, many farmers left the land to work in industry and service enterprises. Furthermore, increasing mechanization saved man-power: In 1950 there were some 1.6 million farms with a total full-time workforce of just under 3.9 million. In 1990 there were only 630,000 farms with just less than 750,000 full-time employees.

As the number of farms and workers dwindled, productivity increased. In 1950 one farm worker produced enough food for only ten people; today the number is 75. In spite of this huge growth in productivity, agriculture has not always kept pace with industry. True, the income gap had been reduced to just under 10% by the late 80s, but it has been widening again as a result of the unfavourable price situation.

Despite the changes family farms still predominate. Over 90% work less than 50 hectares. In contrast to other West European countries, almost half are part-time farms, i.e. the main family income is from activities outside farming. The chief crops in West Germany in terms of proceeds are milk, pork and beef, cereals and sugarbeet. In some regions wine, fruit and vegetables as well as other market-garden products play a major role.

In West Germany livestock farms are generally small. The factory-type holding is the exception. For instance, just under 90% of milking cows are kept on farms with less than 40 animals, and almost 80% of pig-fattening farms have fewer than 600 animals.

In the eastern part of the country the pattern of farming is different. After the Second World War there were about 600,000 holdings which were forced by the communist regime to give up their independence. They were replaced by agricultural production cooperatives which finally numbered about 5,100. They had on average 4,300 hectares under cultivation. Strictly separated from these were the specialized livestock farms with, on average, over 1,650 cows, 11,000 pigs or 500,000 laying hens. Hardly any notice was taken of consumer wishes or production costs. The main consideration for farm managers was keeping to the prescribed target. Nonetheless, consumer prices remained low, simply because the East German regime subsidized staple foodstuffs to the tune of more than 30 billion marks a year.

When the country was united in October 1990 farmland in the former GDR was returned to private ownership. Although there is still considerable uncertainty as regards land and property ownership, some 14,000 farmers had decided by the end of 1991 to run their own farms. At the same time, three quarters of the 4,500 or so production cooperatives were transformed into registered cooperative societies, partnerships or joint-stock companies.

Modern machinery is indispensable for farmers

In order to ease the difficult process of integrating East Germany's farms into the European Community, farmers who establish new holdings or take over old farms receive temporary financial support from the government. Funds are also provided to help convert the former production cooperatives into competitive enterprises.

Apart from maintaining food supplies, farming in the densely populated, highly industrialized Federal Republic of Germany has other increasingly important functions, including nature conservation, looking after the countryside to provide attractive leisure time and recreational areas, and ensuring a continuous supply of agricultural raw materials for industry.

The family farm is best suited to meeting these various requirements since it can adapt to new developments and ensure that foodstuff production is environment-friendly.

The Common Agricultural Policy of the European Community. With the introduction of the common agricultural market of the European Community in the 60s important areas of agricultural policy were transferred to European institutions. This applies in particular to market and price policy and, to an increasing extent, structural policy.

The Community's original objective was to increase agricultural productivity and thus farmers' incomes, to stabilize markets, and to maintain food supplies at reasonable prices. Much has been achieved in the intervening decades, especially as regards increasing production, with the result that supply of major products such as cereals, milk and beef far exceeds demand. Consequently, easing the strain on markets by restricting production has become an urgent priority. A number of such measures have already proved effective, such as quotas for milk and sugar, as well as compensation for farmers who take land out of production and reduce output. But these measures need to be intensified because it is essential to gear agricultural production within the Community to internal consumption.

National farming policy. Although many decisions on agricultural policy are today taken by the European Community, a few important areas of policy are still in the hands of national governments. This applies in particular to agricultural structural policy. Although the Community sets the framework, the national parliament and government provide the substance. The German Government does

Fresh from Germany's farms

so chiefly through its "joint tasks" with the states to improve agricultural structure and coastal preservation. These include water management, the construction of central water supply and sewage treatment facilities, country roads, reallocation of land and village development. The central and regional governments also provide support for individual farmers who wish to rationalize production methods. In addition, funds are provided for underprivileged areas where agriculture is an important economic and social factor.

Food. German consumers have a wide range of high-quality foodstuffs to choose from. Maintaining supply, quality and variety at reasonable prices is the aim of government policy. Much importance also attaches to protecting consumers from hazards to health and fraudulent products. Hence the government issues regulations which require the manufacture and distribution of foodstuffs to be constantly adjusted in the light of scientific findings.

Information on proper nutrition is gaining importance and the Federal Government promotes institutions responsible for consumer education and advice, such as the Deutsche Gesellschaft für Ernährung (German Nutrition Society), the Auswertungs- und Informationsdienst für Ernährung, Landwirtschaft und Forsten (The Food, Agriculture and Forestry Information Service), as well as the regional consumer protection centres. Their information covers not only scientific facts about nutrition but also up-to-date information on products, prices and keeping private stocks of food.

Growing affluence and the wide range of foodstuffs on offer have greatly changed the eating habits of the Germans in recent decades. Compared with the 50s, demand for starchy and vegetable products such as potatoes and cereal products has decreased considerably, whereas consumption of meat, poultry and eggs as well as fruit and vegetables has increased significantly. Nevertheless, consumers are spending less on food: on average family expenditure on food is now only just under 17%, compared with about 35% in 1950.

Forestry. Almost a third of the Federal Republic's total area - 10.7 million hectares - is covered by forest. The state with the largest forest area in proportion to its total size is Rhineland-Palatinate (about 41%), while the one with the least forest - apart from the city-states - is Schleswig-Holstein (10%).

Nearly 40 million cubic metres of timber is felled in Germany every year. This meets about two thirds of domestic demand. In 1990 the country was hit by serious storms which uprooted or damaged almost 17 million cubic metres of timber, the loss running into billions.

Forests are important not only as sources of timber but also as recreation areas for the inhabitants of industrial conurbations. Furthermore, they have a beneficial influence on soil, air and climate in that they retard water runoff, weaken wind impact, clean the air and prevent erosion and landslides. In short, they are a very important environmental protection factor.

A Forest Preservation and Forestry Promotion Act was enacted in 1975. This stipulates that forest land can only be cleared for other uses with approval from the regional authority. The law obliges forest owners to reafforest harvested areas. The foremost aim is to preserve or restore the natural appearance of the forests and ensure their proper management. Since the early 1980s there has been increasing forest depletion. The trees lose their needles or leaves, growth is retarded and they finally die. There are various biotic and abiotic causes of this new type of damage, mainly air pollution caused by industry, the burning of domestic fuel, and also agriculture.

Fisheries. The fishing industry, too, has undergone structural changes in recent decades. Coastal countries worldwide have extended their fishing zones to 200 sea miles, with the result that traditional stocks have been decimated by overfishing, mainly as a result of the excessive use of modern catching methods. This has greatly reduced the Federal Republic's ocean fishing fleet.

Germany's principal fishing areas are the North Sea, the Baltic, and the Atlantic off the British Isles and around Greenland.

The only way the Federal Republic could survive the threat to its fishing industry resulting from the development of international maritime law was within the framework of the European Community. The Federal Government has also helped to keep the fishing fleet going by providing initial and bridging support.

The principles underlying the common fisheries policy which were laid down in 1983 are being reviewed on the basis of an interim report by the European Commission. The main concern is to preserve stocks of fish since there is still considerable overfishing in the North Sea due to excessive catching capacities.

German Farmers' Association:
Deutscher Bauernverband
Godesberger Allee 142-148
5300 Bonn 2

Ocean-fishing in the North Sea

Commerce

Commerce has developed over the past hundred years into an important sector of the national economy. In fulfilling its distribution functions it facilitated the emergence of a modern economy based on division of labour. In the Federal Republic of Germany in 1990 about 4.13 million people were working in approximately 505,600 commercial enterprises (wholesale and retail).

Wholesale trade. Wholesalers sell commercial goods to other traders, processors, industrial users and bulk consumers. They

Consumer markets make shopping easier

Small retailers offer individual customer service

supply production enterprises with capital goods, raw materials and other aids to production, and retailers with consumer items.

Wholesale turnover rose from around DM 50 billion in 1949 to DM 990 billion in 1991. Competition and costs in this sector have grown in recent years, albeit varying in individual branches, forcing smaller and less efficient enterprises out of the market. Rationalization has greatly reduced the wholesaling labour force in recent years. In 1990 it stood at just over a million employed by about 36,600 firms.

Retail trade. As the last link in the distribution system and in direct contact with consumers the retail trade has undergone remarkable development in recent decades. In the presentation and variety of goods as well as in the development of operational forms retail trading underwent revolutionary changes. The advancement of self-service, which began in grocery stores, permitted considerable rationalization. New types of operation, such as discount or consumer markets, came into being.

Today the main characteristics of the retail trade are strong competititon and small profit margins - all to the customer's advantage. In 1949 turnover in the West German retail trade was DM 28 billion. This rose to over 700 billion in 1991, to which must be added the turnover of roughly 100 billion in the new federal states. Rationalization reduced manpower in the West German retail trade to about 2.6 million by the end of the 80s. In the course of German unification, which gave this sector considerable stimulus, the number increased again. In 1990 West German traders had over 2.7 million employees on the payroll, compared with just under 400,000 in the new states.

Wholesale and retail trade in the former GDR was almost entirely state-controlled. Only about 400 businesses were still in private hands. Just before unification East German retail firms had 883,000 employees and a poor range of products.

Increasing motorization and the trend towards bulk buying have favoured the hypermarkets and self-service department stores. As a result many small traders have not been able to compete. From 1962 to 1986 the number of retailers fell from 445,000 to 340,000. However, medium-size retailers can compete with large enterprises where customers are looking for items of their own choice, a wide range of products, expert advice and personalized service. The formation of purchasing associations has helped many of the smaller firms survive. In 1990 only just over 11% of all retailers in Western Germany had not yet joined such an association.

German Retailers' Association:
Hauptgemeinschaft des Deutschen Einzelhandels
Sachsenring 89
5000 Köln 1

Federation of German Wholesale and Export Companies:
Bundesverband des Deutschen Gross- und Aussenhandels
Kaiser-Friedrich-Strasse 13
5300 Bonn 1

Foreign Trade

The Federal Republic of Germany is a highly developed industrial country with a well-trained labour force and an efficient production system, but it lacks raw materials and natural sources of energy. Nor can it produce all the food and feeding stuffs it requires. If only for economic reasons, therefore, it is dependent upon international trade. Germany promotes peaceful cooperation among nations and world economic integration. By consistently pursuing an outward-looking policy it has made itself one of the world's leading trading countries together with the United States and Japan. The main principles of German trade are: international division of labour rather than self-sufficiency; global competition rather than trade restrictions; and reconciliation of interests rather than economic confrontation.

External equilibrium and exports. The total value of the old Federal Republic's imports and exports increased from DM 19.7 billion in 1950 to over DM 1,311 billion in 1990. Since 1952 exports have usually exceeded imports, and this in spite of several revaluations of the mark. Since the early 80s the export surplus has risen constantly, reaching DM 134.5 billion in 1989. In 1991, however, it decreased considerably. One of the reasons is that the huge demand from the new federal states boosted Germany's imports, making her a "locomotive" of world trade.

The Federal Republic's large export surpluses often drew criticism abroad. But they are necessary to offset deficits in other fields - particularly the huge amounts spent by German holidaymakers abroad as well as remittances by foreign workers in Germany to their relatives at home. Moreover, the Federal Republic is one of the largest contributors to international organizations. Nor should one forget that Germany's imports are considerable. The main items imported are farm products and textiles - goods with which the developing countries in particular and young industrial nations are penetrating the world's markets.

Nearly one in three gainfully employed persons in the Federal Republic works directly for export. Germany is one of the world's biggest suppliers of industrial equipment. The principal exports are machinery, chemical and electrical engineering products, motor vehicles, but also iron and steel products. German export companies excel in terms of quality, service and delivery. As a country with high wages Germany has concentrated on high-tech products in order to make up for her disadvantage as regards costs. As a result of her extensive trade relations Germany is affected by disruptions of world trade since they have an impact on jobs, investments, profits and standards of living. Thus a stable world economy, free trade and a well-functioning monetary system are crucial to the German economy.

Trading partners. The progressive economic integration of the European Community (EC) has increased the Federal Republic's

Ready for the world's markets: containers at Bremerhaven

The principal trading partners of the Federal Republic of Germany 1991

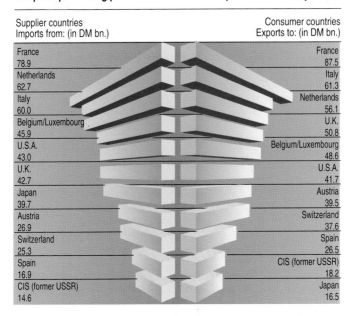

Supplier countries Imports from: (in DM bn.)	Consumer countries Exports to: (in DM bn.)
France 78.9	France 87.5
Netherlands 62.7	Italy 61.3
Italy 60.0	Netherlands 56.1
Belgium/Luxembourg 45.9	U.K. 50.8
U.S.A. 43.0	Belgium/Luxembourg 48.6
U.K. 42.7	U.S.A. 41.7
Japan 39.7	Austria 39.5
Austria 26.9	Switzerland 37.6
Switzerland 25.3	Spain 26.5
Spain 16.9	CIS (former USSR) 18.2
CIS (former USSR) 14.6	Japan 16.5

trade with the other members of the Community far beyond trade with other nations. In 1990 some 55% of German exports went to EC countries.

Germany's main trading partner is France. In 1991 the Federal Republic exported goods and services worth approximately DM 87.5 billion to that country, whereas imports were worth a good DM 78.9 billion. Other major importers of German products are Italy, the United Kingdom, the Netherlands and Belgium/Luxembourg. Next in line are the United States, which in 1991 spent roughly DM 42 billion on goods from Germany.

France also heads the list as far as Germany's imports are concerned, followed by the Netherlands, Italy, Belgium/Luxembourg, the United Kingdom and the United States. Japan, too, is an important trading partner. But although imports from that country reached almost DM 40 billion in 1991, Germany's exports were worth only DM 16.5 billion.

In 1990 the new federal states appeared in Germany's trade statistics for the first time. Trade relations of the former GDR were

Imports and exports of the Federal Republic of Germany
(actual figures, "old" federal states)

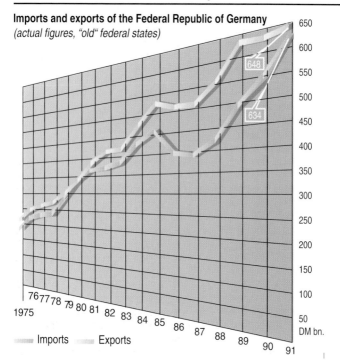

650
600
550
500
450
400
350
300
250
200
150
100
50
DM bn.

648

634

1975 76 77 78 79 80 81 82 83 84 85 86 87 88 89 90 91

▬▬ Imports   ▬▬ Exports

heavily focused on the state-trading countries of the former Eastern bloc. Its main trading partner was the Soviet Union, which continued to feature in united Germany's trade statistics in 1991. In that year Germany exported goods worth roughly DM 18 billion to the Soviet Union, whereas imports were worth DM 14.6 billion.

Investment abroad. After the Second World War the Germans had to start from scratch where foreign investment was concerned. Nearly all German assets abroad had been lost. But by the end of 1990 the total invested abroad was worth approximately DM 221 billion. And other countries have invested in the Federal Republic - up to the end of 1990 well over DM 127 billion.

There are many reasons for investing overseas. Some companies switch production outside Germany because domestic wages are too high. Others have to secure their supplies of raw materials and therefore buy an interest in foreign suppliers. In many cases the aim is to maintain and expand markets abroad. Where trade restrictions or unfavourable exchange rates prove to be a hindrance to direct exports, one way to solve the problem is to produce the goods where they are to be sold.

At any rate, investment abroad helps consolidate international trade. It is conducive to the international division of labour and can help ease acute unemployment problems, especially in developing countries. Moreover, exported German capital is often accompanied by German know-how which thus contributes to the solution of the tasks of the future.

In order to offset possible economic and political risks attaching to investment in developing countries, the Federal Government has introduced special promotional instruments. For instance, it has concluded agreements for the protection of investments with over 70 developing countries and nations in Central and Eastern Europe. These agreements make provision for national and most-favoured nation treatment, the free transfer of capital and profits, fair compensation in the event of expropriation, as well as independent international arbitration.

To guard against political risks the Federal Government also affords financial guarantees for investments it considers worth supporting. The German Finance Company for Investments in Developing Countries (DEG) promotes direct investment in the Third World. Medium-sized German companies receive low-interest loans and grants to help them finance branch establishments in developing countries and the transfer of technology.

Federation of Wholesale and Export Companies:
Bundesverband des Deutchen Gross- und Aussenhandels
Kaiser-Friedrich-Strasse 13
5300 Bonn 1

Raw materials and energy

As stated previously, the Federal Republic has little in the way of raw materials and energy and is therefore largely dependent upon imports. She is the largest consumer of energy in the world and has to buy two thirds of her primary energy from other countries. Her dependence on minerals (copper, bauxite, manganese, titanium, phosphate, wolfram and tin), is very considerable. Germany has few deposits of iron ore and oil. One third of the country's natural gas consumption can be met from local sources. There are large deposits of coal and salt, however, which will last for many decades.

Primary energy consumption
(in Petajoules PJ = 10^{15} J; shares in %, "old" federal states)

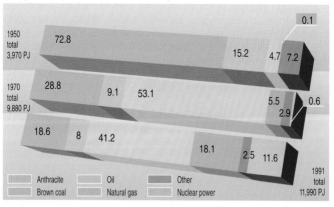

Anthracite	Oil
Brown coal	Natural gas
Other	
Nuclear power	

Mining and oil. The main pitcoal deposits are in the Ruhr region (North-Rhine/Westphalia) and in the Saarland. The reserves total about 24 billion tonnes. There are huge browncoal or lignite deposits in southern Brandenburg, Saxony, Saxony-Anhalt and in the foothills of the Harz Mountains as well as in the lower Rhine area. Here there are over 94 billion tonnes which can be economically extracted.

Coal will continue to meet part of Germany's energy supply, although the amount will be considerably less than in the late 80s. Pitcoal will continue to be required for the steel industry and for power stations, but its geological structure makes extraction expensive, so that production has to be reduced.

Lignite was the main source of energy in the former GDR, but the poor quality and the lack of emission-cleansing facilities in the power stations caused massive air pollution. Furthermore, excessive open-cast mining devastated huge areas. If only for environmental reasons, lignite production in the new federal states is being reduced.

In 1950 pitcoal accounted for 73% of the old Federal Republic's energy consumption. By 1990 it had fallen to just under 19%. But oil, too, is losing ground to other sources of energy, largely on account of the high price. From 55% in 1973 (compared with just 5% in 1950) oil's contribution to energy supply fell to just under 41% in 1990. The oil price explosions in the 70s in particular showed how important uninterrupted energy supplies are for the Federal Republic.

Nearly all of Germany's crude oil must be imported. Her own oil deposits, now down to an estimated 50 million tonnes, are to be found in the North German Plain, the Upper Rhenish Lowlands and the Alpine foothills. The prospects are more favourable with regard to the country's next most important source of energy, natural gas. Following new discoveries in the Emsland region and in the North Sea, natural gas reserves are estimated at up to 500 billion cubic metres. In 1990 gas accounted for about 17.5% of the Federal Republic's primary energy consumption. The Federal Republic also has small deposits of uranium, but all the enriched uranium needed for nuclear energy has to be imported.

Raw materials. Although the Federal Republic's raw material supplies are at present secure, the overall situation necessitates the prospecting of new deposits at home and abroad and measures to reduce consumption. Recycling, the processing and reuse of materials, is becoming increasingly important. The same is true for substitution, the replacement of an expensive or harmful raw material by another that is more environment-friendly.

The Federal Government considers that the best way to secure raw material supplies is to keep world markets functioning. It therefore bases its economic relations with the raw-material-rich but under-industrialized countries on the following principles:

— maintaining world economic growth;

— stabilizing commodity export earnings, particularly of the least developed countries, and securing continuity of raw material supplies;

— accelerating industrialization in the Third World and facilitating technology transfer from industrial to developing countries;

— opening the markets of the industrial countries to imports of finished and semi-finished goods from the developing countries;

— promoting continuous transfer of capital to the developing countries and protecting investors from expropriation;

— increasing transfers of resources from industrial to developing countries.

Energy supply. Secure, environmentally safe and competitive energy supplies are one of the prerequisites for a well-functioning economy and for meeting people's basic needs. The energy industry in the Federal Republic of Germany is mostly in private hands. The state's task is to provide a suitable framework for its activities. This includes an Energy Act and regulations for crisis-prevention and emergency stocking, as well as laws to protect the environment.

Since 1973 conditions on international energy markets have changed fundamentally several times. Two sharp increases in the price of oil have shaken the world economy while the rapid drop in early 1986 caused further insecurity as to price development of the most important energy source. At the same time it has become clear in recent years that where production and consumption of energy are concerned greater care must be taken to protect the environment.

The energy industry in the Federal Republic has taken considerable steps to conserve energy and ensure environment-friendly consumption. In the longer term, however, new shortages and corresponding price increases cannot be ruled out, especially in respect of oil. Hence the energy supply system must remain adaptable.

Energy policy. The main aims of government energy policy are:

— to further reduce environmental pollution caused by energy consumption. The focus is on the climate, i.e. drastically reducing emissions of carbon dioxide;

— to maintain supplies of energy which are competitive, economical and environment-friendly;

— to promote energy conservation and the exploration of long-term alternative sources of energy;

— to seek broad public support for the use of coal and nuclear energy. According to the Federal Government nuclear energy should continue to be a major source of the country's energy. In 1991 the 21 nuclear power stations in the western part of the Federal Republic accounted for some 38% of the country's power supply. The construction and operation of nuclear power stations have been a subject of intensive public debate since 1975. Many people are afraid of the possibility of a nuclear disaster and the damage to the atmosphere this would cause. The Chernobyl disaster of 1986 heightened these fears,which the Federal Government takes very seriously. The people are kept fully informed about the government's energy policy and are told in particular that the continued use of nuclear energy is justifiable and necessary until such time as other reliable, environment-friendly and cheap sources of energy are available.

The Federal Republic's nuclear reactors, as is well known, conform to high safety standards. Ever since nuclear energy has been used for peaceful purposes, the safety of nuclear facilities has been given absolute priority over economic situations. The radioactive waste from these facilities is stored in one of the large salt deposits in

Nuclear power stations supply 38 per cent of Germany's energy

northern Germany, which are considered the safest place since, according to geologists, they have been "stable" for millions of years.

Since German unification the new federal states too have largely been applying the principles of West Germany's energy policy. Hence the strict environmental laws of the West also apply in the former GDR. This has resulted, for instance, in some nuclear reactors being shut down.

Germany's high standards in this field have won international recognition, partly as a result of annual checks carried out by the International Energy Agency. The government's and industry's environment-protection measures have already considerably reduced pollution.

Overland power distribution: an industrial society needs energy

Wind power use is also being encouraged

Money and banking

The basic unit of currency in the Federal Republic of Germany is the Deutsche Mark (DM 1 = 100 Pfennigs). It is freely convertible, i.e. it can be exchanged for any other foreign currency at any time at the going rate. There are no restrictions of capital transactions with other countries. The deutschmark is one of the most stable currencies in the world and the second most important reserve currency after the American dollar.

The German Federal Bank. The Federal Republic of Germany's central bank is the Deutsche Bundesbank (German Federal Bank) in Frankfurt am Main. In exercising its powers it is independent of the Federal Government but must support its general economic policy.

The Federal Bank has a number of state central banks. Its board consists of a president, a vice-president and other members. All are appointed by the Federal President on nomination by the Federal Government. The board and the presidents of the state central banks together form the Central Bank Council. It determines the Federal Bank's monetary and credit policies and draws up general guidelines for its management and administration.

Only the Federal Bank is empowered to issue banknotes. Since 1990 new ones have gradually been introduced, and there is now a DM 200 banknote. The Federal Bank regulates the amount of money in circulation as well as credit supply to industry. It also handles the banking side of domestic and international payment transactions. Under the Treaty on Economic, Monetary and Social Union, which came into effect on 1 July 1990, the currency of the former GDR was converted into deutschmarks. At the same time, the Credit Act also became applicable in Eastern Germany. This and other supervisory laws now cover all 571 banks in the former GDR.

By regulating the supply of money in circulation the Federal Bank keeps the Deutsche Mark stable while at the same time making available the necessary means to finance economic growth. To this end it relies on minimum reserves, refinancing and an open-market policy. The banks are required to keep a certain percentage of their liabilities (minimum reserve) with the Federal Bank, interest-free. By

German banknotes

varying this percentage the central bank can influence the credit-creating scope of the banks.

With its refinancing policy it regulates the allocation of bank credit. It does so by buying bills of exchange and lending money on securities. The discount rate (for bills of exchange) and the Lombard rate (for loans on securities) are important regulatory factors.

The Federal Bank may engage in open-market transactions only to regulate the money market. By buying securities it allows money to flow into the economy, by selling them it withdraws money.

The European Monetary System. The purpose of the European Monetary System (EMS), which was established in 1979, is to stabilize exchange rates between the currencies of member states in the European Community. All EC countries except Spain and Portugal belong to the EMS. There are special arrangements for Britain and Greece. To stabilize exchange rates each member country has fixed a central rate for its currency which is expressed in the European Currency Unit (ECU). The value of the ECU is calculated from a "basket" of the participating currencies. The market rates of each currency may fluctuate up or down from bilateral central rates within a specific margin. If an exchange rate rises or falls outside that margin the Central Bank is obliged to intervene by buying or selling currencies to keep the rate within the currency band. The EMS binds only the exchange rates of the participating currencies. Exchange rates with other currencies, such as the dollar or the yen, fluctuate freely on the currency markets. By the end of the 90s at the latest there will be a uniform European currency. This was decided by the Heads of State and Government of the European Community at their summit meeting in Maastricht, Holland, in December 1991.

Credit institutions. Public, cooperative and private credit institutions operate in the Federal Republic. In 1990 there were 341 lending banks, 11 giro clearing banks, 771 savings banks, 4 cooperative central banks, 3,392 credit cooperatives, 36 mortgage institutions and public mortgage banks, 18 banks with special functions, 20 building societies and 16 postal giro and savings offices.

The private banks include large ones that are joint-stock companies. Giro central banks are the central credit institutions of the public savings banks in the federal states. As house banks of the states they concentrate their activities on regional financing. Most savings banks, which cater mainly for employees and the self-employed, are operated by the municipalities. They are autonomous public enterprises, the local authority being liable. "Zentralkassen" are the regional central institutions of Raiffeisenkassen and Volksbanken, i.e. the rural and commercial credit cooperatives. Nearly 11 million people have shares in these cooperatives.

Mortgage banks are private real-estate credit institutions which give mortgages and local-authority loans and raise the necessary funds by issuing mortgage bonds and local-authority bonds. Among the special credit institutions is the Kreditanstalt für Wiederaufbau (Development Loan Corporation). Buildings societies accept the savings deposits of people who want to build or buy their own homes and give them loans for this purpose after a certain sum is saved.

The activities of all credit institutions in the Federal Republic are supervised by the Bundesaufsichtsamt für das Kreditwesen (Federal Banking Supervisory Office) in Berlin. If in spite of this control a credit institution gets into difficulties, so-called "fire brigade funds" of the banking trade compensate for savers' losses.

Frankfurt Stock Exchange, the biggest in Germany

Financial markets. The total amount of loans provided by banks has risen steadily in recent years. At the end of 1990 banks in the western part of the country had loaned more than two trillion marks (DM 2,000 billion) to private companies and individuals. Private savings, too, have risen continuously, from deposits totalling DM 491 billion in 1980 to DM 678 billion in 1990. Savings still account for the greater proportion of private capital formation, even though interest rates are relatively low. Higher interest rates can be obtained from fixed interest bonds, of which some 1,460 billion were in circulation in 1990. A large proportion of these are government bonds. They include mortgage bonds, which produce a large proportion of the funds required for housing construction.

The public in general are not very interested in stocks and shares. Germany's biggest stock exchange is in Frankfurt on the Main, which handles just under two thirds of all share dealings in Germany. In the world ratings the Frankfurt exchange occupies fourth place behind Tokyo, New York and London.

Accounts and modes of payment. As late as the 60s some German workers were still receiving their wages in cash. Today nearly every employee has a giro or salary account. In addition, over 30 million Germans use Eurocheques, which are accepted in nearly all European countries. Credit cards are becoming increasingly popular. In 1991 over 5.4 million of them were in circulation.

Federation of Commercial Banks:
Bundesverband Deutscher Banken
Mohrenstrasse 35-51
5000 Köln 1

Association of Public Savings and Giro Banks:
Deutscher Sparkassen- und Giroverband
Simrockstrasse 4
5300 Bonn 1

Federation of Cooperative Banks:
Bundesverband der deutschen Volksbanken
und Raiffeisenbanken e.V.
Heussallee 5
5300 Bonn 1

Fairs and exhibitions

Trade fairs developed in the early Middle Ages out of individual markets, often in connection with church festivals. Since they offered good trading prospects and promoted the region's economy they were under the protection of the princes, who granted various towns the right to hold them. Thus the fair in Frankfurt on the Main was first mentioned in the privilege granted in 1240 by Emperor Frederick II. Another granted by the Emperor Maximilian in 1507 established the Leipzig Fair, which has assumed great economic importance.

In Germany the former comprehensive fair has been superseded by the specialized fair. Germany's importance as a location for international fairs is known throughout the world. At present, 107 of the 150 international specialized fairs are held in Germany. In 1991 German fairs and exhibitions attracted more than 9.6 million visitors.

The sites for Germany's fairs are constantly being enlarged. There is considerable investment in new buildings, conversion, and new exhibition concepts. The proportion of foreign exhibitors at German fairs has increased constantly and in 1991 was about 44%. The increasing range of goods and services on offer stimulates competition and makes for even greater international participation.

Fairs and exhibitions in Germany. Apart from the major events, some 130 regional and many small fairs take place every year in Germany. The main German venues are Berlin, Düsseldorf, Essen, Frankfurt am Main, Hamburg, Hanover, Cologne, Leipzig, Munich, Nuremberg and Stuttgart. Of special importance is the Hanover Fair, which has been held every spring since 1947. With a display area of almost 500,000 square metres and about 6,000 German and foreign exhibitors of capital goods and consumer durables, it is the largest fair in the world. Since 1986 Hanover has also been the venue for a separate fair devoted to office, information and communication technology, known as "Cebit".

The spring and autumn consumer goods fairs in Frankfurt am Main focus on ceramics, glassware, china, arts and crafts, jewelry and stationery. Frankfurt is also host to a number of major specialized fairs such as the biennial Sanitation, Heating and Air Conditioning

The Hanover Trade Fair is the world's biggest industrial exhibition

Fair (ISH) or the "interstoff" (clothing textiles). And every autumn publishers and booksellers from all over the world meet at the Frankfurt Book Fair.

Cologne, too, is an important venue for such fairs as "ANUGA" (foodstuffs), "photokina" (photography), an international furniture fair, the "art-cologne" (art fair) and various other fairs for household goods, hardware, bicycles and motor-cycles.

The main events in Berlin are the International Green Week (an agricultural and food exhibition), the International Tourism Exchange, the overseas import fair known as "Partners for Progress", and the International Audiovisual Fair. In 1992, after a break of 60 years, the International Aerospace Exhibition (IFA) returns to Berlin. Important fairs in Düsseldorf are "Drupa" (printing and paper), the "GIFA" (foundries), "INKAMA" (instrumentation), "INTERPAK" (packaging machinery and materials) as well as the fashion fair "IGEDO" which takes place several times a year.

Outstanding events in Munich are the "BAUMA" (construction machinery) and the International Light Industries and Handicrafts Fair. The specialized fairs for the computer industry and electronic components are attracting increasing attention.

German unification has also merged two quite different types of trade fair: the decentralized, specialized type organized in cooperation with the industrial sector concerned in western Germany, and the state-controlled type of the former GDR geared to Leipzig's comprehensive fair. Leipzig has in the meantime changed its concept so that now the traditional spring fair consists

Leipzig has a long tradition as trade fair centre

of several specialized fairs. It is banking on its experience in trade with Eastern Europe and aims to stimulate economic recovery there.

Fairs and exhibitions abroad. The growing integration of the world economy makes it increasingly important for German industry to participate in foreign trade fairs in order to promote exports. For this purpose it has information stands, displays industrial items, designs and models, or runs joint exhibitions with government agencies. In 1990 German firms participated in 136 major fairs abroad. At regular intervals the Federal Republic organizes industrial exhibitions abroad, such as the 1991 "TECHNOGERMA" in Seoul. In 1992 it is participating in the World Exhibition in Seville. Germany will probably be host to a world exhibition in Hanover in the year 2000. Its motto will be "man, nature and technology".

German Council of Trade Fairs and Exhibitions:
Ausstellungs- und Messeausschuß der
Deutschen Wirtschaft (AUMA)
Lindenstrasse 8
5000 Köln 1

Transport

A modern industrial society like the Federal Republic needs a highly developed transport system. It gives people mobility, makes it easier for them to choose where to live and work, and also helps to level out unequal living conditions. Without a well-functioning transport system industry and commerce could not develop the necessary efficiency and flexibility. For a country as greatly dependent on foreign trade as Germany this is particularly important.

The government is confronted with major problems. The transport system in the former GDR must be completely overhauled and expanded. When the European single market starts functioning in 1993 and opens up to Eastern Europe, Germany will become an even more important hub of trade and transport in the heart of Europe.

In the new Kassel-Wilhelmshöhe station: the ICE

"German Unity" transport scheme. Whereas the old federal states have a good transport and communications network, transport infrastructure in the new states has to be rebuilt from scratch and also enlarged. It has been estimated that this will require investment running into billions up to the year 2000. Priority is being given to extending east-west transport links in Germany since they will play a key role in the process of merging the two parts of the country and promoting Eastern Germany's economic recovery. The Federal Government has therefore selected 17 major road, waterway and rail projects known as the "German Unity" transport scheme, which are to be completed as soon as possible. In order to expedite matters the planning and decision-making procedures will be drastically shortened and road and rail projects contracted out to private companies.

Means of transport. Private cars are easily the most popular means of transport in Germany. In 1990 they accounted for some 685 billion passenger kilometres. Buses and local railway systems accounted for 88 billion, the railways 63 and aircraft 18 billion. In the field of freight transport, trucks led the way with 183 billion ton kilometres, followed by the railways (103) and inland shipping (57).

Bundesbahn and Reichsbahn. The biggest transport corporation in the Federal Republic is the Deutsche Bundesbahn (DB). It is the national railway system owned by the state. After it has been merged with the Deutsche Reichsbahn (DR), the rail network in Eastern Germany, German Railways will have a labour force of nearly 500,000. This number will have to be cut, however, in the next few years as a result of rationalization measures, especially where the Reichsbahn is concerned. At present the two systems have a rail network of about 40,900 km, 16,000 km of which are electrified. The 13,000 km of the DR is to be cut back to about 4,800 km.

Since it is a very environment-friendly means of transport, the railways will remain indispensable for the movement of bulk goods and passengers. Modernizing the railway network in the new states alone will cost some 40 billion marks. In 1991 the western DB introduced its first high-speed services. The new ICE trains can travel at up to 250 km/h. Other high-speed routes are planned. The new routes between Hanover and Würzburg and between Mannheim and Stuttgart make the railways even more attractive, especially for businessmen. The aim is to offer an attractive alternative to air and car travel over distances of up to 500 km. As early as 1971 DB was operating Intercity expresses at hourly intervals. Since 1991 more than 630 highly efficient long-distance trains are operating daily between more than 250 cities.

The railways perform an important function in providing local transport in densely populated industrial areas. Attractive services are being provided to induce motorists to switch over to public transport. This would also help ease the burden on the environment. Over the years billions have been spent on modernizing fast metropolitan railway networks (S-Bahn) in Berlin and Hamburg, in the Ruhr district, Frankfurt am Main, Cologne, Nuremberg, Stuttgart and Munich. There are also underground systems, trams and buses.

Metropolitan transit systems embracing all types of transport have proved very successful in nearly all densely populated areas. Passengers may switch from one system to the other using the same ticket. However, local public transport shows a declining percentage of transport overall. The state governments and town councils are trying to reverse this trend, especially as the centres of large towns are becoming increasingly congested by cars.

Roads. There are more cars on Germany's roads than ever. In 1990 there were approximately 42.5 million registered vehicles, including 35.5 million cars (1950, in the old Federal Republic, only 19 million, 1986 approx. 31.7 million). The network of trunk roads has a total length of 221,000 km, including 11,000 km of autobahns (motorways). In size, therefore, it is second only to that of the United States. Leaving aside the situation in the new federal states, the main concern at present is not so much to build new roads as to remove bottlenecks and accident black spots, and to provide more links with regions with little transport infrastructure. On nearly all of Germany's roads there is a graduated speed limit. On national highways, for instance, the maximum speed limit is usually 100 km/h, in built-up areas 50 km/h and in some cases only 30 km/h. Only certain parts of the autobahns have no speed limit.

To many people the car remains an undispensable means of getting to and from work and of enjoying leisure-time pursuits. Rapid goods transport from door to door would not be possible without the use of trucks. The motor vehicle will therefore remain one of the principal means of transport.

In some areas, however, road and rail transport do not compete but rather complement each other. One example of this is the "pick-a-back" system by which trucks are transported over long

Germany has the world's second-largest motorway network

distances on special railway wagons. In container traffic, too, in which the railways are an important link in the transport chain, road and rail work together. This also applies to car-carrying trains.

Although the motor-car means a lot to the individual in terms of mobility and quality of life, it also has its negative aspects. Together with industry and private households, cars are one of the main sources of air pollution. For several years now those who buy low-pollution cars have enjoyed tax concessions. Road safety is constantly being improved, mainly through modern roads, traffic education in schools, and the construction of increasingly safer cars. Although road accidents have continued to increase, it has been possible to substantially reduce the number of fatalities in the old federal states - in spite of the growing traffic density. In the former GDR, where the people suddenly had to adjust to a drastic increase in traffic and faster cars, accident figures have increased sharply. Improving road safety therefore remains a permanent task.

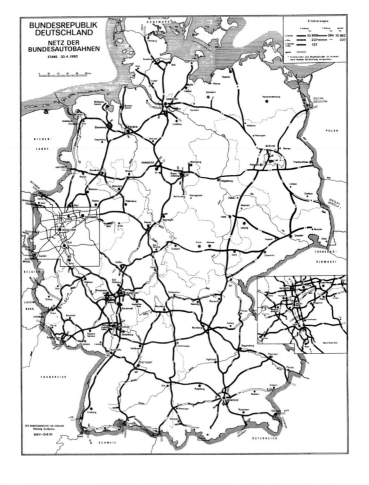

Shipping. As a large exporting and importing country, Germany has a merchant fleet of its own. It comprises 1,066 vessels with a gross registered tonnage of 5.68 million and is one of the most modern and safest in the world. Two thirds of the ships are no older than ten years. Germany is one of the leaders in terms of container and roll-on, roll-off traffic.

Germany's seaports (the largest being Hamburg, Bremen/ Bremerhaven, Wilhelmshaven, Lübeck and Rostock) have been able to hold their own in international competition. Although foreign North Sea ports such as Rotterdam are closer to the West European industrial centres, the German ports have made up for this disadvantage by investing heavily in infrastructure and port facilities. They are now "fast ports" which can turn even large vessels around in a short time. The Baltic Sea ports in Mecklenburg-Western Pomerania expect to benefit from increased traffic with Eastern Europe.

Inland shipping in Germany has an efficient waterways network at its disposal. The main international waterway is the Rhine, which accounts for two thirds of goods transported by inland waterway. Some 3,900 freight vessels ply the country's rivers and canals, which have a total length of 6,700 km. This network will be further enlarged and modernized to serve both internal traffic, as in the case of the Mittelland Canal and the Elbe-Havel Canal, and to increase freight traffic with Eastern Europe via the Rhein-Main-Danube Canal, which forms a continuous link between the North Sea and the Black Sea.

Air transport. The strong growth of international air traffic is making heavy demands on Germany's airports and air traffic control systems. In 1990, 82 million passengers were registered at Germany's airports. In addition, there were nearly 1.8 million tonnes of air freight. The largest airport is Frankfurt am Main; indeed it is one of the principal airports in Europe. Other German airports are Berlin-Tegel and Berlin-Schönefeld, Hamburg, Bremen, Hanover, Düsseldorf, Cologne/Bonn, Munich, Nuremberg, Stuttgart, Saarbrücken, Leipzig, Dresden and Erfurt. Berlin's airports in particular are to be enlarged.

Deutsche Lufthansa is one of the leading international airlines. In 1980 it carried about 22.5 million passengers using a fleet of over 220 airliners. Every year over 15 million holidaymakers fly by Condor, LTU, Hapag-Lloyd, Aero-Lloyd, German Airlines and other smaller companies. Some 90 international airlines maintain regular flights to German airports. From Germany's airports there are direct flights to some 200 destinations in more than 90 countries.

Air traffic centre for Europe: Frankfurt Airport

German airports are operated as private companies but are under public control. Responsible for air traffic control is the Bundesanstalt für Flugsicherheit (Federal Administration of Air Navigation Services). Airport and air safety standards are constantly updated in order to cope with the heavy congestion in Germany's airspace.

Prospects. Experts predict a continuing growth of transport in Germany. They say, for instance, that passenger transport on the roads will increase by about 30% by the year 2010, rail traffic by roughly 40%, and air traffic by more than 100% even. As regards freight traffic, the increases will be even greater. Road haulage, for instance, is expected to grow by 95%, rail freight by 55%. All the more important to make transport systems as environment-friendly and as safe as possible and to make the best possible use of their capacities.

Posts and telecommunications

In 1490 the first teams of horsemen were relaying mail between Innsbruck in Austria and Mechelen in what is now Belgium. That was the birth of the postal service in Germany. The 500th anniversary of that event was celebrated in 1990. Almost at the same time, the postal and telecommunications system in Germany was completely reorganized. Three services formerly controlled by the Federal Ministry of Posts and Telecommunications were transferred to three newly formed public enterprises:

— Deutsche Bundespost POSTDIENST (postal services)
— Deutsche Bundespost POSTBANK (banking services)
— Deutsche Bundespost TELEKOM (telecommunications)

Although there will still be a central administration, the Bundespost, the three new undertakings will have a certain amount of independence and much greater entrepreneurial scope.

The public interest will still be safeguarded by the Federal Ministry of Posts and Telecommunications. The Federal Government has issued regulations and set out political targets to ensure that postal services continue to serve the community as a whole. The ministry also regulates the entire postal and telecommunications market. The three undertakings are being operated in accordance with business principles in order to provide efficient postal, banking and telecommunication services for the public.

The system has been restructured in order to keep postal services competitive in a fast-growing European market. This applies especially to telecommunications, where new technology is being introduced at ever shorter intervals and services have to cater for customer demand.

TELEKOM. This enterprise builds and operates all telecommunication facilities for the exchange of news and data. It includes the telephone network, mobile radio-operated telephone systems, and global satellite communications. Whereas TELEKOM is only responsible for the telephone network, it has to compete with private firms where the sale of equipment and systems to subscribers is concerned. Thus the consumer has a wide choice, from the various

Radio transmitter in Raisting, Bavaria

types of telephone via means of communication such as Eurosignal and telex, to telefax.

All telephone calls in Germany can be dialled by the subscriber direct. This also applies to telephone calls made to 212 countries. A rapidly growing service is telefax. In 1991 900,000 fax machines were in operation.

TELEKOM's telex network, with 110,000 terminals, gives increasing prominence to new text and data services. A fibre-optics network for video conferences, picture telephone and high-speed data transmission is being rapidly extended and is already 500,000 km long.

Cable television has developed into the second largest telecommunication service. In 1991 about nine million households were connected to the cable network. This enables them to receive private and public television and radio programmes.

TELEKOM is faced with the huge task of replacing the obsolete telephone network in the former GDR. In 1990 and 1991 large sections of a completely new digital overlay network were installed and put into operation. The network uses fibre optics and state-of-the-art relay systems and digitalized switching technology. It links the telecommunication centres in the new states among themselves and with the old states in the west. By the end of 1991 500,000 new telephone connections had been installed in the new federal states, priority at first being given to commercial firms and public authorities. In 1991 there were about 33 million telephones in the country as a whole.

POSTDIENST. With a workforce of about 400,000 the Deutsche Bundespost (German Federal Post Office) is the country's largest service enterprise. As a public undertaking it must carry mail and freight to any destination within Germany at a standard rate. This is a highly cost-intensive service. At present the POSTDIENST has to be subsidized by TELEKOM but aims to be out of the red by about 1996. It is competing with private enterprises on the basis of international agreements and is launching an entirely new freight plan to challenge private parcel services. The Post Office's main aim is to ensure that 90 out of 100 letters posted are delivered the next day.

POSTBANK. Although it is forbidden by law to issue loans or deal in securities, the Deutsche Postbank (Post Office Savings Bank) provides a very extensive banking service. Nearly one in three citizens has a Post Office Savings Bank account. Money can be withdrawn or paid into the account at any post office counter. The POSTBANK giro service plays an important role with regard to non-cash payment transactions and intends to improve its service to

Federal Post Office in figures (1990/91)

	Postal service	Telekom	Postal Bank
Employees	390,000	260,000	27,000
Letters	13.87 bn. p. a.		
Goods consignments	327.3 m. p. a.		
Packets	281.9 m. p. a.		
Telephone connections		30.5 m.	
Radio telephone		0.4 m.	
Telefax		0.8 m.	
Cable connections		9 m.	
Postal savings accounts			24 m.
Postal giro accounts			5 m.

attract new customers. Thus since 1991 it has been possible to obtain money from cash dispensers at all post offices using the Postbank card. The POSTBANK also intends to branch out into fixed-term deposits, federal treasury bonds and saving through insurance. It is already Germany's largest savings institution, administering more than five million Post Office Bank giro accounts and nearly 24 million savings accounts.

Tourism

Germany has a remarkable variety of urban areas and landscapes in a comparatively small area. The Federal Republic is popular with German holiday-makers, too, as shown by the fact that nearly half of them stay in their own country. Only 13% of overnight stays are by foreigners (for comparison, in Austria the number is over two thirds). Nevertheless, those foreign visitors spent about DM 17 billion in 1990.

Garmisch-Partenkirchen in winter

The Elb sandstone mountains in the "Sächsische Schweiz"

What Germany has to offer. For centuries the German-speaking regions of Europe were a loose association of many sovereign states with lots of small and large "residencies" or capitals. Nearly all of them had a long and individualistic cultural tradition, as shown by the numerous cathedrals, palaces, castles, libraries, museums, art collections, gardens and theatres all over the country. They are extremely popular with art connoisseurs and art lovers.

But visitors are also attracted by the variety of the landscape. In the north it is the coasts and islands. Tourists also flock to the lakeland areas in Holstein and Mecklenburg, to the central uplands and the Alps. In the south are Lake Constance and the Bavarian lakes. Those looking for romantic scenery choose the Rhine, Main, Moselle, Neckar, Danube and Elbe valleys.

There are more than 80 "tourist routes" which take visitors away from the major traffic arteries, opening up the country's traditional landscapes and providing access to a great variety of tourist attractions. They lead through regions with breath-taking scenery. The best known of these routes is the Romantic Route, which brings to life the Middle Ages, especially in Rothenburg ob der Tauber, Dinkelsbühl and Nördlingen.

The visitor picks up the tracks of the country's long history even in places that are not mentioned in travel guides. In Bavaria he is enveloped by the gaiety of baroque architecture, in the north by brick gothic buildings. In some places time appears to have stood still. The visitor can expect hospitality and the famous "Gemütlichkeit", a word that is difficult to translate but expresses the idea of warmth and friendliness, the "good feeling". The tourist has plenty of opportunities to meet local people at the countless regional and town fairs and traditional festivals.

Cuisine and accommodation have reached a high standard, ranging from cheap rooms on a farm or at a guesthouse to the luxury holiday parks and top-class international hotels. Tourist services are still underdeveloped in some parts of the new federal states but the problems are gradually being solved. These regions are hoping for a strong economic boost from tourism.

Southern Germany has many romantic lakes

The distant horizon: the coastline in Mecklenburg-Western Pomerania

In the restaurant trade experts now speak of the "German culinary miracle". Contrary to the popular belief, the Germans do not only eat knuckle of pork and sauerkraut. For the gourmet there are increasingly more restaurants which compare with their French or Italian rivals. This is borne out by the ratings to be found in the principal international restaurant guides. There is also a wide range of regional specialities. The Germans themselves also appreciate foreign food and the visitor will find Italian or Chinese restaurants, to name only a few, in even small towns and villages.

Apart from the excellent autobahns, there is also a dense network of national highways and local roads. Long-distance rail travel is provided by comfortable trains, all of which have a dining car, and most of the night trains also have a sleeping car. Those who wish can also reserve a seat on car trains. All through the year the Federal Railways offer cheap city tours and other special offers for young people, the elderly and organized groups. For ramblers there are routes of all lengths to choose from. Germany is also easily accessible to the cyclist.

Most formalities for foreign visitors have been simplified. Citizens of many countries can enter Germany as tourists for up to three months without a visa. And there are no restrictions on the amount of foreign exchange which may be brought into or taken out of the country.

Protecting the environment. Like everywhere else in the world, mass tourism is proving harmful to the environment in some regions. One need only mention the burden of traffic, urban sprawl, and air and water pollution. In recent years the government has been taking stronger measures to contain ecological damage. Tourist resorts are increasingly encouraging the kind of tourism that is less of a burden on the environment. For instance, they are trying to halt the spread of tourist facilities and hotels in country areas.

The German Central Tourist Board. Apart from the commercial travel operators there is the German Central Tourist Board (DZT). The DZT is a member of international organizations such as the European Travel Commission. It publishes a wide range of information brochures about the Federal Republic in many languages.

Tourist Board:
Deutsche Zentrale für Tourismus
Beethovenstrasse 69
6000 Frankfurt am Main 1

Tourist Industry Association:
Deutscher Fremdenverkehrsverband e.V.
Niebuhrstrasse 16 b
5300 Bonn 1

Industrial relations

The great majority of the 35.5 million workforce of the Federal Republic of Germany are wage and salary earners, i.e. employees, civil servants and trainees or apprentices. In addition there are 2.5 million self-employed. (These figures relate to the "old" states, that is the western part of the country.) Most of the self-employed also have others on the payroll, in addition to 600,000 helping family members. Employers include private companies, federal, state and local government authorities, and other public institutions.

Employers and employees depend on cooperation with each other. At the same time they have contrasting interests which sometimes lead to confrontation. Employers and workers have the right to bargain and enter collective agreements with each other without state interference. The state does set the general conditions by legislation but it does not lay down how much workers should or may be paid. This and many other things - for example holiday - is left to labour and management representatives, the trade unions and employer associations, to negotiate themselves.

Trade unions. Trade unions in the Federal Republic are few but large. The biggest labour organization is the German Trade Union Federation (Deutscher Gewerkschaftsbund, DGB) with about 10.7 million members in 16 unions. Characteristic of the DGB unions is the principle of "one union, one industry", that is to say they enroll workers of an entire industry, regardless of the kind of work they do. Thus a chauffeur and a bookkeeper working in a printing plant would be in the same Printing and Paper Workers' Union (IG Druck und Papier).

Apart from the DGB there are a number of other trade union organizations. Only the three largest are named here. The German Union of Salaried Employees (Deutsche Angestellten-Gewerkschaft, DAG) with around 575,000 members. It is not an industrial union in the sense outlined, grouping together salaried staff from the most varied branches of industry. The German Civil Servants' Federation (Deutscher Beamtenbund, DBB), with about a million members, is the main organization of permanent civil servants which, on account of the peculiarities of the law on permanent civil servants, is not involved in collective bargaining and cannot call a strike. Otherwise it has all the characteristics of a trade union and has considerable influence. And the Christian Trade Union Federation of Germany (Christlicher Gewerkschaftsbund Deutschlands, CGB), with its affiliated unions, numbers 310,000 members.

As a result of German unification the former Free German Trade Union Federation (Freier Deutscher Gewerkschaftsbund, FDGB) in the former GDR has been dissolved. Its member unions have meanwhile been merged with the corresponding organizations in the west. In the GDR the FDGB was not an independent union but one of the mainstays of the communist regime. In fact it regarded itself as the "school of communism".

The trade unions in the Federal Republic are party-politically and denominationally independent. No one can be forced to join a trade union. The "closed shop" system (where only union members may be employed) prevalent in some countries is unknown in the Federal Republic. The degree of unionization, i.e. the proportion of workers who are members of unions in certain industries, varies greatly but averages less than 50%.

The member unions of the German Trade Union Federation (1990)

Industrial unions/ trade unions (old federal states)	Members (in thousands)	Share in GTUF (%)
Non-metallic minerals	462.7	5.8
Mining and energy	322.8	4.1
Chemicals - paper - ceramics	675.9	8.5
Railway	312.3	3.9
Education and science	189.1	2.4
Gardening, agriculture and forestry	44.1	0.6
Trade, banks and insurance	404.7	5.1
Wood and plastics	152.7	1.9
Leather	42.6	0.5
Media	184.7	2.3
Metal workers	2,726.7	34.4
Food, drink and tobacco — gastronomy	275.2	3.5
Police	162.7	2.1
Post	478.9	6.0
Textiles — clothing	249.8	3.1
Public sector, transportation and traffic	1,252.6	15.8
German Trade Union Federation	7,937.9	100

The unions operate many education facilities for their members. The DGB sponsors the annual Ruhrfestspiele arts festival at Recklinghausen and awards a highly regarded cultural prize every year.

Employers' associations. Employers are grouped in several hundred associations, organized both by region and by industry. Approximately 90% of employers belong to such associations - far in excess of the percentage of employees in trade unions. Their central organization is the Confederation of German Employers' Associations (Bundesvereinigung der Deutschen Arbeitgeberverbände, BDA). The BDA covers all branches of business - industry, crafts, commerce, banking, insurance, agriculture and transport, but it represents entrepreneurs only in their role as employers, i.e. as negotiating partners of the trade unions. All other interests - e.g. taxation or economic policy - are taken care of by other" entrepreneurial organizations. Examples are the Federation of German Industries (Bundesverband der Deutschen Industrie, BDI), the Central Association of German Craft Industry and Trades (Zentralverband des Deutschen Handwerks) and the Federation of German Wholesale and Foreign Traders (Bundesverband des Deutschen Gross- und Aussenhandels).

Collective agreements. A distinction is made between two types of collective agreement. The wage or salary agreement regulates pay and

A shift ends at a car factory in Hesse

in most cases is agreed for a year at a time. The framework or general agreement regulates conditions of employment such as working hours, holidays, minimum notice, overtime rates, bonuses, etc., and often runs for several years. But there are often agreements for special types of work.

Labour and management can negotiate freely provided they meet certain minimum requirements prescribed by law. In actual fact, however, most collective agreements go far beyond these. For instance, although under the law the highest number of work hours is still 48, practically all Germans work less than 40 hours a week, some only 35. Similarly, nearly all workers have a contractual paid vacation of six weeks or more while the law demands only three weeks, and nearly all workers receive additional holiday money and a Christmas bonus on the basis of collective agreements. In many cases actual wages, salaries and other payments are considerably above those laid down in the collective agreement.

Industrial action. In Germany industrial action may only be taken in connection with collective wage agreements. Hence only the parties to those agreements may take such action. A strike may not be called on matters covered by collective agreements where they are still in force. For these and other reasons industrial action has always been kept within limits compared with other industrial countries. Furthermore, in many cases provision has been made for arbitration if the two sides cannot agree. Under the rules of most unions a vote has to be taken among the rank and file. Only if three quarters vote in favour can a strike take place.

The workers' right to strike is counterbalanced by the employers' right to lock them out, that is temporarily to close the plant. Within certain limits, lockouts have been upheld by the Federal Labour Court and the Federal Constitutional Court, but the issue is still controversial. As the state remains neutral in labour disputes, neither strikers nor locked-out workers receive unemployment benefit under the state insurance fund for loss of earnings. Union members receive strike money for loss of earnings, but non-members get nothing. During a strike they must either live on their own resources or apply for national assistance.

Cooperation. Workers and entrepreneurs are not only opponents; they also cooperate in many ways. There is first of all the day-to-day cooperation on the shop floor. But the representatives of both sides'

Employees demonstrating on the Römerberg in Frankfurt

organizations also meet in many contexts. For example, on the committees which hold the final examinations of vocational trainees there are representatives of labour and management. In the labour courts which rule on employment disputes there are lay judges at all levels from both sides. The leaders of various organizations meet frequently when politicians responsible for their field seek their views. These and other forms of cooperation help to foster mutual understanding without blurring the differences in interests.

Codetermination

In the 19th century Germany changed from an agricultural into an industrial society. The rapidly growing new class of industrial workers initially lived in abject misery, almost totally without protection or rights. With the help of their organizations the workers were gradually able considerably to improve their situation and their social security, sometimes only after tenacious struggles. But the workers continued to be totally dependent on their companies until well into this century. The power of the owners was almost limitless.

Works constitution. The Works Constitution Act of the year 1952 governs industrial relations at the workplace. This applies to social welfare and personnel matters, but especially the right of employees, works councils and unions to have a say in practically all areas of company decision-making. The Act thus creates democratic conditions and is conducive to the humanization of the workplace.

The rights of individual workers. The individual employee has specifically defined rights. They include the right to be informed and to express his opinion on matters relating directly to his job. For instance, he can ask to be informed about the effects of new technology on his work, inspect his personal file, and ask for any assessments of his performance and his payslip to be explained to him.

The works council. The works council represents employees in relation to their employers. A works council may be elected in all private companies employing at least five people. Employees under 18 as well as trainees under 25 may elect representatives of their own.

Eligible for election are all employees from the age of 18, provided they have worked for the firm for at least six months. This also includes periods in another branch of the same company. Foreigners too are entitled to vote and hold office.

Members of the works council normally perform their duties in addition to their normal work. Only in large firms must one or several members of the works council be released from their jobs to do council work full-time.

In a single company an overall works council may be established, at group level a group works council.

In government authorities at all levels and other public institutions the equivalent employees' organization is the staff council which is elected in accordance with the Staff Representation Act.

Managerial personnel are not represented by the works council. They include, for instance, a firm's fully authorized officer or comparable staff in leading positions. In firms with at least ten managerial staff a committee of spokesmen may be elected. As in the case of a works council, such spokesmen's committees may also be formed at company and group level but only if on the first ballot the majority of the managerial staff are in favour.

Responsibilities and composition of the works council. The works council must, among other things, ensure that the laws and regulations, accident prevention rules, collective wage agreements and company arrangements applying to employees are observed. It must arrange a shop-floor meeting every three months and report on its activities. Employees attending the meeting may comment on the council's decisions and make proposals of their own.

The size and composition of the works council depends on the size and nature of the workforce. Thus in a company with 5 to 20 voting employees it consists of one person, in companies with 21 to 50 of three, and in companies with between 51 and 150 employees it has five members. The larger the company, the larger the works council.

If one company has several works councils a general works council has to be elected. The same applies to the representative committees of young employees and trainees.

In companies with more than 100 employees an economic affairs committee must be formed. This committee, as the name implies, is a consultative body for economic affairs and keeps employees informed on such matters. Its members are nominated by the works council.

If the works council has at least three members the firm's workers and salaried employees must be represented in proportion to their numerical strength. If the council has nine or more members it forms a works council committee which handles day-to-day business. On certain conditions union representatives may also attend council meetings.

Important codetermination rights cover such matters as company organization, working hours, including the introduction of short-time or overtime, holidays, social facilities confined to the department, company or group, technical controls on the conduct or performance of staff, accident prevention rules, occupational diseases and questions of health protection as prescribed by law, allocation of works-owned housing or termination of tenancy, as well as pay structure, piecework payment or bonus schemes, etc.

The works council has also a considerable say in job descriptions, work processes and the working environment, personnel planning and vocational training.

If the company proposes to introduce changes (e.g. to reduce operations, close down or move to a different location) the works council may under certain conditions draw up a "social plan" which cushions the economic disadvantages to the employees affected.

On all matters concerning personnel, such as appointments, classifications and transfers, the employer must obtain the approval of the works council. This it may refuse to give in certain circumstances governed by law. If the employer intends to carry out the proposed measures even without the council's approval he must seek a decision by the labour court.

The employer must also consult the works council before any dismissal. If he fails to do so the dismissal has no effect. Where a person is to be properly dismissed the works council may lodge a protest. In this case the employer must continue to employ the person dismissed at his request if the works council has objected on grounds prescribed by law and the employee has taken the matter to the labour court. The employer must await the court's decision. In such proceedings a justified complaint by the works council considerably strengthens the employee's position.

The Works Constitution Act and the rules governing elections to works councils also apply in the new federal states. The same holds true for the Spokesmen's Committee Act, which covers the codetermination rights of managerial staff. Such committees are elected in companies with at least ten such staff.

Codetermination. Employee codetermination is one of the main elements of the Federal Republic's social system. It is based on the conviction that democratic legitimation cannot be confined to government but must apply in all sectors of society. Nearly every company decision has an effect on its employees, irrespective of whether it concerns marketing, product development, investment, rationalization, etc. This is why employees should have a say in company decision-making through their representatives.

The willingness of employees to assume a share of the responsibility through their unions has been an important social factor in the Federal Republic's old states. The workforce in medium-sized or large companies (corporations, joint-stock companies, partnerships limited by shares, cooperatives or friendly insurance companies) can influence company policy through their representatives on the supervisory boards. This codetermination is not confined to social affairs but extends to all company activities.

Thus the supervisory board may, for instance, appoint and dismiss the management (board of directors), demand to be informed about all company matters, and make major company decisions, e.g. with regard to major investments or rationalization measures, subject to its approval.

Codetermination in large mining and steel companies has been governed by legislation enacted in 1951 and 1956. Worker participation in the running of large firms in other branches is covered by the Codetermination Act of 1976. Germany's four codetermination laws have been applicable in the new federal states as well since 1 July 1990.

Codetermination in large enterprises. Enterprises other than mining and steel companies which either alone or together with their subsidiaries have a workforce of more than 2,000 are governed by the provisions of the Codetermination Act of 1976. Under this law the supervisory board is made up of equal numbers of representatives of shareholders and employees. However, the shareholders have a slight advantage in the event of a stalemate in that the chairman of the board, who is always a representative of the shareholders, has a second, casting vote. In the appointment of a labour director the employees' representatives have no veto.

Composition of the supervisory board. The supervisory board consists of equal numbers of owner and labour representatives. In enterprises with a workforce of up to 10,000 the board has 12 members (i.e. 6:6), and this increases to 16 (workforce 10,000 to 20,000) or 20 (workforce over 20,000).

The firm's articles may provide that the minimum board size as prescribed by law, i.e. 12 members, may be increased to 16 or 20 members, and one consisting of 16 increased to 20. The labour seats on the supervisory board are allocated to union representatives (two in the case of a 12- or 16-member board, three in the case of a 20-member board).

Election of labour representatives on the supervisory board. All labour members on the supervisory board, i.e. those on the company's payroll and the union representatives, are elected by direct ballot or by delegates. In companies with up to 8,000 employees the law prescribes a ballot, but employees may, with a majority vote, opt to be represented by delegates. In the case of enterprises with a workforce of more than 8,000 the law prescribes elections through delegates. The employees may, however, reverse this procedure, that is to say they can choose by a majority vote to have a direct ballot.

Forms of co-determination and their scope of application

No co-determination		3.4 m. employees	Small firms (less than 5 employees)
Internal co-determination (Staff Representation Act)		3.6 m.	Public sector
Internal co-determination (Labour-Management Relations Act)		9.3 m.	Remaining industry
One-third participation		0.6 m.	Small corporations
Co-determination in coal, iron and steel industries		0.5 m.	Coal, iron and steel sector
Co-determination under the Act of 1976		4.0 m.	Big corporations

Election of shareholder representatives. Shareholder representatives on the supervisory board are elected at the company's annual meeting.

Election of the chairman. The members of the supervisory board elect the chairman and vice-chairman at their constituent meeting. A two-thirds majority is required. Failing this a second vote is taken in which the shareholder representatives elect the chairman and the labour representatives the vice-chairman.

The board of directors. The supervisory board appoints and dismisses members of the board of directors. Here too a two-thirds majority is necessary, otherwise a mediation committee is appointed. Should this too fail to produce an absolute majority a second ballot is taken in which the chairman of the supervisory board has a casting vote.

A labour director with equal rights is chosen according to the same procedure. The labour director is chiefly concerned with personnel and social affairs.

Codetermination in the mining and steel industry. Codetermination in the mining and steel industry is the oldest and most extensive form of work participation. It applies to companies with a workforce of more than 1,000.

The supervisory board. The supervisory board in the mining and steel industry consists of an equal number of shareholder and employee representatives and a "neutral" member. In firms covered by the Codetermination Act the board consists of 11 members (in larger companies it may be increased to 15 or 21). Two of the five employee representatives must work for the company, and three must be proposed by the unions represented in the company (i.e. external members). All employee representatives are first selected by the works council and proposed for election at the general meeting. The election is only a formality since the meeting cannot reject the nominees. The supervisory board then proposes a neutral member, the eleventh, who where a stalemate occurs has the casting vote.

Board of directors, labour director. The members of the board of directors are appointed and dismissed by the supervisory board. One of the members must be a labour director, who cannot be appointed or dismissed against the majority among the employee representatives on the supervisory board. Thus labour directors are in a way the exponents of codetermination at management level.

Codetermination in small enterprises. In companies with 500 to 2,000 employees one third of the members of the supervisory board must be representatives of the workforce. Although this gives them no say in decision-making it provides access to important information.

German Trade Union Federation:
Deutscher Gewerkschaftsbund
Hans-Böckler-Strasse 39
4000 Düsseldorf 30

German Union of Salaried Employees:
Deutsche Angestelltengewerkschaft
Karl-Muck-Platz 1
2000 Hamburg 36

German Civil Servants' Federation:
Deutscher Beamtenbund
Dreizehnmorgenweg 36
5300 Bonn 2

Christian Trade Union Federation:
Christlicher Gewerkschaftsbund Deutschlands
Konstantinstrasse 13
5300 Bonn 2

Confederation of German Employers' Associations:
Bundesvereinigung der Deutschen Arbeitgeberverbände
Gustav-Heinemann-Ufer 72
5000 Köln 1

Social security

The Federal Republic's social security system is the product of many years' growth. Social benefits and services account for nearly 30% of the gross national product and cost in 1990 DM 710 billion. It is a system which is admired by other countries and meets the requirements of the constitution. According to article 20 of the Basic Law, the Federal Republic is a democratic and social federal state and thus under obligation to protect all citizens from social insecurity and ensure social justice. The state has met this obligation by enacting extensive legislation providing for sickness, accident and old-age insurance, as well as child allowances, rent subsidies, unemployment benefits, etc.

Development of social insurance. Social insurance in Germany dates from the Middle Ages when miners first set up common funds to support needy colleagues after accidents at work. But it was not until the end of the 19th century that a comprehensive social insurance scheme emerged. The trigger was Germany's rapid industrial development. It had brought an extraordinary rise in the number of industrial workers who were hardly or not at all able to accumulate assets or save for emergencies. The prime consideration in introducing progressive social welfare legislation was to take the wind out of the sails of a growing labour movement. It is nevertheless recognized nowadays that this legislation became the foundation for a social insurance scheme which also served as a model for other industrial countries.

Laws enacted in 1883, 1884 and 1889 established three branches of insurance which are still the nucleus of the German system: health, accident, invalidity and old age. Pensioners had to be 70 and the maximum annual pension was 190.40 marks.

In 1911 these schemes were merged in the Reich Insurance System, which added pensions for widows and orphans. Invalidity and old age insurance was extended to all salary earners. A separate insurance system was introduced for miners in 1923. Unemployment insurance was established in 1927, and as from 1938 traders and craftsmen, to the extent that they were not privately ensured, were covered by the social insurance scheme.

After the Second World War the system was greatly extended and improved. In 1957, for instance, a statutory old age insurance scheme for farmers was introduced, and in that same year pensions in general were indexed, i.e. adjusted in line with the average increase in incomes. Further reforms were introduced in 1972 and 1992.

Since 1990 the social security system has also benefited pensioners, war victims and physically handicapped persons in the former GDR. The treaties on economic, monetary and social union and on national unification provided that all citizens in the united Germany with its system based on the principles of social justice will enjoy the same benefits after a transitional period.

Pensions insurance. The statutory pensions insurance scheme is one of the central pillars of social security in the Federal Republic of Germany. It ensures that workers will not suffer financial need and are able to maintain an adequate standard of living in retirement.

All wage and salary earners are required by law to be in the scheme. Self-employed persons who are not compulsorily insured by virtue of their membership of certain occupational groups can join the scheme voluntarily. Contributions (currently 17.7% of gross earnings) are levied up to a certain income level. Worker and employer each contribute half the sum. When a person is no longer obliged to be in the insurance scheme voluntary continued membership is possible under certain circumstances.

The scheme pays old-age and invalidity pensions. After the death of an insured person the family dependants retain a certain proportion of the pension. There is a "waiting period", i.e. a minimum membership of the insurance scheme.

As a rule the old-age pension is payable at the age of 65, but under certain conditions it can also be drawn at 63 or 60 (flexible retirement provision). Women can claim a pension when they are 60.

The size of the pension depends on the amount of insured income from employment. The pension reform in 1992 gave older employees a more flexible choice of retirement age. They can now opt for a part-pension, part-work arrangement.

The system has been adjusted in 1992 to meet demographic and economic conditions and to secure the financial basis of pensions beyond the year 2000. The principal objective was to keep pensions related to wages and contributions, to maintain living standards, and to enable pensioners too to benefit from the country's economic progress. For the great majority of employees the statutory pension is the only old-age security. It must therefore maintain the standard of living they have been accustomed to during the many years when they have paid insurance contributions.

Since the 1957 reform, the average pension in West Germany after 45 years is about 70% of the average net income. Thus in 1991 it was approximately DM 1750. And since 1 July 1990 average pensions in the new federal states are about 70% of average incomes in Eastern Germany after 45 insured years. Pensions in the new states increase on an annual basis in line with the wages of the working population there. The aim, therefore, is to bring East German pensions up to the level of West German pensions as soon as possible. As from 1 January 1992 pensions legislation applies to the whole of Germany without distinction.

Over the past century or so the pensions insurance scheme has constantly had to be adapted to new developments. This will continue to be the case. The growing number of elderly people in Germany has sparked a public discussion on the introduction of a separate insurance scheme to provide adequate care for elderly people.

Paying pensions is not the only purpose of the pensions insurance scheme. It also helps to maintain a person's capacity to work or improve or restore that capacity. Thus it covers the cost of treatment at spas and provides support for people who have to retrain for a new job for health reasons.

Company pensions. Company pensions are a valuable supplement to the statutory scheme. Many companies provide them on a voluntary basis. Under the Company Pensions Act of 1974, employees now retain their claim to a company pension even if they leave before retirement age, provided they are at least 35 years old and either their entitlement is ten years old or at least three years if the person concerned has worked for the company for 12 years. Even if the employer becomes insolvent the works pension is still not lost. In such cases it is paid out of a fund established for this purpose.

Health insurance. Nearly all citizens of the Federal Republic have health insurance, whether as compulsory or voluntary members of the statutory health insurance scheme or through private insurance. Under the state scheme insurance is compulsory for all workers, salaried employees and several other categories up to a certain income level. Voluntary insurance is possible under the scheme under certain conditions. The state system also covers pensioners, the unemployed, trainees and students. Employees pay their contributions into their respective health insurance fund (e.g. the district, company or guild fund, the merchant seamen's, miners' or farmers' funds). All insured persons have a free choice of panel doctors and dentists. They pay half of the contributions, their employers the other half. In 1991 the average contribution rate was 12.3% of the proportion of income on which contributions are based.

The health insurance fund pays the cost of medical and dental treatment, drugs and medicines, etc. as well as hospitalization. It pays all or part of the cost of any necessary spa treatment. There are also maternity, family and home-nursing grants. In the event of sickness, employees receive their full wages for up to six weeks, in some cases more. After that period the statutory fund provides sick pay, which amounts to 80% of the regular wage, for up to 78 weeks.

The annual cost of health insurance is staggering. Some services and items paid for by the health insurance fund have had to be

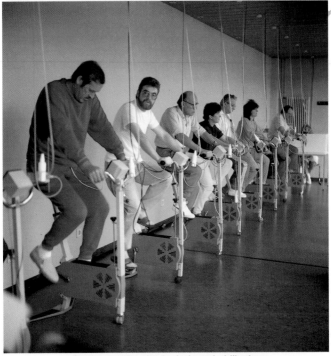

Social security also includes rehabilitation

restricted and people are required to meet a larger proportion of the cost themselves. The funds are also seeking public support for their efforts to reduce costs.

Accident insurance. Protection and support after accidents at work and in the case of occupational diseases is provided by the statutory accident insurance scheme. In the Federal Republic of Germany all employees and farmers are insured by law against accident. Other self-employed people can join the insurance scheme voluntarily. Students, school pupils and kindergarten children are also covered.

The main providers of accident insurance are the professional and trade associations, each of which covers a specific profession or trade in a certain district. The funds are raised by dues paid only by employers. A claim to payment arises from bodily injury or death resulting from a work accident or illness or death resulting from an occupational disease incurred by the insurant. Accidents which occur on the way to and from the place of work count as work accidents.

If an insured person suffers damage the accident insurance fund bears the full cost of treatment. If the worker is incapable of work, injury money is paid. If the insured person becomes incapable of earning a living or dies as a result of an accident or vocational illness the insurance pays a pension or death grant and pension for dependants, as the case may be. Like the other pensions, these are increased in line with general rises in incomes.

The vocational support within the framework of the accident insurance scheme covers vocational rehabilitation training and assistance in obtaining employment. The professional and trade associations are also required to issue regulations on prevention of accidents and control of occupational diseases and to monitor their application in the various enterprises.

Child benefit. The upbringing and education of children is a considerable financial burden on the family. To ease it, a Federal Child Benefit Act was passed. It provides for every parent or guardian to be paid child benefit for every child up to the age of 16, in case of school or vocational training up to the age of 27. The benefit is DM 50 for the first child, DM 130 for the second, 220 for the third, and DM 240 for each additional one. Parents in the higher income brackets receive less child benefit from the second child onwards. Parents with children also enjoy tax relief. Since 1986 the state has been paying a child-raising allowance of DM 600 per month for the first six months. After that the allowance depends on the parents' income. In 1993 this allowance is likely to be extended to cover the first two years.

War victims' benefits (social compensation). The task of the war victims' aid scheme is to compensate, at least financially, the war-disabled, servicemen's widows and war orphans. They are paid index-linked pensions. In addition, the war-disabled can receive therapy and support in starting work and a career. Members of the Bundeswehr and the victims of acts of violence, as well as their bereaved dependents, are taken care of in the same way.

Social Assistance. Every inhabitant of the Federal Republic - native or alien - is entitled to social assistance in times of hardship in the form of maintenance grants or grants to help cope with particular circumstances such as disability, illness or old age. The greater part of social assistance is provided by the states and local authorities. In 1990 the total cost was DM 33 billion. Since 1991 the Federal Social Assistance Act has also been applicable in the new federal states.

Social security (1991, in DM bn.)

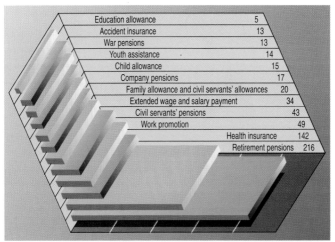

Education allowance	5
Accident insurance	13
War pensions	13
Youth assistance	14
Child allowance	15
Company pensions	17
Family allowance and civil servants' allowances	20
Extended wage and salary payment	34
Civil servants' pensions	43
Work promotion	49
Health insurance	142
Retirement pensions	216

The benefits of the social state are manifest in many other areas of law, such as protection of working mothers and the rehabilitation of disabled persons.

Health

The Federal Republic of Germany has a ramified system of health care backed up by appropriate social measures. Although health care is basically the individual's own responsibility, it is also the concern of society as a whole. All people, regardless of their financial or social situation, should have the same chance to maintain and restore their health. Health care in Germany is a decentralized, pluralist and self-governing system.

The average life expectancy in the Federal Republic has increased steadily over the past 40 years. It is currently 72 for men and 78 for women. This trend is chiefly the result of medical care. The aim is to increase life expectancy further still by reducing the incidence of "civilization" illnesses. There will therefore be a greater concentration on preventive medicine, which includes better health education, regular precautionary examinations, as well as information on healthy living.

The biggest threat to health in Germany, as in all highly developed industrial countries, comes from diseases of the modern world. Half of all deaths are the result of cardiovascular diseases, followed by cancer. Allergies are becoming increasingly prominent, but also those typical of old age such as diseases of the central nervous system. The infectious diseases of earlier generations, such as tuberculosis, cholera, diphtheria and pneumonia, are no longer the threat they once were, thanks to modern medicine. But a new big challenge is AIDS.

Doctors and hospitals. In 1990 there were about 195,000 doctors in the Federal Republic's old states, compared with some 42,000 in the new states. That works out at one to every 321 inhabitants in the west, and one to 379 in the east. Medically, therefore, the Germans are among the best cared-for nations in the world. However, access to doctors and dentists is not equally good everywhere. This is especially true of the distribution of general practitioners, who form the backbone of medical care. In some rural and suburban areas there is still a shortage of doctors, but since the number of doctors is increasing constantly this bottleneck will soon be overcome. Less than half of the nation's doctors are independent. The others work in hospitals or administration or they are engaged in research.

There are about 830,000 beds available in 3,600 hospitals. In this respect the Federal Republic compares well with other countries. Hospitals are operated by the state and local authorities (more than half the beds), charity, mostly church, organizations (more than 40% of the beds) and private enterprises.

Drugs and medicines. The safety of medicines has high priority in the Federal Republic. The Pharmaceuticals Act stipulates that medicines may be given to consumers only after their quality, effectiveness and harmlessness have been tested by a state agency. Even after approval they are kept under constant observation so that dangers are quickly recognized and remedial action can be taken to protect consumers. The Act also sets out detailed safety regulations for the production of pharmaceuticals, and it determines which substances may be sold only in pharmacies and which can only be sold on a doctor's prescription. Anyone whose health is damaged by questionable pharmaceuticals has a claim to compensation from the manufacturer.

Preventive health care. According to the old saying, "prevention is better than cure". Hence preventive health care is becoming increasingly important in health policy. The aim is for every person to maintain their health on their own responsibility by avoiding risks. Preventive or early detection examinations have been introduced in many fields. Many federal and state institutions as well as private non-profit organizations provide information on health education as well as courses and advice on such matters as

— care during pregnancy, health education for infants and school-age children;

— hazards to health such as alcohol, nicotine and drug abuse, overeating, malnutrition, lack of exercise - the well-known causes of cardiovascular diseases which are also a contributory factor in cancer and other frequent diseases;

— programmes to help people who are chronically sick or disabled, and their relatives, to live with their illness or disablement.

Various examinations are offered for the early detection of disease, such as for cancer, which were introduced in 1971. The fight against AIDS (acquired immune deficiency syndrome) is a new task requiring the greatest possible effort. The Federal Government, in collaboration with the World Health Organization and the members of the European Community, is carrying out a programme to protect people from HIV infection and at the same time provide comprehensive advice and care for those infected or showing symptoms. In this respect it is important not to isolate or discriminate against those affected. Until such time as an effective vaccine and treatment are available, education and advice are the best way of preventing this disease from spreading. This programme encourages and enables those concerned to behave responsibly in order to protect themselves and others.

Sick people and their families often need medical care over and above that provided by the medical profession and hospitals. Available for such people is comprehensive counselling as well as the opportunity to discuss their problems with people suffering from the same disease. Opportunities of this kind are afforded by numerous self-help groups which today have an established place in the nation's health system.

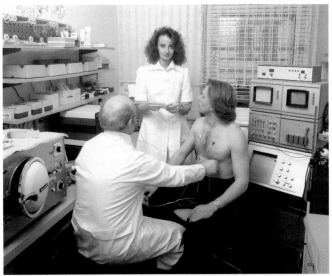

Modern diagnostic appliances in a doctor's surgery

They include:
— Deutsche AIDS-Hilfe (German AIDS Support)
— Deutsche Multiple-Sklerose-Gesellschaft (German Multiple Sclerosis Society)
— Deutsche Rheuma-Liga (German Rheumatism League)
— Frauenselbsthilfe nach Krebs e.V. (Women's Post-Cancer Self-Help Group)

— Angehörigenvereine psychisch Kranker (groups of family members of persons suffering from psychic disorders, e.g. drug-dependent persons)
— Anonyme Alkoholiker (Alcoholics Anonymous)

International activities. Germany plays an active part in the work of international organizations concerned with health. No country can alone cope with the challenges of the most widespread diseases such as AIDS or the hazards posed by environmental pollution. Efforts to combat them, as well as research activities, call for international cooperation. The Federal Republic also feels obliged to give the developing countries professional advice and financial assistance in developing their public health system.

As a member of the World Health Organization (WHO) the Federal Republic is represented on several important bodies. Every year more than 35 international meetings on matters of topical interest are organized in collaboration with WHO. More than 30 scientific institutions have been made into centres for cooperation with this international organization. The Federal Republic is the fourth largest contributor to WHO.

Within the European Community the Federal Republic is actively involved in the development of community health policy. One of the EC's major objectives is to maintain high health standards in member countries. Examples of these joint activities are "Europe Against Cancer", a research programme, the proposed European identity card for emergency cases, an action programme involving an exchange of information on detoxification centres, and cooperation on measures to combat AIDS, alcohol abuse and drug addiction. This cooperation will be greatly intensified as the Community assumes responsibility for health within the framework of the European Political Union.

The cost of health care. Germany's main task at the moment is to build up an efficient public health system in the new federal states. At the same time a solution has to be found to the difficult and perennial problem of finance. Although the reform programme initiated in 1989 helped to stabilize expenditure on health services, the government wishes to improve the economic efficiency of the statutory health insurance system, which covers about 90% of the population. At present the system is costing DM 140 billion a year - about half of total expenditure on public health in Germany's western states.

Protection of the environment

Government, industry and society are confronted with a great challenge. Our natural sources of life are in danger. This is causing growing concern and the great majority of Germans favour intensified efforts to protect the environment. In the old federal states keeping the environment intact is more important than the country's unemployment and housing problems.

Industry, too, has realized the need to reconcile economic progress with ecological protection, for unless the air, water and soil are protected there will in the long run be no basis for industrial production. Industry and commerce are supplying state-of-the-art technology with which to remove environmental pollution. Now more than 4,000 companies specialize in environmental technology. "Environment high-tech made in Germany" has become a new export product.

Environmental policy. The government reacted to environmental danger by establishing a Federal Ministry for Environmental Protection, Nature Conservation and Reactor Safety in 1986. A Federal Environmental Agency had already been set up in Berlin in 1974. Each of the federal states, too, has an environmental department. From the very outset the present Federal Government has sought to stimulate international cooperation in this field, and especially within the European Community. Its policy is based on three principles:
— the preventive principle, i.e. new projects by government and industry are developed in such a way that environmental problems cannot arise;
— the polluter-to-pay principle; and the
— cooperative principle, i.e. government, industry and society join forces to combat environmental problems.

The government's task is to provide the framework for action by companies and individuals to preserve the natural environment. In recent years a broad range of legal instruments has been introduced and these are being constantly developed. But national measures are not sufficient in themselves since polluted air knows no frontiers and contaminated rivers flow through many countries. The Federal Government's aim is to bring protection standards in the new federal states up to the level already achieved in the western part of the country. This will require investment running into billions.

Air pollution. The atmosphere in Germany, as in other industrial countries, is heavily polluted by emissions from power stations, factories, traffic and home-heating systems. This is particularly evident in the damage caused to forests. About 64% of tree stocks are slightly or severely damaged. Only 36% are healthy. Thus human health, the soil, lakes and rivers, buildings and architectural art treasures must be protected from further air pollution.

A comprehensive clean-air programme has been introduced. The aim is to get to grips with pollution at source and reduce it drastically. This applies, for instance, to power stations and district heating plants, as well as car exhaust fumes. Legislation on large furnaces has compelled power station operators to introduce modern technology. Emissions of sulphur dioxide and nitrogene oxide from industry have already been reduced by 20/30% and a further reduction of 40% is hoped for by the mid-90s. Between 1982 and 1990 emissions of sulphur dioxide, for which power stations are principally responsible, were reduced by about 75%.

As far as traffic is concerned, air pollution is being increasingly reduced through the introduction of catalytic converters to remove nitrogen oxides from exhaust fumes. By 1993 at the latest all new motor vehicles in the European Community must be equipped with these converters. Further reductions are achieved by the use of unleaded petrol, which is on sale at all German filling stations.

Ensuring clean air, too, is an international challenge. Half of the sulphur dioxide pollution comes from neighbouring countries, while half of the pollution emitted in the Federal Republic is carried by the wind to other countries. Thus the Geneva Convention on Long-Range Transboundary Air Pollution which came into force in 1983 is of great importance in this respect.

Two of the biggest threats to the world's climate are carbon dioxide, which are one of the causes of the "greenhouse effect", and chlorofluorocarbons (CFCs) which are destroying the earth's ozone layer. Here the Federal Republic is playing a pioneering role in that CFC production is to be stopped altogether in Germany by 1995. Carbon dioxide emissions are to be reduced by 25% by the year 2005.

Protection of rivers, lakes and seas. Major improvements have also been achieved in protecting rivers, lakes and seas, but only through the introduction of tougher legislation and the construction of new, especially biological sewage farms and new sewerage by industrial firms and municipalities. These regulations were designed to prevent organic pollution of surface water in particular. In the early 70s heavily polluted rivers like the Rhine and the Main were, biologically, practically dead, but today they again have several species of fish. The rivers and lakes of the former GDR, however, require a major cleansing operation.

One of the main reasons for this progress is the Effluents Act which requires local authorities and industries to considerably reduce the amount of harmful substances in effluents. Special measures have also been taken to protect the groundwater from toxic plant-protection agents. In 1986 and 1989 strict limits were introduced with regard to drinking water. The use of pesticides, etc., too, is also being reduced.

Many pollutants ultimately end up in the sea via the rivers and the atmosphere unless they are neutralized on land. But shipping and oil extraction, too, contribute to marine pollution. These problems can only be solved through joint action by all littoral states. Steps to reduce pollution of the North Sea have been introduced on Germany's initiative at the International North Sea Conferences of 1984, 1987 and 1990. The aim of these measures is to quickly prevent any discharge of pollutants and also the burning of waste at sea, as has already been achieved in the Federal Republic. Other successes: In 1989 the

Air surveillance of the North Sea

*Modern purification plants like the one at this chemical works
reduce the pollution of rivers and lakes*

dumping of dilute sulphuric acid in the North Sea was stopped altogether. This and similar wastes are now disposed of in special recycling plants on land.

Nature conservation and landscape management. The proportion of land in the western part of the Federal Republic covered by buildings and roads increased from about 8% in the 50s to about 12% in the late 80s. Thus the proportion of natural landscapes was reduced accordingly, making the task of protecting local flora and fauna increasingly more urgent. The Federal Nature Conservation Programme, which forms the basis of landscape planning, has been improved, as have the regulations on protection of species. Ten large regions in Germany requiring special protection have been declared national parks. There are also many nature reserves. International accords such as the European guideline for the protection of birds, the Washington Convention for the protection of species, or the Bern convention for the preservation of Europe's flora and fauna, are strictly observed in Germany.

In many places the soil has been contaminated by heavy metals and chemicals, partly as a result of intensive farming. The government is therefore drawing up comprehensive measures to conserve the soil as a storer and filter of water, but also as a biotope for plants and animals.

Noise and waste. Noise, especially from traffic, has become a serious threat to health in densely populated areas. Noise abatement measures are therefore urgent. Many residential streets have been declared reduced-traffic zones and the noise levels for cars and aircraft have been lowered. Increasingly more roads are being given noise-absorbing surfaces. Efforts are also being made in industry and in the building trade to reduce noise levels.

The 1986 Waste Act introduced modern waste-disposal methods. This law gives the avoidance and recycling of waste priority over traditional methods of disposal. Waste that cannot be recycled must be handled by depots and incinerators. Strict regulations apply to the disposal of "special waste", i.e. toxic or otherwise dangerous waste, for which there are special facilities.

To a country like the Federal Republic which has very limited raw materials, recycling is very important. Part of the household waste destroyed by burning is used for distant-heating purposes. About half of the volume of waste paper and glass is recycled, and to an increasing extent disused cars as well.

Women and society

According to the Basic Law, men and women have equal rights. This constitutional rule is absolutely clear, but in practice it is not quite like that. Old preconceived notions of what women are and what they are not "entitled to" die hard. Women still do not have the same opportunities as men in society, politics and at work. Women are subject to heavy stress through family and work. Nonetheless, their status has gradually improved over the years. And they are in the majority: In Germany there are nearly three million more women than men.

Equality before the law. The principle of equality has only gradually been applied. In 1957 a law was introduced which gave women equal rights where matrimonial property was concerned. Then in 1977 their position with regard to marriage, divorce and family were improved so that, for instance, the question of guilt in divorce cases no longer applied. Now the only criterion is whether the marriage has irreparably broken down. In addition, divorcees now share pension entitlements.

Women in employment. Under a 1980 law requiring men and women to be given equal treatment at work, women may no longer be discriminated against on grounds of sex. Other laws protect pregnant women and prohibit heavy manual work. Women may only be assigned to night work in exceptional cases.

There has been a marked improvement in vocational training for girls and women. All schools and training establishments are open to women. Just under half of all successful candidates in the 1988 final secondary school examination in West Germany were women. Over 40% of all students are women. And the number of women who have completed a course of vocational training has increased significantly since the 50s.

Every second woman between the ages of 15 and 65 is in employment. Women are indispensable in industry, the health system and education. But there is discrimination: They tend to lose their jobs faster than men, and they are offered fewer apprenticeships. Male employees still receive distinctly higher wages than their female counterparts. Women who do the same or similar work to that of men can assert their claim to equal pay in court. Discrimination occurs nonetheless in the differing assessments of the types of work "typically" done by women or "typically" done by men. Women's work is generally downgraded as "physically lighter" employment. In the public service, on the other hand, the principle of "equal wages for equal work" has been put into practice. All civil servants and other public employees are paid according to their respective salary or wage groups with no distinction as to sex.

Discrimination against women at work occurs largely on account of the fact that their working life shows a different pattern. In former times women often went into less demanding trades because they regarded employment merely as an interim occupation before starting a family. But today ever more women want to return to work after a period of child-raising. There are government reintegration programmes to help them. Many choose part-time work and this too is promoted by the government on economic and social grounds. At present, however, there are far too few part-time jobs (only 13%). The Federal Government is preparing legislation to help women combine family duties with employment and thus move closer to the goal of equality.

Women in the family. In Germany nine million out of 27 million marriages are childless. The birthrate is declining. The number of families with three and more children is decreasing while the number with one or two is growing. The government appreciates the social importance of family promotion. It regards work in a family as equal to other employment and introduced legislation providing for child-raising allowances and leave. The state pays DM 600 a month for each child for 18 months. In addition, if one of the parents stays at home to raise the child he or she is entitled to child-raising leave, which from 1993 will be three years for each child. During this period the person concerned is protected from dismissal. Another advantage is that child-raising periods count towards the parent's pension claim.

Women in politics. Women have had the vote and the right to stand for election in Germany since 1918. Although the proportion of politically active women is increasing it is still small. Some of the political parties have introduced quotas to increase the number of female representatives on executive committees.

Lawyer

Line worker

Electrical engineer

Teacher

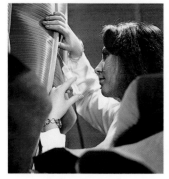

Laboratory worker

Secretary

There has been at least one women minister in every Federal Government since 1961. In the present government there are four. There have been two female presidents (speakers) of the Federal Parliament. Now there is also a separate Federal Ministry for Women and Youth which was established in 1991. All regional governments have women ministers or commissioners for women. Nearly 1,000 municipalities have created "equality posts" specially for women.

Parallel to the statutory measures to establish equality of the sexes, a strong women's movement has developed in Germany. It vehemently opposes any discrimination against women. It has emerged outside the existing women's organizations and has been the driving force in setting up centres for battered wives and their children.

From a legal point of view, equality has almost been achieved 40 years after this principle was incorporated in Germany's Basic Law. There are no longer laws which discriminate directly against women or prescribe a certain role for them. But in some cases they are still disadvantaged socially, largely on account of the way the working world is structured. In their case there is still some leeway to be made up.

The Women's Council:
Deutscher Frauenrat
Simrockstrasse 5
5300 Bonn 1

Youth

Nearly every fourth inhabitant of the Federal Republic is younger than 20, a good 18 million of them, including over two million foreigners. They too are people with different hopes and experiences, and different modes of behaviour. This applies especially since Germany became united. Young people in the former GDR grew up under conditions quite different from those of their counterparts in the western part of the country. However, their general mood and expectations are no less positive than those of young people in the west.

What young people want. Much has been written about young Germans. We read comments like "declining values", the "count-me-out generation", and the "drop-out mentality". But various studies have shown that although young people have assumed new values they nevertheless adhere to the traditional ones as well. They still appreciate such notions as "work", "family" and "loyalty". According to a survey, the main concern of over 90% of young people is to have a secure job, and they consider it particularly important to maintain peace and protect the environment.

Differing concerns. What young people in the new federal states are most afraid of is unemployment and social decline, whereas those in the west show greater fear of environmental pollution and damage. Throughout the country, however, young people have become more critical. In the former GDR many of them helped bring about the peaceful revolution there through their protests and opposition. In east and west they are highly critical but generally not aggressive.

Conflict of generations? One regularly hears about the "generation conflict". In a survey conducted in 1988, however, 90% of young Germans have someone they can discuss their problems with, and in most cases it is their parents. Nevertheless, the dissonance between the generations is perhaps more pronounced than elsewhere because recent German history has been so full of divisions. Some of the population were born at the time of the last emperor, others during the Weimar Republic, yet others during the nazi dictatorship. And then there are those who experienced the difficulties of the immediate post-war years and the East German dictatorship. The in-between generation represent Germany's economic recovery and rise to become one of the leading industrial nations.

The present generation are not, as a rule, short of much and they enjoy the advantages of a modern education system. Technological progress, greater mobility, frequent travel and increasing freedom permit young people to develop their individuality at a much earlier age than in previous generations. This applies to other western industrial countries, too, of course. There were inter-generation conflicts during the first part of the century, too, when the German Youth Movement turned against the middle class lifestyle of adults and sought a closer relationship with nature. And like other western countries, the Federal Republic experienced the youth revolt of the late 60s, which in the 80s developed into the ecological movement, the peace movement and the groups seeking alternative ways of life.

In drawing attention to environmental problems and being strongly committed to peace and a just world order, young Germans are not directing their attacks against the older generation, but they are less

Rock festivals are still extremely popular

compromising and have less confidence in the political establishment. This has produced unrest and protest and constitutes a major
challenge - not only to the government and parliament. A parliamentary commission has looked into the causes and reported that one
of the deeper reasons lies in the incomprehensible and inpersonal
nature of the modern industrial society and bureaucracy.

Youth organizations. There about 80 supraregional youth associations in Germany and an increasing number of self-organized groups.
Most of these organizations are affiliated to the German Federal
Youth Council (Deutscher Bundesjugendring), and include the Young
Protestants Association (Arbeitsgemeinschaft der Evangelischen Jugend), the Federation of German Catholic Youth Associations (Bund
der Deutschen Katholischen Jugend), the youth associations of the
trade unions and the German Boy Scouts Association (Ring Deutscher Pfadfinder). The youth organizations of the political parties belong to the Council of Political Youth Associations (Ring politischer
Jugend). Most youth organizations receive financial support from the
federal, state and local governments. Usually they also welcome
non-members to their functions. Youngsters who do not join a group
but wish to be together with others of their age can do so in various
leisure-time facilities and activities. Usually such establishments employ a social worker.

The German town of Altena in Westphalia has the oldest youth hostel
in the world. It was opened in 1912. There are now 782 youth hostels
in Germany which every year register over ten million overnight stays,
including just under a million by foreigners.

Government policy. The government encourages young people to
develop their character and abilities freely. The aim is that they
should learn to shape their lives on their own responsibility. The state
helps them to enjoy their rights accordingly. This has always been
part of the government's overall social policy, for if young people are
to feel at home in the modern world that world must be given a more
humane countenance.

The state takes care of young people by legislating for their protection and by providing them with social assistance and opportunities
for voluntary activities. It deliberately allows the various organizations, including the churches and other independent institutions, to
take the lead in providing youth assistance. The local authorities offer
a wide range of out-of-school educational opportunities and promote

many non-governmental youth and welfare organizations. Most of the youth assistance funds are provided by the federal, state and local authorities.

A serious problem is youth unemployment, in spite of the fact that there is a downward trend. The government's main instrument for combating unemployment is the Federal Youth Plan (Bundesjugendplan). Under this plan over DM 200 million is spent annually on out-of-school youth activities. These include political and cultural education projects as well as international youth exchanges. For instance, every year more than 100,000 Germans and Frenchmen participate in some 4,000 events organized by the Franco-German Youth Organization. A German-Polish youth exchange programme has also been launched.

The Federal Youth Council:
Deutscher Bundesjugendring
Haager Weg 44
5300 Bonn 1

Sport

Sport is an extremely popular form of leisure-time activity in Germany. This is reflected not only in the popularity of television broadcasts but also in the fact that there are more than 75,000 clubs affiliated to the German Sports Federation (Deutscher Sportbund). A good 21 million people are members of sports clubs, and another 12 million "do their own thing". Sport in Germany is autonomous, the various organizations being self-governing The state only provides support where sports organizations lack the necessary funds. Government policy on sport is based on the principle of cooperation with the various organizations. This also applies in the new federal states, where a start has been made with the building up of independent sports organizations. In Eastern Germany, prior to unification, sport was controlled by the regime. The top sportsmen had an important part to play in the "competition of the systems". Today fair play and partnership come before victory at any price. In East Germany, too, the focus is now on popular sport through clubs and associations.

The German Sports Federation. The central sports organization in Germany is the German Sports Federation (DSB), which embraces 19 regional federations and many individual sports associations. In all the various branches there are over two million people working in an honorary capacity as coaches or officials.

Germany is known abroad as the "world champion at building sports facilities". And it is true that the western part of the country has an extensive network of facilities for mass and competitive sport. There are, for instance, about 50,000 sports grounds, nearly 30,000 gymnasiums, and 7,700 indoor and outdoor swimming-pools. In the new federal states, however, there is still a great shortage of facilities for mass sport. For top competitors there are 44 national training centres and 22 Olympic training facilities, as well as many regional centres.

Popular sports. The German Football Federation (DFB) is far the biggest sports organization in Germany, having more than 5.2 million members. Soccer is played thousands of amateur clubs. It is also a spectator sport, attracting hundreds of thousands to professional games every week. This popularity has increased since the 1990 World Cup in Italy, when the German team won the cup for the third time.

Tennis, golf and horse-riding are becoming increasingly popular. The international success of stars like Steffi Graf, Boris Becker and Michael Stich has made tennis a national sport. Mass sport is largely influenced by the professionals, particularly in soccer, tennis and horse-riding.

The German football team won the World Cup in 1990

Sport in the service of people. Most people who indulge in sport do not do so because they are out to achieve great things. The pleasure of exercise and of taking part in a group activity is the main motive. Sport is good for one's health and makes up for the lack of exercise in a highly technical world. Year by year more and more people are attracted to sport and organized sport is providing increasing opportunities. In the average club these days one can play soccer, handball, volleyball, basketball, tennis and table tennis or take part in track and field events. Water sports, too, are very popular, and there are various possibilities for physically handicapped and elderly people, and for mothers and small children.

Popular and leisure-time sports are also promoted by the DSB programmes "Trimm dich" (Get Fit) and "Sport für alle" (Sport for All) which include popular competitions in running, swimming, cycling, skiing and hiking in which anyone can take part. Millions of people do so every year. Every year about 700,000 have their performance in various sports tested in order to qualify for a "Sports Badge" which is awarded by the DSB. There is a gold, silver and bronze standard.

Professional sport. Top sportsmen must these days undergo intensive training with the full backing of coaches and their organizations and a certain measure of financial security. These problems have been addressed by the "Stiftung Deutsche Sporthilfe" (Sports Aid Foundation) which was established in 1967. It regards itself as a welfare organization and tries to ensure that sportsmen can at least devote themselves to training without having to worry about the financial side. But it also helps them obtain qualifications for the time when they leave competitive sport. The foundation is not a governmental organization. Its funds come from private donors, the sale of special postage stamps on sporting themes, and from a television lottery ("Glücksspirale").

Government promotion. Sports organizations in Germany are supported in many ways by the state. The Federal Government mainly promotes competitive sport. It provides funds for training and competition programmes, medical care for top athletes, the training and employment of coaches, the construction of sports facilities and for scientific research. Talented sportsmen are also promoted in the Armed Forces as well. Sports for the disabled as well as international events by the various sports organizations also qualify for government support. Government money is also spent on sending coaches and advisers to Third World countries.

Marathons are becoming more and more popular

Top competitive sport is promoted in order to help develop sport in general. It also serves to foster the Federal Republic's image abroad, which is why financial support is provided to enable leading sportsmen and sportswomen to be able to participate on an equal footing with their rivals in European and world championships and in the Olympic Games.

Support for popular sport is mainly the responsibility of the regional and local authorities. It focuses on facilities, as well as school, university and club sport.

The German Sports Federation:
Deutscher Sportbund
Otto-Fleck-Schneise
6000 Frankfurt am Main 71

Leisure and holidays

Travel is one of the most popular leisure-time activities in Germany. In 1991 about 70% of Germans over the age of 14 took a holiday away from home of at least five days. The proportion was even greater in the new federal states who, after all, had a lot of catching up to do in this respect. For decades they were permitted to travel to western countries only in very exceptional cases. They were only allowed to travel to Eastern bloc countries.

Growing prosperity and shorter working hours translate into more leisure-time and holidays. In 1991 the average annual number of working hours was only 1,557. It was not always like that. At the turn of the century few workers had any holidays. The first steps in this direction came in 1903 in the metal and brewing industries, when three days leave were given.

By 1930 the average annual holiday was between three and fifteen days. Not until 1974 was the statutory minimum holiday of 18 working days introduced in the old Federal Republic. Today most collective wage agreements provide for holidays of six weeks and more, and most employers pay holiday money as well.

Destinations. Many Germans spend their holidays in their own country, but most prefer the warmer climate of the south. In 1990 they spent over 50 billion marks abroad, compared with about 17 billion spent by foreigners in Germany. The most popular countries for German tourists are Italy, Spain, Austria, France, Switzerland and the United States. They can call on the services of increasing numbers of travel operators. Holiday habits have changed. In former times the emphasis was on rest and sun-bathing, but these days many people prefer an active holiday. They like unspoilt nature, away from environmental pollution. This also applies to weekend leisure-time activities.

Numerous clubs and associations, government institutions, the churches and local authorities offer leisure-time programmes at sports grounds, indoor and outdoor public baths, libraries, hobby courses in evening classes, as well as science and music groups.

According to opinion surveys, the ordinary German family spends about one fifth of its income on leisure-time activities and this propor-

*A camping site on the River Main: many Germans
spend their holidays in Germany*

tion is increasing. The business world has recognized this trend and a thriving "leisure industry" has grown up.

The German Leisure Association (Deutsche Gesellschaft für Freizeit) was established in 1971. It is concerned with the basic research into leisure-time behaviour and provides information, documentation and advice. It has 30 member associations.

The German Leisure Association:
Deutsche Gesellschaft für Freizeit
Bahnstrasse 4
4006 Erkrath 1

Clubs, associations and citizens' action groups

There are few Germans who do not belong to at least one club or association. In Germany there are some 300,000 clubs. Nearly every fourth German is a member of a sports club, and over two million of them are members of choral societies. There are associations of marksmen, stamp collectors, dog breeders and local culture, carnivalists, allotment holders and amateur wireless operators, etc. The members pursue their hobbies but socialize as well.

Some of these associations also play a role in local politics, people with different party affiliation come together in the marksmen's club or the local culture association. They make informal contacts which may have an impact on the life of the community. These associations do not have a defined political role, however.

Associations. It is different with groupings which represent specific material interests of their members. These comprise above all the big labour and employers' associations. In addition to these there are many other organizations which pursue certain vocational, economic, social or other objectives. Thus house owners, tenants, motorists – to name but a few – have associations, some with very big memberships. Minorities, too, have organized themselves and are making their voice heard. These common-interest organizations engage in public relations to win sympathy for their causes and to influence legislation and administration in their favour. Their influence is considerable, but those critics who maintain that the Federal Republic of Germany is "under the rule of the associations" are certainly exaggerating.

Citizens' action groups. A new type of association comprises the citizens' action groups, of which a great number have been formed in the early 70s. Their outstanding characteristic is spontaneity: a few citizens get together without any large organizational input to work towards removal of a grievance because they feel they have been left in the lurch by the authorities, political representatives, parties

Lively discussion in citizens' initiatives is a part of democracy

and associations. In most cases local issues are at stake, for example the preservation of old trees due to be felled to make way for a road, a children's playground or efforts to prevent airport extension. Sometimes action groups pursue contradictory aims, e.g. campaigning for a bypass road to quieten traffic in a residential area, or against such a road for nature conservation reasons. On the whole, however, action groups have achieved many objectives, especially at local level, at least because they were ready to compromise. Meanwhile action groups are operating all over the country. Those most widely known are the movement against the construction of nuclear power stations and the peace movement.

The Federal Government welcomes and supports the activities of groups which draw attention to deficiencies in the modern industrial society. It is a basic right of all Germans to organize and take part in peaceful demonstrations. However, the final decision on controversial matters lies with the democratically elected parliaments and governments. They are required to take the decisions that are best for the community as a whole. This makes it important for individuals and citizens' action groups to become involved as soon as possible in the preparation of government decisions, especially during the planning stage. Some legislation, for instance the Federal Building Act, already provides for such civic participation.

Religion and the churches

"Freedom of faith and conscience as well as freedom of religious or other belief shall be inviolable. The undisturbed practice of religion shall be guaranteed." Everyone in the Federal Republic takes this provision of the Basic Law (article 4) for granted as a fundamental right.

Over 58 million people in Germany belong to a Christian church. Just under 30 million are Protestants, over 28 million are Roman Catholics, and a minority belong to other Christian denominations.

The 1919 Weimar constitution implemented the separation of church and state without, however, completely removing historical ties. The legal situation thus created is by and large the one which obtains today, the post-World War II Basic Law having taken over the corresponding provisions of the Weimar constitution in their original wording.

There is no state church in the Federal Republic. The state is neutral vis-à-vis religions and creeds. But neither are the churches private associations; they have a special status as independent public corporations which are in partnership with the state. Apart from the Basic Law, their relationship to the state is regulated by concordats and agreements. To take care of their interests vis-à-vis the Federal Government and parliament they have high-ranking representatives in the capital.

The churches' property rights are guaranteed. They have a claim to financial allocations from the state which, for example, pays contributions to the salaries of the clergy and assumes, in whole or in part, the cost of certain church facilities, such as kindergartens, hospitals and schools. The churches are empowered to levy taxes on their members, which as a rule are collected by state authorities, the churches paying the administrative cost. To resign from a church a member must make a declaration to a state authority. The clergy are trained mainly at state universities, and the churches have a vested right to influence appointments to chairs of theology at universities.

The work of the churches in running hospitals, old people's and nursing homes, consulting and caring services, schools and training centres represents an almost irreplaceable charitable and social commitment, whose absence from public life would be unthinkable.

Protestant Church conventions receive much attention

The Protestant Church. The Protestant Church in Germany (EKD) is an alliance of 24 for the most part independent Lutheran, Reformed and United churches. Church administrative regions are not identical with the territories of the federal states. The EKD's top legislative body is the Synod, its chief executive body the Council. The Church

Roman Catholic Mass

Office in Hanover is the central administrative department. The Protestant Churches are members of the World Council of Churches and they cooperate closely with the Roman Catholic Church.

The Catholic Church. Up to 1990 the Catholic Church in the Federal Republic consisted of five provinces with 22 bishoprics. At the end of that year, after the union of the Berlin Bishops Conference (founded in 1950) and the German Bishops Conference in the West, three bishoprics and an apostolic administrator in the new federal states were added. Germany's archbishops and bishops consult together in the German Bishops Conference, which has a secretariat in Bonn.

The impetus given by the Second Vatican Council to the involvement of the Catholic laity in church affairs is translated into action by elected lay representatives. The visits to the Federal Republic by Pope John Paul II in 1980 and 1987 met with a big response and stimulated the ecumenical movement and the dialogue between state and church.

Other religious communities. Among the smaller religious communities are in particular the "free churches". Two of the largest Protestant free churches, the Methodists and the Protestant Community (Evangelische Gemeinschaft) joined together in 1968 to form the Protestant Methodist Church (Evangelisch-Methodistische Kirche). In addition there are the Baptists. The Old Catholic Church came into being as a breakaway from the Roman Catholic Church in the 1870s after the First Vatican Council. The Mennonite congregations, the Religious Society of Friends (Quakers) and the Salvation Army are known for their social activities.

In 1933 there were about 530,000 Jews living in the German Reich. Following their persecution and extermination by the nazis, there are now 65 Jewish congregations with 30,000 members, the largest of which are those of Berlin with 6,800 and Frankfurt am Main with just under 5,000 members. In addition, about 15,000 Jews live in the Federal Republic who are not members of the Jewish congregations. The umbrella organization of the Jewish congregations is the Central Council of Jews in Germany. In 1979 a College of Jewish Studies was established in Heidelberg which has won international acclaim.

The presence of many foreign workers and their families has greatly increased the importance of religious communities which previously were hardly represented in Germany. This is the case with the

Greek Orthodox Church and especially with Islam. Today, more than 1.7 million Moslems, mostly Turks, live in the Federal Republic of Germany.

Joint action. In the period from 1933 to 1945 many Protestant and Catholic Christians fought bravely against National Socialism. Two of them were Pastor Martin Niemöller on the Protestant and Bishop Clemens August Count von Galen on the Catholic side. The cooperation in this struggle strengthened interdenominational understanding and awareness of common political responsibility. The churches also played an important part in the peaceful revolution in the GDR.

The churches address the public in many ways, for example in publishing papers on topical issues and other forms of publicity. Worthy of special mention are the two lay movements, the German Catholic Convention and the German Protestant Convention. Charitable works are carried out by the German Caritas Association (Deutscher Caritasverband) on the Catholic side and the Diaconal Service (Diakonisches Werk) on the Protestant side. The churches have put great effort into overseas development aid. Big church aid organizations are funded by voluntary donations. Thus the Protestant "Bread for the World" and the Catholic "Misereor" and "Adveniat" have together collected billions of marks for emergency relief and especially for long-term development measures.

In recent times, the Christian churches have voiced their views, and issued official statements, in the debates on peace and disarmament, policy towards foreigners and political asylum, employment and protection of the environment.

Protestant:
Kirchenamt der Evangelischen Kirche in Deutschland
Herrenhäuser Strasse 12
3000 Hanover 21

Catholic:
Sekretariat der Deutschen Bischofskonferenz
Kaiserstrasse 163
5300 Bonn 1

Jews:
Zentralrat der Juden in Deutschland
Rüngsdorfer Strasse 6
5300 Bonn 2

Mass media and public opinion

Article 5 of the Basic Law guarantees freedom of opinion and freedom of the press and also the right to obtain information from generally accessible sources. There is no censorship. The International Press Institute in London, which is concerned with freedom of the press around the world, describes the Federal Republic as one of the few countries where the state respects the strong position of a free press.

Function of the mass media. The press, and in the broader sense all mass media, has been referred to as the "fourth power" next to the legislature, the executive and the judiciary. And it is true that all mass media in the modern society play an important role. With their wide range of news and opinion they enable the people to understand and keep check on parliament, government and public administration. They thus have a big responsibility. The Federal Constitutional Court noted that "a free press which is not controlled by the state and not subject to censorship is an essential element of a free country. In particular, regular press publications are indispensable to the modern democracy. If the people are to be able to make decisions they must be supplied with the information with which to assess opinions."

Diversity of the media. The people have a choice of many different and competing media. The daily papers alone in the western part of Germany sold about 29 million copies a day towards the end of 1991. At present 25 million television sets and over 28 million radios are officially registered. On average Germans over 14 devote nearly five hours a day to newspapers (half an hour), the radio (2.5 hours) and television (two hours). And supply is increasing constantly.

Only about 5% of the population are not reached by the media at all. The great majority, however, draw their information from two or more media. Most turn to television first for their political information and then read a newspaper for greater detail. For local news people usually consult the local newspaper. Young people read news-

The wealth of information available at a newspaper stand

papers less frequently. But television too is losing some of its public appeal.

Sources of news. The mass media obtain their material from news agencies at home and abroad and from their own correspondents. Radio and television stations have offices in all major cities around the world. This also applies to the big newspapers. The leading domestic news agency is the Deutsche Presse-Agentur (dpa), then the Deutscher Depeschendienst (ddp), Associated Press (AP), Reuter (rtr), Agence France Press (AFP), and the Allgemeine Deutsche Nachrichtendienst (ADN) in eastern Germany which was already functioning in the days of the communist regime there. dpa supplies nearly all German dailies. AP, rtr and AFP can base their German language services on the global networks of their parent companies in the United States, the United Kingdom and France. Good newspapers buy the material offered by at least two of these services, broadcasting networks up to five.

Apart from the general agencies there are various others which specialize. They include the Protestant Press Service (epd), the Catholic News Agency (KNA) and the Sports Information Service (sid). Agencies like the Vereinigte Wirtschaftsdienste (vwd) also provide information for private companies and business organizations.

Various private organizations, public authorities, parties, companies, etc. have their own press departments which, like outside agencies, keep information flowing to the mass media. This is done by means of news conferences, press releases, mailings, picture services and discussions with journalists.

It is part of the journalist's daily routine to research topics of his own choosing. Public authorities in Germany are required to provide journalists with information within the framework of the law. In Bonn alone there are nearly 1,000 accredited correspondents. The 550 Germans among them are members of the Federal Press Conference, and the over 400 journalists belong to the Foreign Press Association. Both are entirely independent of the authorities. The Press and Information Office of the Federal Government (BPA) acts as a mediator between government and public. The head of this public authority is at the same time the government spokesman. Not like in some countries, the government spokesman attends the Federal Press Conference to brief Bonn's journalists. He goes to the press, not vice-versa. This also applies to news conferences given by the Federal Chancellor and ministers in conjunction with the Federal Press Conference. The BPA is also responsible for keeping the Federal President, the Federal Government and the parliament informed about foreign opinion on Germany and about foreign and domestic news. In order to provide this service the BPA evaluates 27 news agencies, over 100 radio programmes and 25 television programmes in German and 22 foreign languages.

Public opinion research. The views expressed in the mass media are also referred to as "published" opinion, which in many instances does not tally with public opinion at large. In some cases they are very far apart. Demoscopy is the scientific study of public opinion. It is based on representative samples, i.e. the opinion of usually 1,000 to 2,000 people as a basis for reliable assessments of public opinion at large.

Public opinion surveys in Germany are carried out by a number of private institutes. Those concerned with political opinion research attract the most public attention. The large German newspapers and periodicals as well as television corporations regularly publish the results of such surveys of the nation's political mood, the image of parties and leading politicians, and of topics of current interest such as nuclear energy, unemployment and political asylum. Since 1989/90 the unification process in both parts of Germany has been on the agenda of public opinion polls constantly. The federal and state governments as well as the political parties use the results of these surveys to keep abreast of changes of opinion, for medium and long-term planning, and as a means of assessing the impact of political measures.

Interest is particularly keen prior to elections, when the parties size up their chances and the demoscopic organizations put their finger on the nation's pulse. Although opinion polls are now very reliable, they are still only "snapshots", as it were. Exact forecasts are difficult, especially where the result is expected to be close.

Exit polls are generally the most accurate. Computer calculations just after the election, however, are based on results from selected districts. With their analysis of changes in these election results according to regions, party strongholds and population groups, the researchers complement the data resulting from their surveys and are in this way able to explain the situation to the public.

The demoscopic know-how acquired over the past quarter of a century is reflected not only in detailed reports, which are required reading for the politician, but is also used by observers in neighbouring countries.

The press

Newspapers enjoy increasing popularity in Germany. They have more than held their own despite the growth of television. In terms of the number of newspapers per 1,000 inhabitants, Germany is in fourth place behind Japan, the United Kingdom and Switzerland.

The newspaper landscape. Local and regional dailies dominate the scene. On workdays about 410 newspapers appear in the old and new federal states. They publish nearly 1,700 local and regional editions in more than 150 offices. The total number of sales is about 28.8 million. Small papers, too, keep their readers informed about the main national and international political, economic, cultural, sporting and local events. More than two thirds of all newspapers are bought by subscription, the rest are sold on the streets. One such streetpaper is the "Bildzeitung" which has the biggest circulation (4.5 million a day). The biggest selling subscription paper is the "Westdeutsche Allgemeine Zeitung" (circulation about 700,000). The large national newspapers have smaller circulations but considerable influence on political and business leaders. These are the "Frankfurter Allgemeine Zeitung" and "Die Welt", the "Süddeutsche Zeitung" and the "Frankfurter Rundschau". Other important national opinion leaders are the weeklies "Die Zeit", "Rheinischer Merkur" and "Deutsches Allgemeines Sonntagsblatt". They offer background information, analysis and reports. There are also Sunday newspapers and special German editions of various foreign newspapers catering for foreigners living in Germany.

Periodicals. More than 20,000 periodicals are published in Germany. The best-known internationally is the news magazine "Der Spiegel", with a circulation of over one million. It was originally modelled on the American "Time" magazine. Another large group are the roughly 600 popular periodicals with a total circulation of over 117 million. These include illustrated magazines such as "Stern", "Bunte" and "Quick", as well as specialized periodicals with radio and television programmes. Special-interest publications are also becoming increasingly popular. They deal with one particular subject comprehensively, whether it be tennis or yachting, computers or electronic instruments. There is a large number of technical journals, though with only a moderate circulation. Others include the political weeklies, church newspapers, customer periodicals, freesheets and official announcements. One third of the periodical market is accounted for by the various organizations and associations. The "ADAC-Motorwelt" published by the Allgemeiner Deutscher Automobilclub has a circulation of nine million, the largest in Germany.

This range of information is rounded off by local freesheets and newspapers published by alternative groups. Also on sale in the cities are foreign newspapers and periodicals.

Press concentration. The number of independent newspapers in Germany has fallen steadily since the mid-50s. The publishers with the greater financial and technical resources have been able to dominate various regional markets. As a result, many towns no longer have two or more local papers to choose from. And many of those still in publication do not have "full news rooms", that is editorial offices which produce their newspapers completely independently. They obtain a substantial proportion of their material from another newspaper or newspaper group. Structural changes have gone hand in hand with technical change due to the introduction of computers and state-of-the-art printing technology. Although this has reduced production costs, newspapers, like nearly all print media, depend on advertising for their economic survival. Advertising covers a large part of the cost.

It is debatable whether the lost of diversity and independence resulting from press mergers jeopardizes freedom of the press.

The major publishing companies. Economic developments have led to the formation of large publishing houses. In the daily press sector the biggest conglomerate is the Axel Springer AG, although its 20% share of the newspaper market is largely due to the high circulation of "Bild". As regards Sunday papers, Axel Springer AG is almost without competition with "Welt am Sonntag" and "Bild am Sonntag". Economic and journalistic power is also concentrated in the publishing groups of the "Westdeutsche Allgemeine Zeitung", Süddeutscher Verlag and Verlag DuMont Schauberg.

Much more important in terms of economic power and journalistic effectiveness are the publishers of periodicals, especially the general interest ones. Leaders in this sector are the Bauer Verlag and the Burda group as well as Axel Springer AG. The media corporation with largest turnover, and in fact the second largest in the world, is Bertelsmann AG, which has worldwide interests and covers book and record clubs, book and periodical publishing, music production enterprises, films, radio and television, and printing.

Press rights. Press rights are subject to state law and include mainly the right of journalists to refuse to disclose their sources of

---

Circulation figures for leading newspapers and magazines

Daily newspapers (1991, in some cases with associated papers)

Bild (Hamburg)	4,506,700
Westdeutsche Allgemeine (Essen)	724,900
Hannoversche Allgemeine (Hanover)	513,000
Sächsische Zeitung (Dresden)	499,400
Rheinische Post (Düsseldorf)	396,000
Frankfurter Allgemeine (Frankfurt)	391,000
Süddeutsche Zeitung (Munich)	389,000
Südwestpresse (Ulm)	370,000
Augsburger Allgemeine (Augsburg)	363,000
Berliner Morgenpost (Berlin)	337,000
B.Z. (Berlin)	336,000
Hessische/Niedersächsische Allgemeine (Kassel)	290,000
Kölner Stadtanzeiger (Cologne)	285,000
Berliner Zeitung (Berlin)	275,000
Rheinpfalz (Ludwigshafen)	247,000
Westdeutsche Zeitung (Düsseldorf)	246,000
Braunschweiger Zeitung (Braunschweig)	240,000
Märkische Allgemeine (Potsdam)	235,000
Ostsee-Zeitung (Rostock)	228,000
Lausitzer Rundschau (Cottbus)	227,000
Ruhr-Nachrichten (Dortmund)	225,000
Die Welt (Bonn)	224,000
Frankfurter Rundschau (Frankfurt)	190,000
Die Tageszeitung (Berlin)	61,000

Weeklies and Sunday newspapers

Bild am Sonntag (Hamburg)	2,665,000
Die Zeit (Hamburg)	495,000
Welt am Sonntag	406,000
Bayernkurier (Munich)	158,000
Rheinischer Merkur (Bonn)	112,000
Deutsches Allg. Sonntagsblatt (Hamburg)	93,000

News magazine

Der Spiegel (Hamburg)	1,083,000

information as well as the right of persons who are the subject of newspaper reporting to have a counter-statement published. Print media are required to indicate the title and address of the publication, the date of issue, names of owners and editors, etc. ("masthead requirement"), and to exercise due care. Publishers and journalists exercise self-control through the German Press Council, which looks into charges of negligence and unethical behaviour. Its views are not binding, however.

Development of a free press in Eastern Germany. In the former GDR the press was an instrument of crucial importance to the ruling Communist Party in manipulating the people. All newspapers were censored. The party's mouthpiece, "Neues Deutschland", ensured that all newspaper reporting was in line with party doctrine. When the wall came down the press in Eastern Germany had developed its own momentum and learned how to make use of its newly won freedom. West German publishing companies and journalists helped in building up a free press. New papers were founded and all former party publications were placed in private hands. Wheras local papers have been able to hold their own in the new situation, nearly all of the former periodicals, and many of the new ones, as well as the old daily newspapers and weeklies, have had to throw in the towel. It will be some time before the newspaper landscape in Eastern Germany is on a solid basis.

Federation of German Newspaper Publishers:
Bundesverband Deutscher Zeitungsverleger
Riemenschneiderstrasse 10
5300 Bonn 2

The German Journalists Association:
Deutscher Journalistenverband
Bennauerstrasse 60
5300 Bonn 1

Radio and television

The broadcasting media, i.e. radio and television, in Germany are not state-controlled. The system, as well as the freedom of broadcasting, are governed by law. The Federal Parliament legislates on posts and telecommunications and is therefore responsible for the technical side of broadcasting. The broadcasting corporations themselves fall within the competence of the federal states, however. Germany has a dual system, that is to say public and commercial systems exist side by side. It is based largely on a 1986 judgement of the Federal Constitutional Court. The court ruled that the public corporations should meet the public's general broadcasting requirements with the private companies playing a supplementary role. For many years Germany had only public corporations, but this changed in 1984 when private television and radio broadcasters were allowed to compete for the first time.

The public corporations. In 1991 Germany had 11 regional broadcasting corporations, two set up under federal law, and a second national television network (Zweites Deutsches Fernsehen – ZDF) based on an agreement between all the federal states. The largest broadcasting station is the Westdeutscher Rundfunk (Cologne) with 4,400 staff, while the smallest is Radio Bremen with 650.

The others are Bayerischer Rundfunk (Munich), Hessischer Rundfunk (Frankfurt am Main), Norddeutscher Runkfunk (Hamburg), Saarländischer Rundfunk (Saarbrücken), Sender Freies Berlin (Berlin), Süddeutscher Rundfunk (Stuttgart), Südwestfunk (Baden-Baden), Ostdeutscher Rundfunk (Potsdam) and Mitteldeutscher Rundfunk (Leipzig). They cater more or less for the regions where they are located, although some supply programmes for several regions. Each broadcasts several radio programmes and the regional corporations form a Standing Conference of Public Broadcasting Corporations (Arbeitsgemeinschaft der öffentlich-rechtlichen Rundfunkanstalten Deutschlands, ARD). Together they operate a nationally transmitted television programme officially called "German Television" but generally referred to as "Channel Two". In addition, they produce regional "Third" TV programmes. The Mainz-based Zweites

Deutsches Fernsehen is a television-only station which transmits the "Channel Two" programme nationwide. It is the largest in Europe.

There are two radio stations with special responsibilities, the Deutschlandfunk (DLF) and Deutsche Welle (DW), both located in Cologne. The DLF is financed by the Federal Government together with the regional broadcasting corporations, whereas the DW is funded entirely by the Federal Government. Prior to the country's unification both stations broadcast Germany-oriented programmes for domestic and foreign consumption. They transmit in German and several dozen foreign languages. Deutsche Welle (Voice of Germany) will continue in this role, though it now incorporates the foreign language departments of the DLF and RIAS television. DLF will focus on a national information programme and function as a subsidiary of ARD and ZDF in Cologne. This also applies to the cultural affairs programme of the Deutschlandsender (DS), which has emerged from the radio broadcasting system in the former GDR. They will be joined by a national information programme produced by the RIAS radio system in Berlin. RIAS used to operate as the "Radio in the American Sector" of Berlin. Although it was under the responsibility of the United States Information Service, it had a German director-general. DLF, DS and RIAS will in future broadcast information programmes jointly.

The broadcasting media in the five new federal states are currently being reorganized. Two new state corporations have been established and temporary arrangements have been made with regard to the former state-controlled broadcasting stations in East Germany. ARD and ZDF have been broadcasting to the whole country since 1990 and have regional studios in the new states. As soon as the new states have their own broadcasting laws and sufficient frequencies are available for private companies, East Germany will be catered for in much the same way as the western states.

Self-government and broadcasting freedom. The public corporations are in general controlled by three bodies: the Radio Council/Television Council, the Administrative Council and the Director-General. The members of the Radio Council (likewise of the Television Council) are representatives of all important political and social groups. They are elected by the state parliaments or nominated by the political parties, religious communities and business and cultural organizations. The Council advises the Director-General on programming and ensures that basic principles are observed.

TV show with audience participation

The Administrative Council draws up the corporation's budget, watches over day-to-day management, and comments on technical aspects. Its members are elected by the Radio/Television Council and they for their part elect the Director-General subject to confirmation by the Broadcasting Council.

The Director-General runs the corporation in accordance with the decisions of the Broadcasting and Administrative Councils. He is responsible for programme content and represents the corporation in its external relations.

This self-administration system guarantees the broadcasting corporations' independence from the state. It does not, however, exclude all political influence. Although the supervisory bodies are not totally composed of representatives of political parties, there has grown in them a kind of party-political power-sharing arrangement which becomes particularly conspicuous when top posts in the corporations – such as those of director-general, programme directors, editors-in-chief and so forth – are up for appointment and draws much public criticism.

The corporations are duty-bound not to favour any side and to maintain editorial balance. This does not prejudice the "freedom of internal broadcasting" that is, the right to express decided points of views. The corporations are, however, required by law grant equal opportunities to express opinions.

Programmes. Each regional corporation runs up to five contrasting radio programmes. They provide a broad variety of entertainment, music, current affairs, sport, regional affairs, drama, opera, and so on. Most networks run scientific and literary series, and special programmes for foreign workers are provided in their own languages. Their orchestras, choirs and ballet ensembles enrich the cultural landscape of many cities.

In the nationally transmitted ARD and ZDF television programmes political reporting, home and foreign affairs documentation, television plays, films and entertainment play a big part. For their foreign coverage both ARD and ZDF have widespread correspondent networks and their own studios in many countries all over the world.

The Channel Three television programmes are transmitted regionally by the ARD corporations and concentrate on regional affairs, such as state politics and regional culture. Third programmes are also of special significance to the education system. Most ARD corporations regularly transmit television for schools and further-education courses at various levels.

Television in the Federal Republic went colour in 1967. The German-developed PAL system is used. More than 80% of the registered receivers are colour sets.

Finance. The public broadcasting corporations obtain most of their funds in the form of listeners' and viewers' licence fees. Television licence revenues are split 70:30 between the ARD corporations and the ZDF. Both corporations are also dependent upon income from commercial advertising. They have much less time for commercial spots than the private companies, with whom they now have to compete for advertising. Television rights, especially for major football and tennis events, have become much more expensive, yet the public corporations cannot increase license fees without the approval of the regional parliaments.

Commercial broadcasting. The public corporations first had to contend with competition in 1985 when "SAT 1" began operating from Mainz as the first commercial television broadcasting company. It was followed in 1986 by "RTL plus Deutschland" (Cologne). Both have meanwhile achieved considerable ratings. At the beginning of 1991 RTL plus reached two thirds of all households and SAT 1 a little more than 62%. Other private broadcasters are "Pro 7" and "Tele 5". RTL plus and SAT 1 are mainly concerned with sport, entertainment and feature films but also offer good political programmes. Pro 7 concentrates mainly on films, whereas Tele 5 specializes in game shows.

Commercial programmes are transmitted via satellite and cable and can also be received via terrestrial frequencies. A number of foreign TV programmes are offered in the same way. The commercial stations are operated by consortia, most of which are publishing companies. Advertising is their only source of revenue.

In 1991 there were already about 100 private radio stations, although only a few of them offer a full programme catering for a whole state. The law requires radio stations to provide a variety of programmes which meet the people's requirements. The Federal Constitutional Court has ruled that, like the public corporations, the commercial companies must not be one-sided, that their programmes must ensure sufficient diversity.

Broadcasting innovation. New technology has considerably changed the broadcasting landscape in Germany. In 1991 some 16 million households were linked up to the broadband cable network which the Post Office has been laying since 1982. Nearly half of these households receive cable, radio and television programmes. The aim in the 90s is to make cabled programmes available to 80% of all 30 million households.

Direct satellite broadcasting has meanwhile become a serious rival to cable. It is an economically viable alternative for everyone, not only those not yet linked up to the cable network. Satellite programmes can be received directly by anyone with a small dish antenna.

Satellite broadcasting raises the question of boundary limitations. It is not yet certain whether national, European, or global concepts will prevail. In 1991 two supranational public and one private organization were operating most of the 15 satellites which supply Europe with about 70 television and radio programmes. One of the satellite programmes is "3sat", a joint undertaking by the ZDF, the Austrian Broadcasting Corporation and the Swiss Radio and Television Company. Another is "1Plus" broadcast by the ARD.

Viewers and listeners in Germany now have an extensive range of programmes to choose from. Among the new media which are available via television are Btx, the Post Office's viewdata system. It enables subscribers to conduct a dialogue with various suppliers via telephone. The possibilities range from stock exchange reports to bank account transactions. The public corporations offer videotex, a service using the normal television signal. Videotex appears on the screen on call and offers news, weather reports, tips for consumers, and much more.

Cultural diversity

Nowhere is the country's federal structure more apparent than in the cultural sphere. Germany never had a cultural metropolis like France's Paris and Britain's London. The considerable cultural autonomy of the regions has led to the formation of small and large cultural centres with different points of emphasis. Thus cultural activity is to be found in even the smallest towns and communities.

In future Berlin, as capital and seat of government of united Germany, will play an important cultural role. But the other cities will retain their standing as cultural centres. The country's federal structure ensures that its cultural diversity will continue to flourish, now enhanced by the rich cultural heritage of the new federal states.

This diversity is apparent from the spread of cultural institutions and activities. The central library of the Federal Republic of Germany is in Frankfurt, where the book trade is also concentrated. Hamburg has the largest concentration of newspaper publishing. Berlin has the most theatres. The central state archives of the Federal Republic are in Koblenz. There are scientific academies in Düsseldorf, Göttingen, Halle, Heidelberg, Leipzig, Mainz and Munich. The major museums are in Berlin, Munich, Nuremberg, Cologne and Stuttgart. The largest literary archives are in the small Württemberg town of Marbach on the Neckar and in Weimar (Thuringia).

It is due to such cultural polycentrism that there are no remote, desolate "provinces" in the Federal Republic. One need not travel hundreds of miles to see good theatre or hear good music. In medium-sized towns one sometimes finds astonishingly valuable libraries or interesting art collections. Be it because the princes of the age of absolutism had the ambition to make their residences centres of culture or because a self-confident middle class patronized the arts and sciences within their walls – Germans today profit from their efforts and enjoy a wide variety of cultural amenities.

The establishment and maintenance of most cultural facilities in the Federal Republic of Germany is the responsibility of local government. Legislation in cultural matters – with few exceptions – is the prerogative of the federal states. Each has a large measure of autonomy in organizing its schools system. And here it becomes apparent that there are also negative aspects to cultural federalism.

Since some schools' curricula and final examination standards vary widely from state to state, problems can arise when families move and the children have trouble adjusting.

But the state governments are cooperating where they can through their Standing Conference of Ministers of Education and Cultural Affairs. The federal and state governments cooperate in planning and financing university building. They also have a joint commission for educational planning and research promotion. Within this framework they promote pilot projects in all fields of education.

The purpose of these bodies is to ensure the degree of standardization necessary for a modern, efficient education system without abandoning the rich diversity of German cultural life.

Schools

Everyone has the right freely to develop his personality and to choose his place of education and profession or occupation. This is a fundamental right guaranteed by the Basic Law. As a result, the government is required to provide all citizens with the best possible opportunities to receive the kind of education that is commensurate with their abilities and interests. Such educational opportunities should be available throughout life so that young people will become emancipated and able to play their part in the country's democratic system. As an industrial country short of raw materials, the Federal Republic relies heavily on its skilled labour and therefore spends heavily on education. In 1989 the federal and state governments and local authorities, together with industry, spent about DM 156 billion on education in the western part of the country. That is nearly 7% of the gross national product.

The education system. Education in Germany is largely the responsibility of the federal states. This applies especially to general and vocational education, continuing education and higher education.

School attendance is compulsory from the ages of six to 18, i.e. for 12 years, during which full-time attendance is required for nine years and part-time attendance at vocational school thereafter. In some states ten years of full-time schooling are compulsory. Attendance at all state schools is free. Materials, in particular textbooks, are also put at the pupils' disposal, some of them free of charge.

The Basic Law demands that religious instruction be a regular subject. From the age of 14 pupils may drop it if they wish. Denominational schools have lost importance in recent decades. Most states have "interdenominational schools oriented to Christian principles", that is schools based on Christian culture in which only religious instruction is given in denominationally separate classes. As a rule girls and boys are in mixed classes. There are also various private schools which receive state grants.

Kindergarten. Kindergarten is a German institution adopted by many countries – the very word, in fact, has become assimilated in many languages. It develops personality, the ability of children to express themselves fluently, teaching them to become useful members of society. Most children spend only the morning in kindergarten, but there are also many all-day kindergartens, which are for families where both parents are in employment.

The kindergartens are not part of the state school system. Attendance is voluntary and usually parents have to contribute to the cost. In West Germany there are over 24,000 operated by local government, churches, associations, firms or private people. More than 80% of all three to six-year-olds attend kindergartens. In the former GDR nearly 95% of children attended kindergarten, most of them run by the state. There were also crèches for children up to the age of three. The reason for this extensive provision of kindergarten facilities is that there was a very large proportion of working mothers in East Germany.

The school system. At the age of six children enter primary school (Grundschule). In general it lasts four years, in Berlin six. In most federal states childrens' work in the first two years at school is not graded but assessed. After four years at primary school they attend one of the other schools available to them according to their ability. Here the fifth and sixth school years are known as the "orientation phase" when children and their parents can revise their choice of school.

About one third of the children pass from the primary school to the junior secondary school (Hauptschule). Most of those who leave at the age of 15 or 16 take a course of vocational training, which includes attendance at a vocational school until the age of 18. Successful completion of Hauptschule opens the way to many occupations for which formal training is required. The range of subjects taught at Hauptschule has been substantially improved. For example, nowadays almost every pupil is instructed in a foreign language, mostly English, and gets vocational orientation to ease the transition from school to working life.

Intermediate school (Realschule) as a rule takes six years, from year 5 to year 10. Realschule leads to a graduating certificate at intermediate level between Hauptschule and senior high school (Gymnasium). The intermediate certificate qualifies pupils to attend a technical school (Fachschule or Fachoberschule), specialized schools offering vocational training at upper secondary level. The intermediate certificate is also regarded as a prerequisite for a medium-level career in business and administration. A third of all pupils obtain the intermediate certificate.

The nine-year Gymnasium (5th to 13th school years) is the traditional grammar or senior high school in Germany. The former classification into ancient-language, modern-language and natural-sciences Gymnasium is rare nowadays. Today the so-called

German educational system in diagram form

Further training
(general/vocational further training in diverse forms)

Graduate-level vocational qualification

Vocational qualification	General higher education qualification	University/Technical university Teacher training college Polytechnic Administrative college Art college Comprehensive university
Technical school	**Evening grammar school/college**	

	Vocational training qualification intermediate vocational qualification		Polytechnic qualification		General higher education qualification	
13					**Higher grammar school level**	13
12	**Vocational training in firm and vocational school (dual system)**	**Vocational extension school**	**Full-time – vocational school**	**Technical – secondary school**	(grammar school, vocational grammar school, comprehensive school)	12
11						11
10	Basic vocational training year					10

Elementary school qualifications after 9 or 10 years/secondary school qualification

		10th school year					10
10							10
9							9
8	Special school	**Elementary school**	**Secondary school**	**Grammar school**	Compre-hensive school	8
7						7
6			Orientation level				6
5			(dependent on/independent of type of school)				5

4				4
3	Special school	**Primary school**		3
2				2
1				1

School year	Special Kinder-garten	**Kindergarten**

"reformed upper phase" (11th to 13th years) is the rule; under this system courses have replaced the conventional classes. In these courses students concentrate on the subjects they are most interested in. This is intended to facilitate the transition to university. Some Gymnasiums specialize in business or technical studies.

Graduation from the Gymnasium, the so-called "maturity certificate" ("Reifezeugnis" or "Abitur") is the prerequisite for study at university. However, the number of Gymnasium graduates has increased to such an extent that not all those who wish to study can get university places. Certain restrictions have had to be introduced (numerus clausus).

The three-level school system has often been criticized. It is argued that for many children the direction is determined too early. This problem is remedied in the orientation or promotion phase so that pupils can choose the right school in the 7th school year. Another model is the comprehensive school, which amalgamates the hitherto separate types of school and normally provides classes for years 5 to 10. Some comprehensive schools have their own senior grades akin to those of the Gymnasium. According to ability, pupils have the option of taking courses with higher or lower standards. Vocational

Schools, classes and pupils in institutions of general education in the 1989/school year

Type of school	Schools	Classes	Pupils		Percentage share of fe-male pupils
			Number	Shares(%)	
Old Federal Republic					
Preclasses, school kindergardens	3,249	4,854	67,512	1.0	42.6
Primary schools	13,585	112,264	2,449,711	36.4	49.0
Orientation level	1,124	9,045	210,085	3.1	48.6
Elementary schools	5,889	49,496	1,043,976	15.5	45.3
Secondary schools	2,573	35,380	857,218	12.7	52.4
Grammar schools	2,462	40,600	1,545,577	23.0	51.0
Integrated comprehensive schools	314	8,129	224,536	3.3	46.6
Free Waldorf schools	108	1,459	48,465	0.7	51.9
Special schools	2,762	25,369	246,278	3.7	38.1
Evening schools/colleges	246	294	41,137	0.6	50.5
Total	32,313	286,890	6,734,495	100.0	48.8
Former GDR					
Polytechnic high schools	5,226	93,206	1,986,314	93.8	49.4
Extended polytechnic high schools	223	2,394	39,626	1.9	57.8
Special schools	479	6,663	63,614	3.0	37.0
People's high school courses	–	–	28,166	1.3	46.3
Total	5,928	102,263	2,117,720	100.0	49.1

familiarization instruction is part of the syllabus. The graduation certificates of comprehensive schools are recognized in all federal states.

Physically or mentally handicapped children whose needs are not adequately catered for at general education schools attend special schools.

Anyone who for any reason has missed out on educational opportunities can catch up via the "second route". Evening colleges give working people the chance to prepare for Gymnasium graduation in courses lasting three to six years, which they attend in addition to their daily work. In the same way one can achieve final Hauptschule or Realschule certificates through evening classes. But it is hard and demands great sacrifice from the student.

Teachers. For every type of school there are specially trained teachers. Academic study is obligatory for all but its contents and duration vary. Generally speaking the future Grundschule and Hauptschule teachers study for six semesters (three years). Longer university study is required for Realschule, Sonderschule, Gymnasium and vocational school teachers.

All applicants for the teaching profession have to sit an examination after completion of their studies. This is followed by a period of practical training and a second examination. Those who find employment are as a rule appointed civil servants for life.

New schools in the new states. One of the biggest tasks in the next few years is to introduce the western school system in the new federal states. In the former GDR the state polytechnic secondary school was compulsory for ten years. It was totally oriented to socialist doctrine. Following unification curricula there are now being depoliticized and the new states are adopting various school models from the west. It has still not yet been decided whether elements of the old system should be retained, e.g. the shorter overall school period of twelve years. Although the teachers from the old system in Eastern Germany were kept on after unification they have not automatically been made civil servants. Whether they will remain in the school system will be decided on a case-by-case basis.

Vocational education

Ninety per cent of the youngsters who end their general schooling at junior secondary or intermediate level go into vocational training, most of them in the "dual system". This comprises practical, on-the-job learning with theoretical instruction in vocational school. That means private enterprise and government are jointly responsible for vocational training. On the government side, the federation is responsible for the training regulations, while the vocational schools are the responsibility of the state governments. There are about 400 recognized occupations for which formal training is required. Their popularity with young people varies. Almost 35% of the male trainees are concentrated in 10 preferred vocations and among the female trainees it is more than 55%. The favourite occupations of boys are motor mechanic, electrician, office clerk, fitter, painter and carpenter; the girls' favourites are hairstylist, sales assistant, office clerk and doctor's or dentist's assistant.

The computer is part of many training courses

Training on a drilling machine

On-the-job training. Practical on-the-job training, usually called apprenticeship, takes from two to three and a half years, depending on the occupation, but in most cases three years. The apprentice is paid "training remuneration" which increases annually. What has to be learned, and finally tested, for a vocation is set out in training regulations. These are issued by the responsible federal ministries and are based on proposals from the business associations, employers' organizations and trade unions.

The training concludes with an examination held by the self-governing business organizations, such as a chamber of industry and commerce or crafts or other institutions. On the examination board are representatives of the employers, labour and vocational schools, and teachers.

Over 500,000 firms in all branches of the economy, including the free professions and the public service, provide vocational training. Large enterprises have their own training workshops, but a large part of the training takes place on the job. More than half the trainees learn in smaller firms, most of which are too specialized to be able to impart all the necessary knowledge. This is why inter-company training centres have been set up where trainees can broaden their vocational skills.

Vocational schools. In addition to on-the-job learning, the trainee has to attend vocational school on one or two days a week for three years. The schools teach general subjects and the theory which a young person is better able to learn in a school than at the place of employment. Vocational schools are, however, not only attended by trainees. They are also obligatory for all under-18s who attend no other type of school.

Other forms of vocational training. Apart from apprenticeship and vocational school there are a number of other vocational training systems being used by ever more young people. There is the full-time specialized vocational school whose courses last at least one year. Where they are longer, they can be counted as an apprenticeship or part of it.

The specialized secondary school (Fachoberschule) admits pupils with an intermediate certificate. Successful graduation from the Fachoberschule (after two years) qualifies young people for study at colleges of higher education (Fachhochschulen).

Preparation for working life. In principle, no young person in Germany should begin working life without a vocational training. Here the dual system has proved its value. It has even been copied by a number of other countries. For demographic reasons demand for training places was very heavy in the 80s. In 1990, by comparison, the western part of the country had 659,000 places available for only about 560,000 trainees. In the new federal states, too, all 140,000 young people seeking an apprenticeship found one. This has been made possible by massive efforts on the part of all concerned – industry, the federal and state governments, the Federal Institute for Employment, and the Trust Agency (Treuhandanstalt). 10,000 training places were offered by federal agencies. All small firms (i.e. those with up to 20 employees) who took on a new apprentice in 1991 received a grant of DM 5,000. The first inter-company training centres were established. Under the Unification Treaty, vocational training qualifications were recognized in both parts of the country. This makes for greater mobility among young people.

Higher education

German universities have a long history. The Federal Republic's oldest university, at Heidelberg, was founded in 1386. Several others have had 500-year jubilees, including Leipzig (founded 1409) and Rostock (1419). But apart from these venerable institutions there are very young universities, more than 20 having been founded since 1960.

For more than a century the educational ideal of German universities was that which Wilhelm von Humboldt tried to realize at the Berlin University founded in 1810. The Humboldt type of university was conceived for a relatively small number of students. It was to be a place of pure science, non-purposive research and teaching, and only secondarily serve to prepare students for a profession. In time this ideal clashed more and more with the requirements of a modern industrial society. In addition to the traditional universities there came into being technical universities, teacher-training colleges and specialized colleges, the latter especially in the 70s and 80s. Education policy also changed. The demand for the best possible educational opportunities for all young people found general recognition.

Whereas in 1960 only 8% of an age group took up academic studies, nowadays nearly every third seeks a university place. The number of students rose to more than 1,700,000 in 1990/91. In that year alone there were 318,000 freshmen. The state tried to meet this increasing demand by expanding existing universities and building new ones, doubling teaching staff and increasing university funding several times over. New courses of study were introduced and efforts were made to orientate study more than before to later vocational practice.

University organization. The universities in the Federal Republic of Germany (apart from church-owned universities and colleges of the armed forces) are state facilities. The federation controls only the general principles of the university system and research financing, contributing funds to university construction and research projects.

The universities are self-governing. Within the framework of the law, each university draws up its own constitution. Nowadays universities are headed by a full-time rector or president elected for several years. All groups - professors, academic staff, students and employees - play their part. In most states the student community manage their own affairs.

Types of universities. The mainstay of the tertiary education system are the academic universities and similar institutions of higher education. Courses culminate in a Master's degree ("Magister"), a "Diplom" or a public-service degree ("Staatsexamen"). After that, further qualification is possible up to doctorate level.

Another type of tertiary college is the "Fachhochschule", a specialized higher technical college or polytechnic. It provides a more practical education, especially in engineering, business administration, social science, design and agriculture, concluding with a degree examination ("Diplomprüfung"). Today nearly every third new student enrolls at a Fachhochschule.

In two states comprehensive universities (Gesamthochschulen) were established in the early 1970s as entirely new or amalgamated institutions. The comprehensive university combines the various tertiary forms under one roof and offers corresponding integrated studies. It is a model which has not spread widely.

Also new in the Federal Republic is the distance-learning university in Hagen, Westphalia, which opened in 1976. It now has nearly 50,000 students who, in addition to their correspondence courses, also attend regional centres.

Courses and students. A few figures may show how successful efforts to open tertiary study to all strata of the population have been.

Students at universities and colleges by faculty
(old Federal Republic 1989/1990)

Law, economics and social sciences	427,000	(28.3%)
Engineering sciences	320,000	(21.3%)
Languages, the arts and sport	304,000	(20.3%)
Mathematics, natural sciences	215,000	(14.3%)
Medicine	105 000	(7,0%)
Art, art sciences, design	68,000	(4.5%)
Agriculture, forestry and nutritional sciences	36,000	(2.4%)

In a a lecture hall: student numbers are large

In the 1952/53 winter semester 4% of the freshmen came from wage-earner families, compared with 19% in the 1987 summer semester. In 1952 one fifth of students were women, today it is about 40%.

The federal and state governments also want foreigners to study in Germany. In 1991 the number was about 76,000. The assistance they receive is regarded as a contribution to international understanding.

Traditionally students are quite free to shape their own courses of study. Although for many courses curricula are recommended and interim examinations are obligatory, in many others students are still free to choose between certain subjects and lectures.

No study fees are charged at the Federal Republic's universities. If neither the student nor their parents are able to pay for their living expenses the state helps. Under the Federal Education Promotion Act (BAFöG) students can obtain financial assistance. Half the amount is a grant, the other half a loan which has to be repaid when the graduate enters a profession.

In 1991 three fifths of new students in East Germany claimed BAFöG loans, compared with one fifth in the west. The universities have student welfare organizations. They have refectories, which are state-subsidized, and hostels.

In the new federal states just under 70% of all students are at present accommodated in hostels. About 40% of all freshmen are still living with their parents. Rents on the open market are a serious problem for many students. But at least there is cheap insurance. All are covered by the statutory accident insurance scheme and they are charged little for health insurance under the state scheme.

The problem of student numbers. Despite considerable expansion of the university system the enormous growth in the number of people wanting to study has led to admission restrictions (numerus clausus) having to be introduced for some subjects. The available university places are distributed by a central authority in Dortmund (Zentralstelle für die Vergabe von Studienplätzen). For the particularly attractive subjects such as medicine, dentistry and veterinary science there is a selection procedure which takes account of the applicant's average high school graduation ("Abitur") mark and the time spent waiting for admission. There are also tests and interviews. Special consideration is given to hardship cases. In such courses as economics, law, industrial management and computer science available places are distributed. Every applicant is assigned to a particular university, where possible according to choice.

Reforms have been under discussion for some time, principally with a view to reducing the length of courses. Today students spend on average 14 semesters (seven years) at university, much longer than in other countries. Many of them have even served an apprenticeship or in the armed forces before going to university. As a result, freshmen are getting increasingly older. The fact that they begin earning their living comparatively late in life is a serious disadvantage, also in view of the competition from other countries.

In spite of the difficulties new entrants are optimistic about the future. In 1991 most of them thought they would have good prospects after completing their courses.

The situation in the new federal states. The universities in the former GDR are being reorganized in line with the recommendations of the Science Council. Some of the research carried out at academies is being reintegrated into the universities and partly transferred to extramural research establishments financed jointly by the federal and the state governments. Suitable professors and lecturers with an untainted political past are being incorporated in the public service. The reorganization process is to be completed by the mid-90s and is being financed to the amount of DM 1.8 billion from a fund for the renewal of higher education and research which runs until 1996.

The University Rectors' Conference:
Hochschulrektorenkonferenz
Ahrstrasse 395
5300 Bonn 2

Adult education

Every year ten million people in Germany take advantage of the many opportunities for further education. Continuing education is necessary in a modern industrial society in view of the fact that the demands of work are becoming greater and changing all the time. Many people have to change occupations several times in their life. But further education is also an important leisure-time factor. It has a political function as well since the individual can only have a say in matters if he is capable of making his own judgement in various fields.

Adult education centres. Adult education centres were introduced towards the end of the 19th century, based on the Scandinavian model. They impart mainly practical but also theoretical knowledge. Today the subjects range from astronomy via language courses to Zen meditation. There are some 850 such centres in the Federal Republic and about 3,800 sub-centres. They are generally run by local authorities or registered associations. Funds are contributed by the state governments. Adult education centres are non-partisan and non-denominational. Most of them take the form of evening classes, but there are also residential centres which offer courses lasting several days or weeks.

In 1989 alone, they ran nearly 400,000 courses which were attended by 5.5 million people (in 1965 there were 78,000 courses and 1.7 million participants). Four million took part in 87,000 individual events.

For a number of years certificates have been awarded in various subjects such as languages, mathematics, science and technology. In 1989 some 15,000 students sat for examinations. This widely varying education work is done by some 5,600 full-time teachers and nearly 130,000 part-time course leaders.

Further vocational training. Industry spends more than DM 10 billion every year on further training for the labour force. There are 11 supraregional training institutes run by industry and 30 further-

There are also courses in foreign laguages, such as Spanish

education institutes. Large enterprises additionally run courses of their own for their own employees. The participants are meant either to achieve a higher vocational qualification (promotion qualification), refresh their skills in their own occupation (adaptation training) or learn a completely new job (retraining). Three out of four participants in further-training schemes report that they obtained better jobs.

The state provides roughly DM 5.5 billion a year on further training promotion. During the course trainees receive grants or loans. The cost of tuition and learning materials can be wholly or partly borne by the state.

Unemployed people in particular are making ever more use of further education to improve their employment prospects. Three quarters of the unemployed participants who finish courses successfully find work within six months.

The armed forces provide further training for servicemen in their own technical schools. There they can work for all school certificates up to the university entrance qualification (Abitur). The services provide initial courses, retraining measures and further training. So far over 300,000 of its members have obtained vocational qualifications in their institutions.

Wide selection of courses. The trade unions also run a large further-education programme. The Volkshochschulen and the German Trade Union Federation (Deutscher Gewerkschaftsbund, DGB) are linked in a working group called "Arbeit und Leben" (Work and Life). This provides workers with courses in economic and social affairs, works constitution, insurance and labour law and much more. Works council members and other labour representatives can take courses at special DGB colleges and academies.

The churches, too, are active in the field of adult education. The Protestant Church maintains 15 academies, where it holds seminars on topical issues. In the foreground of Catholic further-education work are family and marriage problems and theological and cultural themes. Finally, there are also a number of foundations, closely allied to the political parties, which have further-education programmes: Friedrich-Ebert-Stiftung (SPD), Friedrich-Naumann-Stiftung (FDP), Konrad-Adenauer-Stiftung (CDU), Hanns-Seidel-Stiftung (CSU), and Stiftungsverband Regenbogen (The Greens). Private distance-learning organizations also offer about 1,000 courses of further education. In 1989 there were 140,000 participants, including 40,000 from the new states. There the continuing education facilities still have to be brought up to the western level.

German Adult Education Federation:
Deutscher Volkshochschulverband e.V.
Rheinallee 1
5300 Bonn 2

Scholarship and research

The 1991 Nobel Prize for Medicine was awarded to Erwin Neher and Bert Sakmann for their work in the field of cellular biology. In 1989 the Nobel Prize for Physics was shared by the physicist Wolfgang Paul and two American colleagues, and in 1988 the Nobel Prize for Chemistry was shared by Johann Deisenhofer, Robert Huber and Hartmut Michel. Thus if one takes Nobel Prizes as the yardstick, Germany is holding its own in fields of advanced research.

Germany used to be known as the "land of science". German universities led the world in many areas of scholarship. Up to the Second World War ten out of 45 Nobel Prizes for physics and 16 out of 44 for chemistry went to Germans. But after 1933 the nazis drove many of the country's best brains abroad. A good number of them went to the United States, where they proved of inestimable value to the country's scientific institutions. Germany had a hard task making up for this brain drain after 1945 and it was a long time before she caught up with the world's leaders. Today there is a problem of a different kind: how to integrate the scientists and research institutions of the former GDR meaningfully into an efficient research organization spanning the whole country.

Research institutes. Most research in the Federal Republic is done by the universities, non-university research institutes and industry. Research by university teachers has a long tradition in Germany. "The unity of research and teaching" has been a pillar of German academic life since Wilhelm von Humboldt reformed the Prussian universities in the early 19th century. At the universities one still frequently finds the traditional type of scholar working alone or within a small group on a subject of his choice.

But certain research projects, especially in the natural sciences, are too vast for this type of approach. They can be coped with only by big teams and large-scale installations; their funding can run into billions. Such large-scale research is best done in the government-funded centres for new sources of energy, aerospace, medicine, molecular biology, environmental and polar research.

In the western part of Germany some 420,000 people have jobs connected with science and research - one third scientists, one third technical and one third other personnel. Added to this number are those in the former GDR.

In 1990 the Federal Republic spent about 2.9% of the gross national product on research and development (Japan 2.9 to 3%, the United States 2.8%).

Sponsors of research. The universities focus mainly on basic research. In fields of applied research and development they cooperate with other institutes and industrial laboratories. This speeds up the practical application of their theoretical findings.

Closely linked with the universities are the five academies of science in Düsseldorf, Göttingen, Heidelberg, Mainz and Munich. They are centres of scientific communication and mainly support long-term scholarly projects such as the publication of enzyclopaedias etc. Essential support for university research comes from the German Research Foundation.

The Max Planck Society for the Promotion of the Sciences has an international reputation. It is the largest research organization outside the universities and its 60 or so facilities are financed from public funds. The Max Planck Society engages in basic research which is either not done by the universities or requires particularly large facilities, such as observatories for astronomy or experimental facilities in the field of plasma physics.

The 16 big-science institutions are another important instrument of government research policy. They receive 90% of their funds from the Federal Ministry for Research and Technology and 10% from the government of the state where they are located. Their research ranges from microparticles via aerospace to cancer, environment and climate research.

Spending on research and development
(old federal states, in billions of DM)

Research sector	1971	1981	1989
Non-university research institutions	3.01	5.78	8.40
Universities and colleges	4.27	5.87	9.09
Private industry	10.70	26.60	47.30
Research abroad	0.79	1.07	1.88
Total	18.77	39.32	66.67

1991 Nobel Prize for Erwin Neher (left) and Bert Sakmann

An important link between research and its practical application is the Fraunhofer Society for the Advancement of Applied Research. In its various institutes it carries out commissioned projects. Other significant contributions are made by the Fritz Thyssen, Robert Bosch and Volkswagen Foundations. They and the Donors Association for German Science (Stifterverband für die Deutsche Wissenschaft) are much in demand for research projects, especially in collaboration with the universities. The Alexander von Humboldt Foundation, which receives financial support from the government, enables foreign scientists to do research in Germany and pays for research trips by outstanding foreign scientists.

Many of the tasks facing the government today cannot be accomplished without scientific preliminary work and consultation. Such activities are in the responsibility of the many research institutions of the federal and state governments, such as the Institute for Current Affairs (Institut für Zeitgeschichte), the Heinrich Hertz Institute for Communication Technology (Heinrich-Hertz-Institut für Nachrichtentechnik), the Federal Health Office (Bundesgesundheitsamt), or the Federal Environmental Agency (Umweltbundesamt).

International cooperation. Germany has concluded agreements on scientific and technological cooperation with over 30 countries. Within the European Community it plays an active part in joint European research projects. This work is carried out by institutions with large-scale facilities beyond the means of individual countries. They include the high energy accelerator of the European Nuclear Research Organization (CERN) in Geneva, the very high flux reactor of the Max von Laue - Paul Langevin Institute (ILL) in Grenoble, or the European Molecular Biology Laboratory (EMBL) in Heidelberg. Germany is also involved in space research through the European Space Agency in Paris.

She also attaches great importance to the research and development programme of the European Community. She contributes also to the EUREKA programme of European cooperation in the field of high technology. EUREKA is the outcome of a Franco-German initiative in 1985.

Research policy. Research in Germany is determined by the freedom of teaching and research as anchored in the Basic Law, and by the country's federal structure by which responsibility is divided between the federal and state governments. Primarily it is the scientific institutions themselves who decide what research to undertake and assess the results, especially in the field of basic research.

Every four years the Federal Government submits a research report in which it informs the public and parliament about the aims and focus of financial support for research and development. Although private companies choose their own research projects, the government can provide incentives in the form of tax concessions or grants. It can, for instance, promote large-scale pro-

A plankton sample is taken for ocean research purposes

jects which are in the public interest but are too costly for an individual company.

Literature

The oldest testimony to German literature is the Song of Hildebrand, a story about how Hildebrand has to fight and kill his son Hadubrand for honour's sake. The Song of Hildebrand was sung at court by wandering minstrels. The names of German authors began to emerge in the 12th century. They included Wolfram von Eschenbach, Walther von der Vogelweide and Gottfried von Strassburg who wrote poems and epic stories, often in the French style.

German literature has always borrowed from abroad. The humanists of the Renaissance discovered Greek and Roman literature. Martin Luther translated the Bible into the vernacular and made it accessible to all German-speaking people. He thus laid the foundation for common high German.

Not until the 17th century did writers like Martin Opitz start creating a German national literature. But it could not be kept within national confines. Its medium, the German language, was never limited by natural boundaries. Whether someone writing in German is an Austrian, Swiss or German is of little concern to the reader. The poets Rainer Maria Rilke, who was born in Prague, and Hugo von Hofmannsthal, born in Vienna, are just as much a part of German literature as the writers Robert Musil from Klagenfurt, Thomas Mann from Lübeck and Franz Kafka from Prague. And what would German literature be without the Swiss Gottfried Keller or Max Frisch, the Austrians Adalbert Stifter or Thomas Bernhard, or the lyricist Paul Celan, who was born in Romania? The works of all these authors are contributions to German literature. However, the following brief survey will largely be confined to the literature of East and West Germany.

Highlights of the past. In the 18th century, the Age of Enlightenment, Storm and Stress, Classicism and Romanticism, writers and thinkers were primarily concerned with the struggle of ideas. Later, against the backdrop of wars of liberation, they were also concerned with developing a German or cosmopolitan literature.

Gotthold Ephraim Lessing was the first to have commoners appear in a tragedy and to extol humanistic ideals. In Riga, Johann Gottfried Herder developed concepts of a new national German literature and made Shakespeare, among others, his model. Not long afterwards the "Storm and Stress" writers gathered around Johann Wolfgang von Goethe.

Goethe and Friedrich Schiller are Germany's classical writers. For half a century their ideal, a harmony of self and world, sentiment and reason, bound by a strict form, dominated German literature. The French Revolution of 1789 was a break in that very fruitful period.

The romantic poets strived after quite different ideals. Many of them were driven by patriotic sentiments. The romantics of Jena and Heidelberg renounced the ideals of the Enlightenment. They wanted not to improve the world but to spiritualize, to poeticize it. Introspection, the reverse glorification of the Middle Ages, as well as the romantic longing for national heritage competed with the desire to open up new worlds, new vistas. Thus emerged collections of folklore in the form of songs, fairy-tales and sagas by Clemens Brentano, Achim von Arnim and the brothers Grimm. The response was considerable and long-lasting. Georg Büchner incorporated fairy-tales in his ironic, realistic dramas, and Heinrich Heine's "Lorelei", the most frequently quoted German poem, is a saga of the Rhine.

But this was also the time when great works of international fame were translated into German. The translations by Ludwig Tieck and the Schlegel brothers of Shakespeare and Cervantes became very famous and provided the stimulus for many more translations of great works, from the Romance and old Nordic languages, and later from Oriental and Indian literature.

The great 19th century writers are still widely read today: Adalbert Stifter, Theodor Storm, Wilhelm Raabe, Theodor Fontane. Thomas and Heinrich Mann count among this century's greats, and works by Rainer Maria Rilke, Gottfried Benn, Hermann Hesse and Bertolt Brecht can be had in any bookshop.

During the twelve-year nazi dictatorship many German authors went into exile. Whilst in Marseilles, Anna Seghers described in "Transit" how people persecuted by the nazi regime desperately tried to flee Europe. In Denmark Bertolt Brecht complained about the "Dark Times" (Finstere Zeiten), and Thomas Mann wrote his "Doktor Faustus" in the United States. Only a few writers (including Gottfried Benn, Hans Carossa, Ernst and Friedrich Georg Jünger, Erich Kästner and Ernst Wiechert) stuck it out in the "Internal Emigration", some of them being banned from writing or producing material that was non-commital.

The new beginning after 1945. After the Second World War German writers made a fresh start. They first tried to fill the vacuum with works in the foreign mould. They tried Hemingway's neo-realism and Jean-Paul Sartre's existentialism. One spoke of "Trümmerliteratur" (literature of the ruins) and of "Zero Hour" literature.

The most radical example is "Draussen vor der Tür" (Outside the Door) which the author himself, Wolfgang Borchert, described as "a play which no theatre wants to stage and no public wants to see". This, like other works of that period, reflects the author's strong political commitment. Writers like Günter Eich, Peter Huchel or Hans Erich Nossack considered it their task to influence politics by literary means.

In the 50s and early 60s this attitude largely gave way to a different approach. Some authors criticized society on moral grounds. Their uneasiness about the negative aspects of the economic upswing, about the egotism and materialism of the affluent society, found articulation, for example, in novels like "Das Treibhaus" (The Greenhouse) by Wolfgang Koeppen or "Billard um halb zehn" (Billiards at Nine-thirty) by Heinrich Böll, whose short stories, too, deal with the legacy of National Socialism, a theme which dominated German literature in the 50s and 60s, as in Alfred Andersch's "Sansibar oder der letzte Grund" (Zanzibar or the Abyss) or the "Blechtrommel" (The Tin Drum) by Günter Grass.

Many writers began to reflect on the artistic essence of literature (Uwe Johnson, Peter Härtling) and the language became a subject in itself. They spoke of the "reprivatization" of literature. The most prominent German playwrights of that era were the Swiss Friedrich Dürrenmatt "Der Besuch der alten Dame" (Visit from an Old Lady), "Die Physiker" (The Physicists) and Max Frisch ("Andorra").

The late 60s. The new turning-point came in the late 60s. Literature focused on its social function. The stimulus was provided above all by the student movement of that period (the "68ers"). Literature was to serve the political cause. Poets (F. C. Delius, Erich Fried, Yaak Karsunke) and playwrights (Rolf Hochhuth: "Der Stellvertreter" [The Deputy]), Heinar Kipphardt: "In der Sache J. Robert Oppenheimer" [Re. J. Robert Oppenheimer]) and Peter Weiss: "Die Ermittlung" [The Investigation]) deal with contemporary topics or bring day-to-day happenings onto the stage (Martin Sperr: "Jagdszenen aus Niederbayern" [Hunting Scenes from Lower Bavaria]), (Franz Xaver Kroetz: "Wildwechsel" [Watch Out for Game]).

Many writers of the 60s, too, saw themselves as political authors, especially Heinrich Böll ("Ansichten eines Clowns" [Opinions of a Clown]); "Gruppenbild mit Dame" [Group Picture with Lady]), Günter Grass ("Hundejahre" [Dog Years]), Martin Walser ("Halbzeit" [Half

Siegfried Lenz

Martin Walser

Botho Strauß

Ulla Hahn

Heiner Müller

Christa Wolf

Time]), Siegfried Lenz ("Deutschstunde" [German Lesson]), all of them members of Group 47, a fluctuating group of writers brought together by Hans Werner Richter with the aim of "gathering together and encouraging young writers".

Uwe Johnson was the one to concern himself most with the division of Germany ("Mutmassungen über Jakob" [Conjecture about James]). Group 61, on the other hand, depicted the working world (Max von der Grün: "Irrlicht und Feuer" [Will-o'-the-Wisp and Fire]); Günter Wallraff: ("Wir brauchen dich" [We Need You]). Yet another group focus on the old principle of "L'art pour l'art" and "Concrete poetry" as a question of language per se. Prominent among them are Ernst Jandl, Friederike Mayröcker, Helmut Heisenbüttel and Franz Mon. In 1968 the "Kursbuch" (The Time-table), a literary magazine by Hans Magnus Enzensberger, proclaimed the "death of literature".

The rediscovery of the self. In the 70s many German-language authors made their personal feelings the subject of their works: Max Frisch: "Tagebuch" (Diary); Wolfgang Koeppen: "Jugend" (Youth); Thomas Bernhard: "Die Ursache" (The Cause), "Der Atem" (Breath), "Die Kälte" (The Cold); Elias Canetti: "Die gerettete Zunge" (The Rescued Tongue). Since the mid-70s there has been a separate body of women's literature - Carin Struck: "Klassenliebe" (Classroom Love); Verena Stephan: "Häutungen" (Skinnings); Brigitte Schwaiger: "Wie kommt das Salz ins Meer" (How does the Salt get into the Sea), which is still trying to establish itself. In the field of documentary literature, there is a mixture of political pretentiousness and self-reflection (Uwe Johnson: "Jahrestage" [Anniversaries]); Walter Kempowski: "Tadellöser & Wolf"; Günter Wallraff: "Ganz unten" [Right down at the bottom]).

Ordinary, day-to-day events are reflected more strongly in the lyricism (Wolf Wondratschek, Nicolas Born, Ulla Hahn) and drama of those years (Botho Strauss: "Trilogie des Wiedersehens" [The Wiedersehen Trilogy]) than in novels. But again and again there is the "flight into poetry".

In the late 80s works by the "old masters" were a pleasant change from the "production literature" of this period (newspaper articles, reviews and other ways of making a living by the pen). Heinrich Böll, who won the 1972 Nobel Prize for Literature, wrote "Frauen vor Flusslandschaft" (Women against a River Landscape) and Grass "Die Rättin" (The Female Rat).

Production literature. Johannes Mario Simmel and Willi Heinrich, Heinz G. Konsalik and Utta Danella - the number of writers of light literature in Germany is legion. The same is true of the authors of screenplays, stories for periodicals and novelettes. A man who reviews literary works with "papal authority" is Marcel Reich-Ranicki, almost a household name and a controversial figure. His reviews have "made" many of today's authors, and much of his criticism is itself literature. For in the process of distributing modern literature discussion groups on books often made up of writers reviewing the works of colleagues are still a path to literary success, although they are constantly loosing ground on account of the financial power of the big publishing monopolies as reflected in their persistent advertising of current books in the media.

Separate trend in the east. In the former GDR post-1945 writers were required to extol Soviet-style "socialist realism". Most of the works produced in the 50s were later described as "construction" literature. The subjects were land reform, distribution of large estates to refugees and farmworkers, or the redevelopment of farm holdings. The enemy-image was obvious. The good people, including the party secretary, take up the struggle with the bad people, the big landowners, the "bourgeois scholars", the disguised western agents. And of course everyone knew who was going to win.

The GDR leadership rejected any external influence on the state's literature. "Take up your pen, friend, the socialist national culture needs you!" was the slogan at the first Bitterfeld conference of 1959. The second conference, however, held in 1964, had to concede that the results had fallen far short of expectations.

In the 60s most authors still believed they could improve the political system. A kind of critical, subjective writing emerged. "Construction" literature was superseded by the "arrival" literature. Novels such as Jurek Becker's "Jakob der Lügner" (James the Liar), Hermann Kant: "Die Aula" (The Hall), the prose and poems of Johannes Bobrowski: "Levins Mühle" (Levin's Mill) and "Litauische Claviere" (Lithuanian Pianos), the stories of Franz Fühmann: "Das Judenauto" (The Jew's Car), and the plays of Peter Hack, Heiner Müller and Volker Braun caused a stir in the Federal Republic at that time. Many of them were first or only published in the Federal Republic and were instrumental in gaining recognition for the GDR as a "cultural state". Many authors returning from exile (e.g. Anna Seghers, Arnold Zweig, Johannes R. Becher) wrote books that were in line with the communist system or wrote very little at all.

Soon more or less concealed rejections of "socialist realism" began to appear. Christa Wolf coined the term "subjective authenticity" ("Nachdenken über Christa T." [Reflections on Christa

T.]). In the 70s Wolf Biermann, the singer/songwriter who had been critical of the system, was banned from appearing on stage and in 1976 was deprived of his citizenship and forced to leave the country. His courageous example was followed by others. Stefan Heym: "Der König-David-Bericht" (The King David Report), Ulrich Plenzdorf: "Die neuen Leiden des jungen W." (The New Suffering of Young W.), Franz Fühmann: "22 Tage oder Die Hälfte des Lebens" (22 Days or Half a Life), Reiner Kunze: "Die wunderbaren Jahre" (The Wonderful Years) and Günter de Bruyn: "Märkische Forschungen" (Studies in the March), criticized the GDR and its system of informers which they themselves could hardly escape. Among those who did leave East Germany were Günter Kunert, Sarah Kirsch, Reiner Kunze and Joachim Schädlich.

East German literature was faced with a crisis and began to take up subjects that had hitherto been taboo, such as utopian literature and women's topics. Indeed, some even looked at the darker side of the socialist society, such as those who had made good out of the system (Günter de Bruyn: "Neue Herrlichkeit" [New Glory]), conformists (Christoph Hein: "Der fremde Freund/Drachenblut" [The Alien Friend/Dragon's Blood]), the contradictions between rulers and ruled (Volker Braun: "Hinze-Kunze-Roman" [Tom, Dick and Harry Novel]), and real life in the GDR (Wolfgang Hilbig: "Die Weiber" [The Womenfolk]); "Alte Abdeckerei" [The Old Flaying House]).

The literary scene following German unification. The removal of the Berlin wall, which had been the subject of many novels and stories, changed life in Germany overnight and also many an artist's "view of the world". The country's reunification also marks a new phase in the nation's literary evolution. Many authors, especially from the former GDR, are still trying to come to terms with the past, also with regard to their personal lives, some of them as victims, others as fellow-travellers. For they were after all, despite their opposition, in many ways caught up in the power system.

Writers need time to digest and reproduce reality. It remains to be seen which authors from the former GDR will continue to write and how they go about it. But it will also be seen how the changed political circumstances are mirrored by West German authors as well. The reading public are full of expectancy. Never before has there been "so much beginning" as at the beginning of the 90s, in Germany and beyond. It is a time for new literary talent.

The book trade and libraries

The first book to be printed with movable type was published in Mainz in 1455. The inventor, Johannes Gutenberg, was printer and publisher in one. Thus the birth of the new technology coincided with the beginning of German book publishing and selling. For a long time the leading publishing centre was Frankfurt am Main. In the 18th century it was surpassed by Leipzig, which held the position until World War II. Now several cities share the leadership in the publishing field in the Federal Republic of Germany - Munich, Berlin, Hamburg, Stuttgart, Frankfurt, Cologne and, since 1989, Leipzig once again. In terms of book production Germany comes second to the United States. In 1990 there were over 70,000 first and new editions. Nearly 600,000 titles were available in German bookshops.

There are over 2,000 publishers in the Federal Republic. About 75 of them have an annual turnover of DM 10 million or more, but none of them dominates the market. There are also many small companies who contribute to the variety of literature available to the public. After the war book clubs attracted a wider readership. They derived their origin from the idea of "national education". One of them, the Gutenberg Book Guild (Büchergilde Gutenberg) was founded by the

Book production by field

(first and new editions 1990, old federal states)

Titles	Area	%
4,738	General	7.8
3,053	Philosophy, psychology	5.0
3,385	Religion, theology	5.5
12,978	Social sciences	21.3
3,342	Mathematics, natural sciences	5.5
8,629	Applied sciences, medicine technology	14.1
4,740	Art, art and crafts, photography, sport, games	7.8
11,563	Linguistics and literature, fiction	19.0
8,542	Geography, history	14.0

The Gutenberg monument in Mainz

trade unions. Today there are ten book clubs with about six million members. Subscription on this scale makes books cheaper.

In 1990 total turnover of books and journals came to about DM 12.7 billion, a record which was chiefly due to heavy demand from the new federal states. In statistical terms, the average price of a book in 1990 was about DM 36.60, though paperbacks are much cheaper. The book trade is the only branch of commerce in Germany still permitted to dictate retail prices. Bookshops have to sell every book at the price set by the publisher, who argues that prices have to be maintained in order to ensure that small bookshops too can make a living. This is a controversial issue.

Mergers have taken place in the book trade as well. In the 70s the smaller shops with a selling space of up to 500 sq m were in the majority. Today it is the larger bookstores that are taking over, especially in city centres. Wholesale chains from France and the United Kingdom are also acquiring a larger share of the market. Most of the 577 bookstores in the former GDR, which in the old days were run as "people's enterprises", have meanwhile been privatized. Two thirds of them have been sold in eastern Germany, the rest to buyers in the west. Many famous publishing houses who opened new establishments in the west when Germany was divided have since been reunited with their parent companies in Eastern Germany, one of these being the Reclam-Verlag.

Book Trade Association and Book Fair. The professional organization of publishers and sellers is the Börsenverein des Deutschen Buchhandels (Book Trade Association) in Frankfurt. This

In one of the big new bookstores

organization launched the Frankfurt Book Fair, which is held every autumn. Apart from the commercial side, it is also the book trade's "window on the world" and a major cultural event. Every year it has a different theme. In 1991 it was Spain. In that year nearly 8,300 publishers from 95 countries exhibited their products. The fair culminates in the award of the Peace Prize of the German Book Trade Association. Recent prizewinners are Léopold Sédar Senghor, Max Frisch, Yehudi Menuhin, Teddy Kollek, Vladislav Bartoszewski, Hans Jonas, Václav Havel and György Konrád. Germany's second most important book fair is the spring fair in Leipzig, which sees its role partly as that of intermediary with the countries of eastern Europe.

Libraries. Unlike other countries Germany has no ancient national library. It was not until 1913 that the new German Library in Leipzig brought together all German-language literature under one roof. Today that library holds 6.8 million volumes. The division of Germany after the Second World War led to the foundation of the German Library in Frankfurt am Main in 1947. It had the same function as the Leipzig library. It was founded by the book trade and since 1969 has been operated by the government. In addition to all German-language literature published since 1945, it collects the "exile literature", that is works produced between 1933 and 1945 by German writers who fled the country to escape the nazi regime. It contains 3.9 million volumes.

Gütersloh City Library

A trade magazine for book sellers

One of the country's principal libraries is the Bayerische Staatsbibliothek in Munich (5.5 million books), another the Staatsbibliothek Preussischer Kulturbesitz in Berlin (3.7 million). In addition to the general libraries (mostly state and university libraries) there are specialized libraries such as the central medical library in Cologne. A library with an outstanding reputation is the Herzog-August-Bibliothek in Wolfenbüttel, which has over 660,000 volumes, including 12,000 priceless medieval handwritten books.

In western Germany there are also 15,000 public libraries with over 30 million volumes. Most of them are owned by the local authorities and churches. In the former GDR there were about 9,500 public and union libraries. Since 1990 the latter have either been split up or converted into public libraries.

The German Book Trade Association:
Börsenverein des Deutschen Buchhandels
Grosser Hirschgraben 17—21
6000 Frankfurt am Main

The arts

When, in 1947, one of the first post-war art exhibitions opened in Augsburg under the motto "Extreme Art", it evoked little enthusiasm. The public weren't used to abstract art. Under National Socialism most schools of modern art had been declared "degenerate". This was the regime's catchword for a campaign to destroy everything in art that was too critical or too abstract. Thus the German expressionists and abstract painters were affected. Great contemporary painters such as Oskar Kokoschka (1886-1980), Max Beckmann (1884-1950) or Vassily Kandinsky (1866-1944) were taboo. In 1937 alone, 1,052 paintings were confiscated from German galleries. As a result, German artists lost touch with international trends.

Developments since 1945. After the Second World War the gap was closed with remarkable speed. Painting followed pre-war trends and owed much to Paul Klee (1879-1940) and Vassily Kandinsky, who had already moved towards abstract art before the First World War. Also still alive were the great "degenerate" artists Oskar Kokoschka, Max Beckmann, Max Pechstein (1881-1955), Emil Nolde (1876-1956), Erich Heckel (1883-1970) and Karl Schmidt-Rottluff (1884-1976). Their task was to bring back the modern art that already seemed almost history. The abstract expressionism which evolved in France under the influence of the Germans Wols (Wolfgang Schulze, 1913-51) and Hans Hartung (1904-67) established itself. Its main exponents were Willi Baumeister (1889-1955), Ernst Wilhelm Nay (1902-68) and Fritz Winter (1905-76).

In the early 60s the Düsseldorf group "Zero" proclaimed a new beginning. It was in the Op-Art category, which had its roots in, among other things, the experimental tradition of Bauhaus. The best-known members of this group are Otto Piene (born 1928), Günther Uecker (born 1930) and Heinz Mack (born 1931). They did not regard art as a platform of pathetic humanity but turned to natural phenomena - light, movement and space. They directed attention to the objective, technologically influenced environment and its significance to mankind. This aim is apparent in the fire and smoke pictures of Piene, Uecker's nail pictures and Mack's light steles and dynamos.

The Pop-Art which came from the United Kingdom and the United States found little response in Germany, while "Signal Art" and Hard-Edge painting were taken up by Günter Fruhtrunk (1923-82), Karl Georg Pfahler (born 1926) and Winfred Gaul (born 1928) and became very popular.

Thus whereas artists in the Federal Republic were able to follow existing traditions and draw on new currents flowing from western Europe and the United States, their colleagues in the former GDR were tied to the "socialist realism" prescribed for them. They were permitted to do nothing more than portrait a favourable picture of the socialist society and its kind of people. Until the late 60s the artistic creation promoted by the regime's functionaries was predominantly a description of working life under the socialist system.

New trends in painting came mainly from the Leipzig Academy of Art. Among its best-known artists were Werner Tübke (born 1929) and Bernhard Heisig (born 1925), whose monumental paintings, though still tied to historical or social themes, shed the sterility of the 50s and 60s. Wolfgang Mattheuer (born 1927), also a member of the Leipzig Academy, went much further in his efforts to derive more out of realistic painting. His pictures, such as Snow White as the Statue of Liberty are more a synthesis of post-expressionist new objectivity and "magic realism" than a testimony to socialist realism. A. R. Penck (born 1939) chose as his theme idols of the Stone Age. The works of these painters were very much in demand by western galleries in the late 70s.

The artists of today. "Informel", new in the 50s, is still not yet outmoded. It turned visual art into action, used new, unusual materials. Paint was applied thickly, and sometimes the artist departed from the traditional rectangular shape. The result was "happenings", "critical realism", the "New Wild Ones" who lived life to the full in neo-expressionism. There were also light displays, rotating elements, collages, posters, and above all action art, which usually takes place outside the artist's studio.

Joseph Beuys (1921-86) set the trend. He no longer attached importance to "immortal" works but staged art as action. For instance, he had himself taken across the river Rhine in a dugout. He spared no expense to "bring art to society". HA Schult, the action artist from Cologne, also has a liking for the spectacular. His action theme is "fetish car", to the amusement of the general public. In Cologne, for instance, he had a car monument raised onto a medieval tower. Action of this kind is also appreciated by the American Jonathan

HA Schult's "car fetish" in Cologne

Borofsky, who in Germany likes to decorate the "city as an artistic space" with moving objects. One of his works is the "Hammering Man", a black giant with a slow hammering motion, to be seen in front of the exhibition hall in Frankfurt on the Main.

Anselm Kiefer before one of his "pictorial objects"

At present there is a trend towards mammoth objects, though there is still considerable variety. Anselm Kiefer (born 1945) shapes massive works of art in his studios, which are like shop floors in factories. They are made mostly of lead but also include aircraft in their original size. "Zweistromland" is the name of a 32-ton sculpture consisting of 200 books made of lead on shelves eight metres long. He calls his pictures, many of which are inspired by mythology, "picture bodies" because he attaches various materials to them such as dust, flower petals, ash or roots.

But between action art, the giant silhouettes in the townscape, and Kiefer's lead objects, there are in Germany countless types of artistic experiment in which the artists are prepared to try any form, any material. There is much arte povera and realistic, surrealistic or

Borofsky's "Hammering Man" at the Frankfurt Trade Fair Centre

13. 6. — 20. 9. **KASSEL** 1992

DOCUMENTA IX

Poster for Documenta 1992 in Kassel

expressionistic elements. Rebecca Horn (born 1944) presents sculptures as "performances" and uses them in her own films. Gerhard Richter (born 1932) is a master of ambiguity on the border between abstract and non-abstract art. Georg Baselitz (born 1938), who has won many awards and has an international reputation, expresses in his upside-down pictures the misery of the human creature. Sigmar Polke (born 1941) represents the occult trend but also enjoys practical jokes: "Dürer will be here in a moment", is the name of one of his objects. Huge dolomite blocks and the Heinrich Heine monument in Bonn bear the signature of Ulrich Rückriem (born 1938). Günter Uecker today celebrates the "poetry of destruction". Jörg Immendorf (born 1945) is a kind of modern historical painter. In his picture "Café Deutschland" the storm of history blows the Berlin wall away.

Galleries and exhibitions. Most works of art are to be found in the museums and galleries of the big cities. Painters like Max Ernst, Otto Dix, Chagall, Picasso, Dalí and other "classic artists" still draw visitors in their thousands. Avant-garde works are particularly prominent in Cologne and Düsseldorf, home to the most experimental artists. In Berlin the Grisebach auction centre is on the way to becoming as famous as Sotheby's in London.

The most spectacular exhibition is the "documenta" which takes place in Kassel every five years. At this "international exhibition of contemporary art" the avant-garde are on display for 100 days, shocking, provoking or amusing some half a million visitors.

Beethoven sculpture "Beethon" by Klaus Kammerichs
outside the Beethoven Hall in Bonn

Promotion of the arts. Few painters and sculptors can live on the proceeds from the works they have sold. They receive government grants and assistance from private companies. The "Kunstfonds e.V.", founded in 1980, helps recognized artists finance ambitious projects. The fund has DM 1.7 million a year for artistic purposes. Of this amount DM 1.3 million is provided by the Federal Government, the other DM 400,000 coming from publications on contemporary art.

Well-known places of cultural activity are the artists colony at Worpswede in northern Germany, the Villa Massimo and the Villa Romana in Italy. At these centres scholarship holders can work without disturbance and free from financial worry. Industry, too, promotes art. For over 40 years the cultural section of the Federation of German Industry, for instance, has been awarding prizes to painters and sculptors.

"Art on buildings" is also encouraged. It is now normal for companies to set aside 1% of their building costs for artistic decoration. As a result one sees paintings in the corridors of high-rise buildings of large banks, and action artists leave their stamp in front of the buildings of government departments or private companies.

Architecture

German architects of the 20th century have been trend-setters. This applies especially to Walter Gropius (1883-1969) and Ludwig Mies van der Rohe (1886-1969), two of the leading figures of the Bauhaus style of the 20s, whose functional approach won worldwide recognition. Masterpieces of this synthesis of art and technology are to be seen on all continents.

For a long time the situation after 1945 was a great disadvantage. The destroyed towns and cities had to be redeveloped and cheap housing was needed for millions of people. In those days little consideration could be given to architectural quality. In later years there were bitter complaints about the monotonous architecture of satellite townships and the dull fronts of department stores and administrative buildings. This was particularly true of the former GDR. There valuable old buildings were destroyed and scarce resources used to build massive housing estates, all constructed in the same prefabricated mould.

Today architects are experimenting more and more but at the same time providing buildings that meet human needs. While the success of many projects is still attributable to the Bauhaus style and philosophy, new trends, such as the post-modern, have produced some remarkable buildings. German architects are also gaining prominence abroad with their bold designs, for instance Helmut Jahn, who is based in Chicago, a city of modern, high-rise buildings. He built the 254-meter high tower at Frankfurt's exhibition site.

Outstanding structures. Germany has some fine examples of prestige building. The skeleton high-rise, all-glass construction type, as exemplified by Mies van der Rohe's Seagram building in New York, found variance in the Federal Republic in the three-sectional Thyssen House in Düsseldorf (built by Helmut Hentrich, 1960) and the administration building of the Hamburg Electricity Works (Arne Jacobsen and Otto Weitling, 1969).

An example of unconventional, dynamic architecture is the central office of the BMW car-making firm in Munich, with its striking cylindrical form (Karl Schwanzer, 1972), or the Bahlsen biscuit fac-

The Art and Crafts Museum in Frankfurt am Main

tory in Hanover with its interlocking cubist forms (Dieter Bahlo, Jörn Köhnke, Klaus Stosberg, 1974).

Another striking landmark is Stuttgart's television tower with restaurant and observation platform (Fritz Leonhardt, 1956). The tent-like structures (Günter Behnisch, 1972) designed for the 1972 Olympic Games in Munich has become world famous. The sports facilities are situated in a park which continues to be a popular area for leisure pursuits.

Original ideas have also materialized in cultural buildings in the narrower sense. The most famous of these are Berlin's new Philharmonie by Hans Scharoun (1964) with its vineyard-like terraced auditorium constructed around the centrally placed orchestra. Münster's Stadttheater, on the other hand, incorporates a classical ruin. Stuttgart's Liederhalle and Mannheim's multi-purpose hall at Herzogenriedpark are fine examples of assembly hall architecture.

Museums which integrate well into the local townscape were built by Hans Hollein in Mönchengladbach (1982) and Gottfried Haberer, who created Cologne's Wallraff-Richartz-Museum/Museum Ludwig (1986). James Stirling's Neue Staatsgalerie in Stuttgart has also been received with much acclaim (1983). Another outstanding piece of architecture is the new Museum für Kunsthandwerk (Arts and Crafts Museum) in Frankfurt am Main, which was designed by Richard Meier (1985). University buildings, too, reveal some interesting examples, for instance the University of Constance, whose buildings fit asymmetrically into the terrain. And the Filderklinik in Filderstadt near Stuttgart demonstrates how a hospital can be organically merged with the landscape.

Many churches, too, have been built in Germany since the Second World War. The architects had plenty of scope for experimentation. Worthy of mention are Berlin's Memorial Church (Gedächtniskirche), which had been destroyed during the war. Egon Eiermann fused the old ruin with a new steel construction with large glass sections (1963). Also outstanding is the fortress-like pilgrimage church at Neviges by Gottfried Böhm (1967).

Urban planning. Present-day architecture must also make allowance for the needs of urban planning. During the reconstruction phase in Germany much historical substance was sacrificed. Old

The restored Saarbrücken Castle with its new middle tract

A modern religious building: the Church of Reconciliation in Kaiserslautern

residential buildings, from the late 19th century, for instance, were not considered worth preserving. But in the meantime people's attitudes have changed. The historical value of buildings is now appreciated. New buildings are integrated as far as possible into the local environment, the utility structures of department stores built in the 50s and 60s are no longer wanted. A greater awareness for the natural growth of town centres is reflected, for instance, in the Schneider department store in Freiburg (Heinz Mohl, 1976) or Würzburg's Kaufhaus by Alexander von Branca. The "Alte Oper" in Frankfurt on the Main is a magnificent building from the late 19th century. Its exterior was completely reconstructed in 1981 and it now houses an ultra-modern concert hall and congress centre.

More and more houses and groups of old or historical buildings as well as entire streets are being listed as protected objects. This also applies to industrial buildings such as the foundry in Bendorf on the Rhine or the pithead tower in the German Mining Museum in Bochum. The city has begun renovating the old houses in the centre. This will provide additional accommodation and is in keeping with the current trend of encouraging people from the outskirts back into the city.

The task of urban redevelopment will continue for long time, especially in town centres in the former GDR. In that part of the country there is much building substance worth preserving in the historical quarters, which are in a state of decay through decades of neglect.

Museums, collections, exhibitions

There are more than 3,000 museums in the Federal Republic of Germany: state, municipal, association and private museums, museums of church and cathedral treasures, residential, castle, palace and outdoor museums. They have grown up over the centuries out of royal, church, and later civic collections.

Princely collections were, of course, not intended for the erudition of the general public. Their owners wanted to show admiring visitors all their wonderful possessions. In Munich, for instance, which was an international art centre as early as the 16th century, Bavarian dukes collected not only works of art but also machinery, craftsmen's tools, musical instruments, minerals and exotic objects from distant lands. The "Grünes Gewölbe" of the Saxon electors of Dresden was probably the largest treasure house in Europe in the 17th century. It eventually became an art gallery, but also a mathematics and physics museum and a minerology museum.

Not only rulers but many wealthy citizens had private collections. As a result, there was a museum in Germany for all fields of art, all types of activity. Every large museum tried to display as much as possible and in many cases there was fruitful competition. Nearly everything was exhibited: from Rembrandt and Picasso to tapestries (Kassel), from wine-making equipment (Koblenz) to meteorites (Marburg), from mummies from the moors (Schleswig) to optical instruments (Oberkochen) or the oldest boat in the world reconstructed from original parts (Bremerhaven).

Art lovers and patrons. German museums of today have lost their oft-criticized pseudo-religious character. The educational mission which museums used to carry out very rigidly is now fulfilled in many cases by means of the living experience, and to this end the museums are equipped with video equipment and have cafeterias and very light rooms. The museum becomes a place of contact and discussion and the exhibits are related to the present. The result is that Germans today visit the museum as casually as they used to go to a cinema.

Year in, year out over 100 million people visit Germany's museums, which in some cities occupy a whole district. Examples are the Main embankment in Frankfurt, or Berlin, where the Stiftung Preussischer Kulturbesitz (Foundation for Prussian Cultural Property), established in 1951, can fill whole museums with its collections from Prussian days.

As in former times, wealthy private citizens are partly responsible for the museum boom through their sponsorship. Peter Ludwig, a businessman in the Rhineland, is one of the best-known. He supports mainly modern art galleries up and down the country. The latest to receive his help is the Ludwig-Forum in Aachen, a former umbrella factory which also puts on exhibitions of art from the former GDR.

Several other museums are under construction. One of them is the Haus der Geschichte der Bundesrepublik Deutschland (Centre for the History of the Federal Republic of Germany) in Bonn, while in Berlin the Deutsches Historisches Museum (German Historical Museum) presents German history in its entirety right up to the present time.

An important role is played by art and anthropological museums on account of the broad range of their displays. The Deutsches Museum in Munich, for instance, has originals and models depicting the development of technology and science, while the Germanisches Nationalmuseum in Nuremberg has the largest collection on the

The work table of Otto Hahn in the German Museum in Munich

*An item on display at the "Jewish Worlds" exhibition
in the Gropiusbau, Berlin*

history of German art and culture from prehistory to the 20th century. Also unique is the large number of ethnological museums in a country which was only briefly a colonial power but nevertheless produced many outstanding discoverers and scholars who were concerned with foreign cultures. In addition to the Berlin museums, the Linden-Museum in Stuttgart deserves special mention in this respect.

The Pergamon altar in the Pergamon Museum, Berlin

Special exhibitions are increasingly in demand. Those held in 1989 alone drew 4.2 million visitors. On such occasions the museums and galleries can draw on their extensive stocks. Historical exhibitions such as "Die Welt der Staufer" commemorating the medieval imperial Hohenstaufen dynasty, held in Stuttgart in 1977, or "Preussen - Versuch einer Bilanz" (Prussia - An Appraisal), which took place in Berlin in 1981, arouse considerable interest. Also extremely popular were comprehensive retrospectives such as the Darmstadt Jugendstil (Art Nouveau) exhibition "Ein Dokument deutscher Kunst" (1976).

It has also been possible to bring major international itinerant exhibitions to Germany, such as the Tutenchamun exhibition and a display of treasures from San Marco in Venice. Art from non-European countries attracts considerable interest in Germany. The exhibition "Die Frau im alten Ägypten" (Women of Ancient Egypt) attracted 250,000 visitors to Cologne. The city of Aachen presented "Vergessene Städte am Indus" (Forgotten Cities on the Indus), and Munich staged an exhibition of Mongolian culture.

The largest festival of modern art in the world is Kassel's "documenta", which takes place every five years and draws up to half a million visitors.

Museum variety. The broad regional distribution of Germany's museums makes them accessible to large numbers of people. There is no central government "museum policy", but museums cooperate with one another in many fields, such as restoration and museum security, central documentation and research. Such activities are coordinated by the Deutscher Museumsbund (German Museums Association), which was established in 1917 and embraces all German museums. A similar task is performed by the Institut für Museumskunde of the State Museums of Prussian Cultural Property in Berlin.

Museum architecture, too, shows great variety, ranging from the 19th century art "temples" to such ultra-modern buildings as the Neue Staatsgalerie in Stuttgart or the Architekturmuseum (Museum of Architecture) in Frankfurt am Main. Many museums were destroyed during the Second World War, but their collections were stored in safe places. There are still traces of war damage. It took over 30 years to rebuild Munich's Neue Pinakothek.

Major museums

Art
Aachen: Domschatzkammer, Neue Galerie
Berlin: Staatliche Museen Preussischer Kulturbesitz, darunter
   Gemäldegalerie und Nationalgalerie
Bonn: Städtische Kunstsammlungen
Braunschweig: Herzog-Anton-Ulrich-Museum
Dessau: Bauhaus-Archiv
Dresden: Gemäldegalerie Alte und Neue Meister, "Grünes Gewölbe"
Essen: Museum Folkwang
Frankfurt am Main: Städelsches Kunstinstitut, Museum für moderne
   Kunst
Hamburg: Kunsthalle
Hanover: Niedersächsisches Landesmuseum, Kestner-Museum
Hildesheim: Roemer-Pelizaeus-Museum
Karlsruhe: Staatliche Kunstsammlungen
Kassel: Staatliche Kunstsammlungen
Cologne: Wallraf-Richartz-Museum/Museum Ludwig
Leipzig: Museum der Bildenden Künste
Munich: Alte Pinakothek, Neue Pinakothek
Regensburg: Museum Ostdeutsche Galerie
Stuttgart: Staatsgalerie

Cultural history
Bonn: Rheinisches Landesmuseum
Cologne: Römisch-Germanisches Museum
Mainz: Gutenberg-Museum; Römisch-Germanisches
    Zentralmuseum
Munich: Bayerisches Nationalmuseum
Nuremberg: Germanisches Nationalmuseum
Würzburg: Mainfränkisches Museum

Science and technology
Berlin: Museum für Technik und Verkehr
Bochum: Deutsches Bergbau-Museum
Bonn: Zoologisches Forschungsinstitut und Museum Alexander
    Koenig
Braunschweig: Staatliches Naturhistorisches Museum
Bremerhaven: Deutsches Schiffahrtsmuseum
Dortmund: Museum für Naturkunde
Frankfurt am Main: Naturmuseum und Forschungsinstitut Sencken-
    berg
Mannheim: Museum für Technik und Arbeit
Munich: Deutsches Museum
Stuttgart: Staatliches Museum für Naturkunde

Anthropology
In: Berlin, Frankfurt, Göttingen, Hamburg, Kiel, Cologne, Lübeck,
    Munich and Stuttgart.

Music

From Beethoven to Stockhausen, from Claudio Abbado to Udo Lindenberg, from the Magic Flute to Cats, from the huge concert hall to concerts in the barn - music is always in the air and always on offer all over Germany. Most cities have orchestras and opera houses of their own. And even provincial towns offer high-standard performances. Over 100 local and regional music festivals are held on a regular, usually annual, basis. Conductors, orchestras and soloists from all over the world appreciate the music scene in Germany, which is very prone to experimentation.

Opera houses and orchestras. In united Germany there are 95 government-sponsored opera houses and concert halls and 195 professional orchestras. The country's oldest opera house is in Hamburg, having been built in 1678. The most modern are in Cologne and Frankfurt am Main. Berlin has three opera houses. Among the most beautiful are the Nationaltheater in Munich and the Semper-Oper in Dresden, both of which were built in the Italian renaissance style. The leading orchestra is the Berlin Philharmonic Orchestra, the "masters of perfect sound". But others with international names are the Munich Philharmonic Orchestra, the Bamberg Symphony Orchestra, the Leipzig Gewandhaus Orchestra, Dresden's Staatskapelle, and several radio symphony orchestras.

Conductors and soloists. In Germany there is a regular exchange of international artists and promising new names. Concerts and opera performances are often studied with stars from all over the world. The Berlin Philharmonic Orchestra is conducted by the Italian Claudio Abbado, successor to Herbert von Karajan, who died in 1989. Conversely, German conductors have engagements in many foreign countries. One of them, Kurt Masur, is conductor of the New York Philharmonic Orchestra, while Christoph von Dohnányi is chief conductor of the Cleveland Orchestra. German soloists such as the violinist Anne-Sophie Mutter, singers such as Hildegard Behrens, Dietrich Fischer-Dieskau, Peter Hofmann, René Kollo, Peter

Schreier, Hermann Prey and Edda Moser count among the best in the world.

The repertoire. The great classical works are popular in many parts of the country. There are also traditional festivals devoted to the works of individual composers, such as Ludwig van Beethoven (whose birthplace in Bonn attracts visitors from all over the world) or Georg Friedrich Händel. The Wagner Festival in Bayreuth is still a major attraction. Helmut Rilling, founder and director of the Gäching Choir and of the "International Bach Academy", as well as several ensembles in Leipzig, specialize in the works of Johann Sebastian Bach.

The world of ballet in Germany experienced a "miracle" in the 60s. This was due above all to the outstanding work of the South African John Cranko with the Stuttgart State Ballet, whose current director and prima ballerina is Marcia Haydée. The name Pina Bausch and her Wuppertal Tanztheater, too, stands for outstanding ballet productions. One of the traditional centres of musical review is the Friedrichstadtpalast in Berlin.

There are also regular programmes of works by modern classical

Main Concert Hall in the Neues Gewandhaus, Leipzig

Kurt Masur conducts the New York Philharmonic Orchestra

composers such as Paul Hindemith, Igor Stravinsky, Arnold Schönberg and Béla Bartók, as well as Boris Blacher, Wolfgang Fortner, Werner Egk and Carl Orff who, with his world famous "Schulwerk", encouraged children to take up music. Bernd Alois Zimmermann, an audacious avant-gardist, established his place in musical history with his opera "Die Soldaten".

Today's composers try to win public support for music outside the realm of familiar harmony by using the most unusual effects in large theatres. In 1990, Hans Werner Henze offered a kind of wild action theatre with his opera "Das verratene Meer" (The Betrayed Sea) based on the novel by the Japanese writer Yukio Mishima. Aribert Reimann, who experiments with cords of 20, 30 and more notes, presented his opera "Lear" in Munich as a ghastly psychodrama. Karlheinz Stockhausen stages visionary opera in Wagnerian dimensions. Mauricio Kagel, an Argentinian living in Cologne and for

Rock and pop: the singer Udo Lindenberg

many years a leading composer in Germany, regards himself as a "complete art maker" in that he uses his body as a musical instrument. The American John Cage has obtained his music from computers, and Wolfgang Rihm used sheet metal and drums in his "Oedipus".

The fact that less spectacular contemporary music has also received attention is to be attributed chiefly to the broadcasting networks, who include in their programmes concerts of works by modern composers and also commission works. Workshop performances, too, have helped to promote modern music. The best-known among them are the "Donaueschinger Musiktage" and the "Internationale Ferienkurse für Neue Musik" in Darmstadt.

"German Kraut Rock". Jazz, Rock and Pop received little attention in Germany until "German Kraut Rock" came along as the "New German Wave" with often scurrilous songs and German lyrics. Nina Hagen, the punk singer with the shrill voice, and Udo Lindenberg with his "Panic Orchestra", attracted a considerable following. The

German jazz scene, which in the 50s was more of a protest movement, now has musicians of stature: the trombonist Albert Mangelsdorff is one of the best exponents of Free Jazz. Klaus Doldinger tries to link up rock and jazz with his group known as "Passport". And the Cologne group BAP are conspicuous for their dialect songs.

By comparison, German pop singers are underrepresented. Dance orchestras like those of Bert Kaempfert, James Last, Max Greger and Paul Kuhn won international fame. Other singers who have gained prominence are Peter Maffay and Marius Müller-Westernhagen. Then there are the singer-songwriters Franz Joseph Degenhardt, Wolf Biermann and Hannes Wader, each of them with his own original style.

Music for all. There are various competitions to promote young talented musicians. The best-known among them is "Jugend musiziert" (Youngsters Make Music). Music is also greatly encouraged at school. In western Germany alone there are over 700 public music schools as well as about 15,000 choirs. Nearly every second German child plays a musical instrument, the principal ones being the flute and guitar. Listening to music is much more popular with the younger generation than watching television. The music branch is flourishing. Every year over 200 million records, cassettes and CDs are sold in Germany. Only the United States can boast of more.

Theatre

Berlin, Munich and Hamburg especially are cities which haven't been "seen" unless one has been to the theatre. Germany has 30 of them, including the "Deutsches Theater" and the "Schiller-Theater". But other cities too have remarkable repertoires. Bochum is a good address for those who prefer the unusual, and Mannheim comes to mind because it produces the most plays.

Germany has no "theatrical capital" which attracts all the best talents. This makes for a highly varied theatrical landscape. There is plenty of theatre in the provinces, too: in Veitshöchheim or Memmingen in Bavaria, in Massbach in Franconia, or Meiningen in Thuringia. This variety is traditional. In the 17th and 18th centuries many of the sovereign German princes set up splendid court theatres in their capitals. In the 19th century many towns and cities, having acquired more civic rights, made the theatre a public institution. And that is more or less how the situation has remained to this day.

Monument to Goethe and Schiller
in front of the German National Theatre in Weimar

Ballet in Hanover-Herrenhausen

The theatres. Every season Germany's theatres are subsidized to the tune of over two billion marks or the equivalent of about DM 100 for each ticket. Most public support goes to the state or municipal theatres, but most private ensembles can also expect some financial support. Very few of the 420 German theatre companies could survive without subsidies. Public funding is meeting with growing criticism, however, partly on account of the great cost of rebuilding East Germany's economy. Most of the 67 theatres in the former GDR are in a poor state and badly equipped. On top of that the staff are generally too old.

Drastic economies and closures can hardly be avoided. In view of this situation many producers are looking for new sources of finance, and this applies not only to companies in eastern Germany. Whereas in the past art and commerce were strictly separated, theatre directors court industrial sponsors - as indeed do those responsible for production in other branches of art.

Theatre-goers. The theatre is extremly popular in Germany, especially among the older generation. In the 1989/90 season some 34 million people attended plays and festivals. These include six million who attended non-subsidized musical productions in Bochum and Hamburg. The theatres have a subscription system which enables theatre lovers to buy tickets for ten or twelve plays, operas or concerts etc. in advance. This saves them the trouble of queuing at the box office.

"Thinking in images": director Peter Stein

Dramatists. German theatres have a preference for classical works, often in bold modern or politicized productions. Extremly popular are the major German comedies, especially Kleist's "Der zerbrochene Krug", which was seen by over 125,000 in the 1989/90 season. Not far behind are Brecht and Shakespeare. Most in demand among Brecht's works is the "Dreigroschenoper", while "Hamlet" and "King Lear" lead for Shakespeare.

Contemporary playwrights are not nearly so popular, but some have aroused feeling among theatre-goers. One of them, Rolf Hochhuth, has dealt with controversial subjects in such plays as "Stellvertreter" (The Deputy) written in 1964. And Harald Mueller, with his "Totenfloss", written after the Chernobyl disaster of 1986, develops a daunting apocalyptical scenario. Tankred Dorst, who in 1990 was awarded the Georg Büchner Prize (one of the most highly esteemed literary prizes in Germany), wrote a psychological narrative play with his "Deutsche Trilogie". Heiner Müller takes his themes from historical disasters. Botho Strauss depicts the upper middle class, often with a mythical strangeness. Klaus Pohl, on the other hand, has supplied the theatre with murder stories. Since Brecht, Franz Xaver Kroetz, author, director and actor, is the most popular German dramatist worldwide. He has written about 40 plays, most of which take a critical look at society. They have been translated into more than 40 languages.

The producers. In many cases the real theatre stars are the producers. Many of them seek to provoke the public. They leave hardly any classical play as the author wrote it. Some of them claim that their productions are their own work, which led someone to coin the term "producer theatre". Names like Jürgen Flimm, Klaus Michael Grüber, Peter Zadek, Luc Bondy and Robert Wilson fall into this category. Peter Stein is the man who invented "Thinking in Pictures". The suggestive imagery of his productions have been impressing critics and audiences alike since the early 80s. Indeed, his production of Anton Chekov's "Drei Schwestern" (Three Sisters) was shown in Moscow. Today Stein produces in Paris, Milan and London, but he regularly returns to Berlin and to some of the smaller German theatres.

Cinema

German films once enjoyed world fame. That was mainly in the 20s and 30s when Fritz Lang, Ernst Lubitsch and Friedrich Wilhelm Murnau were at their best. In those days half the world loved Marlene Dietrich and the Blue Angel. But the nazi regime ended it all. Most of the great directors and many actors went into exile. The legendary Ufa film company lost its artistic vitality and was eventually reduced to the level of making nazi propaganda films.

After the war German film makers had difficulty catching up with the rest of the world. And today they are also having to struggle in the face of powerful competition in the form of television, which is siphoning off not only cinema-goers but also directors and actors. Expensive Hollywood films dominate most cinema programmes. Foreign productions also benefit from the fact that foreign-language films are nearly always dubbed in German.

This makes life difficult for the German film industry, but there have been notable exceptions such as Doris Dörrie's "Männer" (Men) and Wolfgang Petersen's war film "Das Boot" (The Boat), and films of high artistic standard are appearing regularly, largely due to heavy government subsidies and support from television, which occasionally cofinances feature films.

Cinemas and cinema-goers. Germany's cinemas were most popular in the 50s when television was still in its infancy. In those days over 800 million people a year went to the cinema. Today it's hardly 100 million, 70% of whom are between 15 and 30. The biggest attractions are the mammoth Hollywood productions, which in 1990 cornered 84% of the German market. German films had to be content with no more than 9%.

In 1990 Germany's 3,754 cinemas had a turnover of over DM 351 million in a highly competitive market. In the second half of the 80s alone, 450 independent cinemas went bankrupt. Competition from television is growing constantly. Ever more feature films are being televized, a fact which is making the private networks increasingly popular. It is not yet possible to say what effect the huge growth of cable and satellite television, video productions and pay-TV, will have on

A new "Cinedrome" in Cologne

the cinema. One of the aims of government promotion is to give cinemas a fair crack of the whip in this highly competitive branch of industry.

Of late, however, international cinema groups have been coming to the fore which hoped to achieve a renaissance of the cinema in Germany. They are reversing the trend towards the small studio type of cinema and building the huge palaces of former times. The new supercinemas containing sometimes more than a dozen cinemas, restaurants, offices and shops, all under one roof, are designed to attract new cinema goers. Projects of this kind are scheduled for Berlin, Frankfurt am Main, Dresden and Leipzig. The Hollywood firm of United Cinemas International, the largest cinema chain in the world, intends to build 40 of these Cinedoms in Germany.

Germany's young film makers. In the 60s and 70s the film industry in West Germany experienced a revival. Directors in the former GDR were forced by the regime to glorify life under socialism. Despite this some of them produced interesting films. Young directors in the Federal Republic had a much easier time. Having tired of the timid comedies and folklore films, they produced a series of remarkable films with financial support from the Federal Ministry of the Interior. Alexander Kluge, for instance, in his film "Abschied von gestern" (Farewell to yesterday), skilfully mixed fiction with documentary material. Werner Herzog, in "Jeder für sich, Gott gegen alle" (Every man for himself, God against all), sensitively depicted the life and suffering of the enigmatic foundling Kaspar Hauser. Bernhard Sinkel and Alf Brustellin directed "Lina Braake", perhaps the best comedy of the new German films. Rainer Werner Fassbinder provided impressive insights into German society with films like "Katzelmacher", "Die Ehe der Maria Braun" and that big Berlin story "Berlin Alexanderplatz". In only 13 years Fassbinder, who died in 1982, produced 41 television series and films, including "Die Sehnsucht der Veronika Voss", for which he received the Golden Bear at the Berlin festival in 1982. And it was Fassbinder's films in particular that made the Munich actress Hanna Schygulla an international star.

These early commercial successes inspired unusual productions. Wim Wenders (born 1945) described taciturn heroes in films like "Paris, Texas" or "Der Stand der Dinge", for which he was awarded the Golden Palm at the Cannes film festival of 1982 and the Federal Film Prize in 1983. In 1988 he surprised the film world with his "Der Himmel über Berlin" (Heaven over Berlin), in which an angel in Berlin falls in love with a trapeze artist. This film, which won the Federal Film

SAM SHEPARD
HOMO FABER
EIN VOLKER SCHLÖNDORFF FILM
Nach dem Roman von Max Frisch

Scene from Schlöndorff's "Homo Faber"

Prize and then the prize for best director at the Cannes festival, was also a success in Japan.

The actress Margarete von Trotta attracted attention through her portrayal of famous women. "Rosa Luxemburg" is regarded as her best film. Werner Herzog (born 1942) offered exciting action films with unusual heroes, subjects and locations. At the Cannes festival Herzog won the prize for best director for his film "Fitzcarraldo", the story of a fanatic opera fan bent on building an opera house in the jungle.

Filmed literature. German directors are particularly ambitious and often successful as well when it comes to filming major literary works. The best among them is Volker Schlöndorff (born 1939). He filmed Robert Musil's "Der junge Törless" and Heinrich Böll's "Die verlorene Ehre der Katharina Blum". For his adaptation of Günter Grass' bestseller "Die Blechtrommel" (The Tin Drum) Schlöndorff received the Golden Palm at the Cannes film festival of 1979. And in 1980 the Blechtrommel was awarded an Oscar as the best foreign film.

Novels are still greatly valued as material for films. Petersen's world success "Das Boot" was based on the novel of the same name by Lothar Günther Buchheim. Doris Dörrie, currently Germany's best-known woman director, based her "Ich und Er" (Me and Him) on Alberto Moravia's novel, whereas Schlöndorff brought Arthur Miller's "Death of a Salesman" and Margaret Atwood's "The Story of a Servant" to the big screen. His adaptation of Max Frisch's novel "Homo

Scene from "Herbstmilch" by Joseph Vilsmaier

Faber" with Tom Shepard in the main roll was particularly successful. For this film he received the Silver Film Band in Berlin.

The Golden Film Band went to another literary film in the same year: "Malina" by Werner Schroeter. With the French actress Isabelle Huppert in the title roll, it is a story of self-destruction and is based on a coded autobiography by the Austrian writer Ingeborg Bachmann. A model example of the new realism local culture film is "Herbstmilch" (Autumn Milk) by Joseph Vilsmaier. This film, of the bestselling autobiography of the same name by a Bavarian country woman Anna Wimschneider, was one of the most pleasant surprises.

German film makers are more and more ready to try their hand at the difficult art of comedy and satire. Loriot, Germany's most satirical humorist, brings out the comedy of every-day situations in his films "Ödipussi" and "Pappa ante portas". And director Michael Schaack, in his cartoon "Werner Beinhart" presents us with a comic hero. Otto Waalkes appears in his films as a shrill-voiced comic.

Financial support. New creative films have emerged partly as a result of support from the "Kuratorium junger deutscher Film", a public agency which awards prizes for first films (in the case of newcomers also second films) of artistic value. The curatorium is an agency of the federal states. There is also a general agreement between the film industry and the television operations under which the latter provide considerable funds for coproductions. Under this arrangement such jointly produced films may not be broadcast on television until at least two years have lapsed. The Film Promotion Act of 1968 provides for financial assistance not only for film production but also for cinemas known as "programme cinemas" which specialize in films of artistic value. The funds are obtained by means of a levy on all cinemas and the video industry.

Since 1951 the Federal Ministry of the Interior has been awarding an annual German Film Prize. Its categories are the Golden Bowl, which is worth one million marks, and Film Ribbons in Gold and Silver with prizes of up to DM 900,000. The ministry also awards prizes to help cover production and distribution costs.

A Film Assessment Agency, which was established in 1951 by agreement among the federal states, issues ratings for feature and short films: "wertvoll" (valuable) and "besonders wertvoll" (especially valuable). These ratings translate into tax exceptions or reductions, as well as subsidies under the Film Promotion Act. They also provide guidance for the public.

Umbrella organization of the film industry:
Spitzenorganisation der Filmwirtschaft
Langenbeckstrasse 9
6200 Wiesbaden

Festivals

In Germany you never have far to travel to the next festival. That cities have festivals is no surprise, but there are also charming small towns, like Schwetzingen with its rococo theatre, that are also able to offer something special.

There are over 100 music festivals alone. Every three years Bonn stages its International Beethoven Festival in September, while in August and September Augsburg stages Mozart concerts in a rococo atmosphere. Eutin celebrates Carl Maria von Weber, who was born there, whilst Halle and Göttingen focus their festival on Georg Friedrich Händel. Munich and Garmisch-Partenkirchen, on the other hand, have a festival devoted to Richard Strauss. The Richard Wagner Festival in Bayreuth has been an annual event since 1876. For Wagner fans this festival is like a magnet for nowhere else can they see such extraordinary productions.

Hardly any city does not have a music festival. Munich has its opera festival (July), Frankfurt am Main the Frankfurt Festival (September),

Bayreuth Festival 1991: "The Flying Dutchman"

Schleswig-Holstein Festival: music in a barn

Stuttgart the European Music Festival (August and September), and Berlin the Jazz Festival (November). Every year in August Heidelberg offers its romantic Castle Festival. The Schleswig-Holstein Festival founded by the pianist Justus Frantz in 1986 brings internationally famous musicians to this northernmost state of the Federal Republic and became extremely popular. It is a big musical event in a provincial setting.

Those more interested in the theatre can enjoy Berlin's Theatre Festival, which every May produces the best German language plays. The Ruhr Festival in Recklinghausen, likewise in May, tailors its classical and modern repertoire mainly to a working-class public in the middle of the Ruhr district. And then there are numerous towns like Bad Hersfeld, Schwetzingen, Schwäbisch Hall or Jagsthausen, whose historical castles, palaces and churches provide a charming backdrop for productions of mainly classical works.

The oldest festival takes the form of the Passion Plays at Oberammergau (Upper Bavaria) which is held every ten years in fulfilment of a pledge to God by the people of the village for having been delivered from the plague.

Berlin is an excellent address for directors and actors. There every February the International Film Festival is held and the Golden and

The Bach Week in Ansbach

Silver Bears are awarded. Another interesting event is the Nordic Film Festival held every November in Lübeck, and Mannheim's International Film Week in October.

Germany's festival organizers like their events to have an international flair. Bayreuth, for instance, in addition to staging its famous Wagner Festival, has also been staging the International Youth Festival since 1950. And Berlin has its "Horizonte", a festival of world cultures.

Index

(D) = diagram (M) = map (P) = picture

Picture Sources

Presse- und Informationsamt der Bundesregierung, Bildstelle (53); Stiftung Preußischer Kulturbesitz (6); Max-Planck-Gesellschaft (1); Deutsches Museum (1); Landesbildstelle Rheinland-Pfalz (1); Bertelsmann Lexikon-Verlag (5); Stief PICTURES (35); Stief/Bahnsen (1); Stief/Acaluso (1); Stief/Ford (1); Stief/Vogel (1); Stief/Walz (1); Bildagentur Mauritius (24); Bildagentur Schuster (4); Bildagentur VISUM (5); Bildagentur Bilderberg (5); Vario-press (2); Hessische Polizei (1); Stiftung Warentest (1); RTL Plus (1); CMA (1); Gewandhaus Leipzig (1); Deutsches Filminstitut (2); Bildagentur Helga Lade (2); Sachbuchverlag Karin Mader (1); BASF AG (2); Hoechst AG (3); Buchhandlung Hugendubel, Frankfurt (1); Adam Opel AG (1); Volkswagen AG (1); Daimler Benz AG (1); Wonge Bergmann, Frankfurt (1); Reinhold Dallendörfer (3); Bundesministerium für Post- und Fernmeldewesen (1); Bundesministerium für Verkehr (1); Bundesministerium für wirtschaftliche Zusammenarbeit (3); Bundesministerium für Verteidigung (1); FAG: Foto M. Skaryd (1); Stadt Frankfurt/Brieker (1); dpa (14); Bayreuther Festspiele Bayreuth (1); Polydor (1); Documenta Kassel (1); Deutsche Zentrale für Tourismus (1); KNA (1); EPD (1); Deutsche Bundesbank (1); Frankfurter Börse (1); Erhard Pansegrau (3); Jürgen Müller-Schneck (1); Klaus Lehnartz (1); Verkehrsamt Stuttgart (1); M. Zadek (1).
Cover photographs: dpa (3); Bundesbildstelle (1); Mercedes-Benz AG (1); Johann Scheibner (1); Fritz Mader (1); Koshofer (1).
Maps: Westermann Schulbuchverlag GmbH, Braunschweig

Editor: A. Hoffmann
Translator: Gerard Finan
Layout: Peter Lenz
Correct as at May 15, 1992

© Societäts-Verlag, Frankfurt/Main
All rights reserved
Typesetting and conversion work: Societätsdruck, Frankfurt/Main
Cover and diagrams: Icon, Bonn
Reproductions: Gehringer, Kaiserslautern
Printed by Westermann, Braunschweig
Printed in Germany 1992
ISBN 3-7973-0522-2